Multicultural Care

Psychologists in Independent Practice

Michael J. Murphy, Series Editor

Leon VandeCreek, Series Editor

Multicultural Care

A Clinician's Guide to Cultural Competence

Lillian Comas-Díaz

American Psychological Association

Washington, DC

Second Printing, May 2015

Published by
American Psychological Association
750 First Street, NE
Washington, DC 20002
www.apa.org

To order
APA Order Department
P.O. Box 92984
Washington, DC 20090-2984
Tel: (800) 374-2721; Direct: (202) 336-5510
Fax: (202) 336-5502; TDD/TTY: (202) 336-6123
Online: www.apa.org/pubs/books
E-mail: order@apa.org

In the U.K., Europe, Africa, and the Middle East, copies may be ordered from
American Psychological Association
3 Henrietta Street
Covent Garden, London
WC2E 8LU England

Typeset in Minion by Circle Graphics, Inc., Columbia, MD

Printer: Maple-Vail Book Manufacturing Group, York, PA
Cover Designer: Minker Design, Sarasota, FL

The opinions and statements published are the responsibility of the authors, and such opinions and statements do not necessarily represent the policies of the American Psychological Association.

Library of Congress Cataloging-in-Publication Data

Comas-Díaz, Lillian.
  Multicultural care: a clinician's guide to cultural competence / Lillian Comas-Díaz.
—1st ed.
   p. cm.
Includes bibliographical references and index.
ISBN-13: 978-1-4338-1068-8
ISBN-10: 1-4338-1068-9
1. Cultural psychiatry. 2. Psychiatry, Transcultural. I. American Psychological Association. II. Title.
RC455.4.E8C65 2012
616.89—dc23

                                        2011035902

British Library Cataloguing-in-Publication Data
A CIP record is available from the British Library.

Printed in the United States of America
First Edition

DOI: 10.1037/13491-000

To A. Toy Caldwell-Colbert, PhD, American Board of
Professional Psychology member (1951–2008),
a multicultural caring clinician.

Contents

Acknowledgments

I am part of all that I have met.
—"Ulysses" (Alfred, Lord Tennyson, 1842)

Like Tennyson's "Ulysses," this book is part of all that I have met. Family, friends, teachers, mentors, significant others, colleagues, artists, and guides accompany me on the cultural competence journey. Although their names are written in my heart, space limitations do not allow me to list them here. Likewise, I am indebted to numerous multicultural clinicians and scholars who paved the way toward the improvement of clinical services for all individuals. Definitively, the development of cultural competence is a collective effort. In this spirit, I acknowledge the intellectual contributions of all of the authors cited in this book's reference section.

I gratefully recognize Josephine (Jo) Johnson, Michael Murphy, and Manuel (Manny) Casas for their insights and helpful comments on an earlier version of this book. I extend my gratitude to Louise Silverstein for her help with genogram programs, Scott Browning for letting me see his genogram adaptation, and Amber L. Knott for lending me her library. A special thanks goes to the American Psychological Association editors Beth Hatch for contributions well beyond her duties, Susan Reynolds for her support and patience, Nikki Seifert for her superb technical editing, and Jessica Kamish for her outstanding assistance with the construction of the cultural genogram.

I also wish to thank A. Toy Caldwell-Colbert for working with me to develop the supplementary online course "Applying the APA Multicultural Guidelines to Psychological Practice" (see http://www.42online.org/continuing-education/multicultural). The royalties from the sale of this book will be donated to the scholarship that bears her name, the A. Toy Caldwell-Colbert Distinguished Student Service Award, established by the Society for the Psychological Study of Ethnic Minority Issues (Division 45 of the American Psychological Association).

Muchas gracias to Judith A. Nowak for witnessing and to Carol Spindel for teaching. My heartfelt appreciation goes to Frederick M. Jacobsen for his ongoing encouragement. Last, but certainly not least, I humbly thank my clients. They are the soul of this book.

Multicultural Care

Introduction: Multicultural Care in Clinical Practice

L ike the air people breathe, culture permeates life. Culture influences how people become distressed, interpret their maladies, seek help, and eventually, heal. Similarly, culture shapes how clinicians view themselves, their clients, and their clinical practice.

Culture is the proverbial elephant sitting in the middle of one's consulting room. If one ignores this elephant, he or she runs the risk of collision. Notably, if one approaches culture from a reductionistic perspective, he or she may reenact the fable of the blind men touching different parts of the elephant and misidentifying the animal. In other words, the clinician ends up misinterpreting the effects of culture on clinical practice. Instead, when one recognizes the role of culture, he or she develops an approach to clinical care that examines the impact of context on clients, ourselves, and the world.

My intention in writing this book is to help clinicians increase their clinical cultural competence. Although there are numerous resources on cultural competence, they tend to emphasize the training of graduate students as opposed to the continuing education of practicing clinicians (Rogers-Sirin, 2008). I intend for this book to bridge this gap by offering resources to graduate students, clinicians in training, novice therapists, and seasoned practitioners alike.

To facilitate the journey toward cultural competence, I propose the adoption of a *multicultural care* perspective. This approach involves enhancing understanding of clients' contexts, developing a multicultural therapeutic relationship, and adapting the healing approach to clients' needs. As a clinician, you already have most of what you need to endorse a multicultural care approach. You can become a multicultural caring clinician without abandoning your theoretical orientation. At the core of multicultural care is a desire to work with multicultural clients. Although all people have cultures, I use the term *multicultural individuals* to refer to culturally different individuals and/or people of color.

Multicultural care is a reflective practice that involves a continuous analysis of cultural embeddedness. As a cultural reciprocal learning experience, multicultural care advances a position of "knowing that you don't know." That is, instead of knowing facts, multicultural caring clinicians focus on understanding significant processes that occur during healing interactions. Clinicians can combine this approach with a commitment to cultural competence as a developmental process. This means that when they commit to cultural competence, they can enhance the knowledge, attitudes, and skills that enable them to engage in effective multicultural practice (Betancourt, Green, Carrillo, & Ananch-Firempong, 2003).

To achieve these goals, multicultural caring clinicians engage in an ongoing cultural self-assessment to critically examine multiple interacting contexts. Such a reflexive examination helps one recognize cultural complexities; enhances multicultural awareness; and fosters the development of *cultural empathy,* that is, the ability to connect with clients' cultural orientations. Multicultural care fosters the use of a cultural analysis to guide clinical encounters. Because every clinical encounter is a cross-cultural interaction (Comas-Diaz & Griffith, 1988), enhancing cultural competence increases clinical effectiveness with all clients. Consequently, the concept of clinical competence can be replaced with that of *cultural competence* because the latter is more inclusive and superordinate than the traditional notion of clinical competence (D. W. Sue, 2001; D. W. Sue & Sue, 2008).

Multicultural caring clinicians are also willing to integrate diverse and pluralistic healing approaches into their practice. Because many culturally diverse individuals have historical or contemporary experiences, or both, with oppression, a multicultural care perspective fosters empowerment. This viewpoint embraces the notion of *cultural humility,* or the lifelong commitment to develop empowering relationships through self-evaluation and self-critique (Tervalon & Murray-Garcia, 1998).

MULTICULTURAL CARE AND ETHICS

Ethical considerations mandate cultural competence in clinical practice (Arredondo & Toporek, 2004; R. L. Hall & Greene, 1995). The American Psychological Association's (APA) "Ethical Principles and Code of Conduct" (APA, 2010b), Principle E (Respect for People's Rights and Dignity), states:

> Psychologists are aware of and respect cultural, individual, and role differences, including those based on age, gender, gender identity, race, ethnicity, culture, national origin, religion, sexual orientation, disability, language, and socioeconomic status and consider these factors when working with members of such groups.

Moreover, Standard 2.01a (Boundaries of Competence; APA, 2010b), of the APA Ethics Code highlights the importance of cultural competence and asks psychologists to avoid harm by restricting their work with populations and in areas in which they have not gained appropriate competencies. Along these lines, Standard 2.03 (Maintaining Competence) urges psychologists to undertake ongoing attempts to maintain their competence.

As I discuss later in this book, I recommend applying a cultural analysis to ethical dilemmas. In Chapter 4, I discuss the application of such an analysis to specific dilemmas, such as personal disclosure, gifts from clients, and activities outside of therapy.

MULTICULTURAL CARE AND THE
APA MULTICULTURAL GUIDELINES

Although different mental health fields, such as counseling (Arredondo et al., 1996; D. W. Sue, Arredondo, & McDavis, 1992) and social work (National Association of Social Workers, 2001), have developed guidelines for cultural competence, the material in this book is anchored by APA's *Guidelines on Multicultural Education, Training, Research, Practice, and Organizational Change for Psychologists* (hereinafter referred to as the *APA Multicultural Guidelines;* APA, 2003). These guidelines are aspirational because they are not mandatory or exhaustive, and they may not be applicable to every practice-oriented situation. They highlight the respect and inclusiveness for the heritage of all cultural groups; the recognition of cultural contexts of individuals' and groups' experiences; and the role of external forces, such as history, economics, sociology, politics, geography, and ecology, in people's lives.

The *APA Multicultural Guidelines* (APA, 2003) have evolved, and continue to evolve, with time. Although developed for psychologists, these guidelines can inform the clinical work of other mental health practitioners. In brief, the *APA Multicultural Guidelines* encourage psychologists to (a) recognize that people are cultural beings, (b) value cultural sensitivity and awareness, (c) use multicultural constructs in education, (d) conduct culture-centered and ethical psychological research with culturally diverse individuals, (e) use culturally appropriate skills in applied psychological practices, and (f) implement organizational change processes to support culturally informed organizational practices and policy. The six specific multicultural guidelines are listed below.

Commitment to Cultural Awareness and Knowledge of Self and Others
1. "Psychologists are encouraged to recognize that, as cultural beings, they may hold attitudes and beliefs that can detrimentally influence their perceptions of and interactions with individuals who are ethnically and racially different from themselves."
2. "Psychologists are encouraged to recognize the importance of multicultural sensitivity/responsiveness, knowledge of, and understanding about ethnically and racially different individuals."

Education

3. "As educators, psychologists are encouraged to employ the constructs of multiculturalism and diversity in psychological education."

Research

4. "Culturally sensitive psychological researchers are encouraged to recognize the importance of conducting culture-centered and ethical psychological research among persons from ethnic, linguistic, and racial minority backgrounds."

Practice

5. "Psychologists are encouraged to apply culturally appropriate skills in clinical and other applied psychological practices."

Organizational Change and Policy Development

6. "Psychologists are encouraged to use organizational change processes to support culturally informed organizational (policy) development and practices."

Readers can access the complete text of the *APA Multicultural Guidelines,* including research basis and examples, at http://www.apastyle.org/manual/related/guidelines-multicultural-education.pdf.

Although all *APA Multicultural Guidelines* (APA, 2003) are relevant to practitioners, three areas are of particular significance to clinical practice: (a) commitment to cultural awareness and knowledge of self and others, (b) guidelines related to psychological practice, and (c) organizational change and policy development.

SUPPLEMENTARY ONLINE COURSE

A continuing education online course, "Applying the *APA Multicultural Guidelines* to Psychological Practice" (Comas-Diaz & Caldwell-Colbert, 2006), complements this book. Psychologists in Independent Practice (Division 42 of APA) sponsored the development of this online course in conjunction with the Society for the Psychological Study of Ethnic Minority Issues (Division 45 of APA) and the Society of Counseling Psychology (Division 17 of APA). The online course educational objectives are to

- apply the *APA Multicultural Guidelines* to improve psychological practice;
- identify the effect of culture on practice;
- implement strategies to compare the worldviews of clients from cultures different from that of the clinician;
- discuss the usefulness of developmental models and theories, such as ethnic racial identity and multicultural sensitivity on psychological practice;
- adjust psychological practice to provide cultural competent services;
- become familiar with resources available to clinicians on cultural competence; and
- develop at least one culturally competent psychological skill consistent with the lifestyle of culturally diverse clients.

This online course is available at http://www.42online.org/continuing-education/multicultural.

Although the online continuing education course offers a guideline-by-guideline explanation of the *APA Multicultural Guidelines* (APA, 2003), this book takes a more holistic approach that draws from, but does not focus on, the *APA Multicultural Guidelines*. It expands on the online course's content by weaving an extensive literature review and research findings with ample clinical material. In this fashion, the scholarship and clinical material that I present in this book inform each other. As a consequence, the clinical vignettes are grounded in cultural, theoretical, practical, and empirical evidence. Finally, because no one can be an expert on all cultures, this book helps readers to go beyond the knowledge-based culture specific constructs. In other words, it helps them to focus on the processes needed for working with multicultural individuals.

ORGANIZATION OF THIS BOOK

To facilitate the reading of this book, I organized the material around aspects of clinical practice. Each chapter demonstrates the application of cultural competence to a different aspect of clinical practice: self-awareness, engagement, assessment, analysis, therapeutic relationship, psychopharmacology and testing, treatment, and general multicultural consciousness.

In Chapter 1, I discuss multicultural awareness as an initial developmental stage in the journey toward cultural competence. I introduce cultural self-assessment as a means to enhance multicultural sensitivity and reflective practice. Although self-assessment is the focus of Chapter 1, self-assessment exercises appear throughout subsequent chapters because they are a fundamental component of cultural competence.

In Chapter 2, I argue for the importance of the initial engagement and listening to multicultural clients. My aim is to enhance clinicians' ability to connect with clients by listening with a multicultural ear to their stories of distress. Because culture shapes the stories clients tell and modulates the voice they use in storytelling, Chapter 2 offers practical suggestions to enhance cross-cultural communication. Moreover, I illustrate the use of the explanatory model of distress through clinical material. I offer practical mnemonic devices to assist clinicians in listening to their clients' stories. I end the chapter with a discussion of engagement as a clinical consultation.

In Chapter 3, I discuss multicultural assessment. Similar to Chapter 2, Chapter 3 covers asking clients about their backgrounds, problems, and strengths. However, unlike Chapter 2—which emphasizes helpful listening during the initial contact—Chapter 3 focuses on gathering information for diagnosis and treatment purposes. It offers practical strategies to conduct a process-oriented clinical assessment, taking context into consideration. Numerous areas of examination are presented, organized under client's ethnocultural heritage, journey, self-adjustment, and relations. Clinical material illustrates the use of tools such as a multicultural interpersonal inventory, cultural genograms, culturagrams, and sociopolitical timetables.

I devote Chapter 4 to the application of a cultural analysis to assessment and treatment. A cultural analysis can facilitate the understanding of a client's culturally situated reality. In other words, it helps clinicians to see through a multicultural lens to help them "enter" their clients' lives. I illustrate the use of cultural formulation and analysis through the presentation of case vignettes. I conclude by exploring selected collectivistic values and applying a cultural analysis to the ethics of multicultural care.

In Chapter 5, I discuss the multicultural therapeutic relationship as a central component of multicultural care. Because research has documented that a good working relationship is characterized by therapists' respect, support, understanding, skill, and care for their clients (Hersoug, Hoglend, Monsen, & Havik, 2001), I focus on the multicultural caring healing relationship as a mirror of the self in the other. I present multicultural clients' expectations of psychotherapy and therapist, as well as the cultural and sociopolitical parameters of transference and countertransference.

In Chapter 6, I advocate for cultural critical thinking in multicultural care. Specifically, I discuss the use of cultural critical thinking in the application of psychopharmacology and psychological tests to multicultural individuals, and I offer suggestions to enhance clients' psychopharmacological treatment. Furthermore, I discuss ways of decreasing cultural bias in the administration and interpretation of psychological tests.

The next two chapters deal with multicultural treatment. In Chapter 7, I discuss the incorporation of empowerment approaches into multicultural treatment. Readers will find a clinical illustration of the application of multicultural care with empowerment approaches, culturally adapted trauma therapy, a cultural genogram, a culturagram, and a sociopolitical timeline. I then present culture specific healing approaches in Chapter 8. I emphasize how clinicians can enhance their practices by learning from holistic and syncretistic healing orientations, such as ethnic psychotherapies and folk healing.

In Chapter 9, I conclude the book with a discussion of multicultural consciousness as a way to promote cultural competence in organizations, communities, and society. Following this final chapter, readers will find a glossary and a list of resources on cultural competence.

Throughout the book, I provide practical clinical suggestions, including multicultural tools and resources to complement therapeutic practice. Each chapter begins with a clinical vignette and cultural self-assessment questions and ends with a summary of multicultural clinical strategies. My intention is to help clinicians to complement their clinical style with these suggestions. Moreover, I structured this book to enhance readers' reflective practice through the use of cultural self-assessment. Clinical material illustrates the main concepts in multicultural care. The clinical vignettes intend to enrich the book's practical relevance. Although the vignettes are based on various clinical examples, I disguised the material to protect clients' and therapists' identities. However, I attempted to keep the clinical richness through a composite of real therapeutic material.

I invite readers to envision this book as a roadmap into their journey of becoming culturally competent. The suggestions presented are geared toward enhancing clinical effectiveness. As clinicians develop their cultural competence, they will become better clinicians.

1

Cultural Self-Assessment: Knowing Others, Knowing Yourself

To know others is wisdom; to know yourself is enlightenment.

—Tao Te Ching

Sonia: I'll castrate him.

Dr. Jenkins: What?

Sonia: Dale won't abuse me anymore. [*Opens her purse.*] Got a light?

Dr. Jenkins: Sorry. I don't allow smoking in my office.

Sonia: Don't you see I'm upset? [*Crosses her legs.*] Can you do something?

Dr. Jenkins: [*Swallows hard as she stares at the dressed-for-success Colombian American woman sitting in front of her.*] What would you like me to do?

Sonia: Just do something.

Dr. Jenkins: Let's try some deep breathing. [*Teaches Sonia a deep breathing technique.*]

Sonia: Thanks, I feel better.

Dr. Jenkins: Are you upset enough to harm Dale? [*Tries to assess Sonia's violence potential.*]

Sonia: Whose side are you on? [*Eyes begin to mist.*]

Dr. Jenkins: If you tell me that you intend to hurt someone, I need to inquire.

Sonia: You got to be kidding. [*Tears wash her rouge from her checks.*] I can't believe you're taking me literally.

Dr. Jenkins: What did you mean when you said you wanted to castrate Dale?

Sonia: Do you remember Lorena Bobbitt?

Dr. Jenkins: The woman who cut off her husband's penis? [*Caresses the gold band adorning her ring finger in her left hand.*]

Sonia: Real men don't hit their wives. If they do, they're not *machos*. [*Uncrosses her legs.*] Lorena cut her husband because he didn't deserve to be a man.

Dr. Jenkins: What do you mean?

Sonia: Don't you get it?

Dr. Jenkins: Are you seeking revenge for Dale's abuse?

Sonia: No. [*Crosses her legs.*] You just don't understand.

How do you feel about this clinical encounter? The issues Dr. Jenkins must deal with? Did Dr. Jenkins misunderstand Sonia? Did she demonstrate cultural awareness toward Sonia's situation? How would you approach Sonia's behavior if she were your client?

As I discuss later in this chapter, Dr. Jenkins's apparent lack of multicultural awareness may have contributed to a therapeutic impasse: "You just don't understand." To understand one's clients, one needs to interpret their behavior in a cultural context. Being aware of clients' culture improves clinical communication, promotes the emergence of a therapeutic alliance, and facilitates clients' participation in treatment. Certainly, knowing oneself fosters multicultural awareness and sensitivity.

In this chapter, I discuss how to conduct a cultural self-assessment to increase one's *cultural self-awareness*. Succinctly put, cultural self-awareness involves becoming conscious of one's reactions to culturally different individuals. It entails being cognizant of similarities and differences among cultural groups, as well as being aware of the cultural differences that exist among seemingly homogenous cultural communities. Cultural self-awareness helps you to enhance your knowledge of self and others to promote sensitivity and responsiveness to culturally different clients.

One can engage in a cultural self-assessment to facilitate self-awareness. A building block of multicultural awareness, a cultural self-assessment is a useful clinical method to examine the cultural differences and similarities between clinician and client. This tool entails an ongoing process of critically examining one's culture, history, ancestry, and context.

ASSESSING WORLDVIEW

A cultural self-assessment helps to unearth one's *worldview.* The concept of worldview refers to the personal attitudes, beliefs, and behaviors that may unconsciously or consciously influence interactions with individuals of any cultural background.

Like all people, clinicians approach human interactions within the limits of their worldview. Differences in worldview between clients and clinicians may lead to communication problems, misdiagnosis, premature treatment termination by the client, or all of these. To illustrate, the U.S. surgeon general's report on culture and mental health (as cited in Satcher, 2001) notes that cultural misunderstandings between clinicians and their clients may prevent ethnic minorities from using mental health services and receiving appropriate treatment. The demographic changes and the mental health needs of diverse populations intensify the relevance of clinicians' multicultural awareness in addressing and eliminating the mental health disparities addressed in the surgeon general's report. Regrettably, clinicians unaware of the differences between their worldview and their clients' may help to foster this disparity gap (Caldwell-Colbert, 2003).

You can begin self-assessing your worldview using Kluckholn and Strodt-beck's (1961) cultural framework. According to this classic model, you can examine your worldview orientation by answering the following questions:

- What do I believe is the innate character of human nature? (good, evil, or mixed)
- What is my relationship with nature? (subjugation, harmony, or mastery)
- What is my temporal focus? (past, present, or future)
- What is my preferred form of self-expression? (being, being–becoming, or doing)
- What are my preferred social relations? (lineal, collateral, or individual)

According to Kluckholn and Strodtbeck (1961), White Americans tend to subscribe to a *mastery* over nature orientation, endorse a *doing* activity, are *future* time oriented, and support *individual* social relations. Readers can ask themselves how they compare with this White American cultural baseline. Given that Kluckholn and Strodtbeck's research was 50 years ago, does this baseline remain the same today? Have these cultural orientations changed? For example, does the current ecological, "green" movement affect the relationship between people and nature (i.e., shift from mastery over nature to harmony with nature)?

In addition, you can engage in a cultural self-assessment when you examine their worldview using an individualism–collectivism orientation continuum. Triandis (1995) classified worldviews into *collectivistic* or *individualistic* according to how people view the relationship between self and other: individualistic members frequently view themselves independently from others and from context. Consequently, they tend to define themselves primarily in terms of internal features such as traits, attitudes, abilities, and agencies (Rhee, Uleman, Lee, & Roman, 1995). Accordingly, individualistic people value personal agencies, such as assertiveness, competition, self-assurance, self-sufficiency, and self-efficiency (Church & Lonner, 1998). In contrast, members of collectivistic societies tend to value communal welfare, develop a relational self-identity, and form strong social and emotional connections with others. As such, the collectivistic worldview allows individuals to place themselves and their lives within a larger context. (See Chapter 4 of this volume for a discussion of the collectivist values of familism, contextualism, and syncretistic spirituality.) Because collectivistic members attribute importance to relationships, they tend to prefer relational values, such as interdependence and harmony; to favor communication that minimizes conflict; to tolerate the views of significant others; and to share resources (Triandis, 1995). Research findings seem to verify these assertions: Individualistic persons tend to process stimuli as if they were unaffected by the context, in contrast to collectivistic members, who tend to process information while paying attention to their surrounding context (Berry, 1991; Kühnen, Hannover, & Shubert, 2001).

Although most multicultural individuals espouse a collectivistic worldview, they also adhere to individualism, depending on the specific context. For example, a Latina in the United States may exhibit individualism at work by being assertive, and she may subscribe to collectivism at home by tolerating the traditional views of her parents. Nonetheless, mainstream clinical practice in the United States mostly reflects individualistic cultural values. Unfortunately, if clinicians have limited multicultural awareness regarding their clients' worldview, they risk colliding with a cultural iceberg.

THE CULTURAL ICEBERG

Culture is an internal representation (Gehrie, 1979) that has been compared to an iceberg (E. T. Hall, 1976). Like an iceberg, most of culture's content lies below the surface (Weaver, 1998). Consequently, clinicians may see only a very small portion of clients' culture, and the rest is hidden deep below the surface. In clinical practice, the superficial culture, or the small portion of the iceberg, includes visible characteristics, such as clients' dress, manner, language, and other easily recognizable aspects. Superficial culture has a relatively low emotional load. Conversely, the majority of the cultural iceberg, or the *deep culture,* is unconscious and tends to have a high emotional valence— the kind of issues addressed in psychotherapy. Deep culture influences worldview, perception, and behavior. It frequently involves unspoken rules, such as norms that regulate family relations, intimacy, identity, relationships, boundaries, emotional space, and many others psychological areas. Such a cultural unconscious (Hoffman, 1989) permeates people's lives. When clinicians are unaware of a client's deep culture and cultural unconscious, they run the risk of colliding with cultural icebergs and, consequently, limit the development of a therapeutic alliance. Multicultural care offers a map to help clinicians navigate the cross-cultural waters. You can begin this journey by examining your own cultural iceberg. Such a self-assessment explores the following questions (Locke, 1992; Pinderhughes, 1989):

Surface culture:

- What is the cultural connotation of my name?
- Does my physique bear a cultural meaning?
- Does my appearance (e.g., clothes, hairstyle) convey a cultural nuance?
- Does my skin color have an ethnic, racial, and/or cultural significance?
- Do my language (formal, informal) and speech (e.g., accent, modulation, style) have cultural implications?

Deep culture:

- What is my cultural heritage?
- What was the culture of my parents and ancestors?
- What cultural group(s) do I identify with?
- What is my worldview orientation (i.e., values, beliefs, opinions, and attitudes)?
- What aspects of my worldview are congruent with the dominant culture's worldview? Which are incongruent?

Professional/theoretical culture iceberg:

- How did I decide to become a clinician?
- How was I professionally socialized?
- What professional socialization do I maintain?
- How does my theoretical orientation influence my worldview?
- What do I believe to be the relationship between culture and clinical practice?
- What abilities, expectations, and limitations do I have that might influence how I relate to culturally diverse clients?
- How do I feel about the cultural differences between my clients and me?
- How do I feel about the cultural similarities between my clients and me?

Cultural icebergs interfere with your ability to recognize the existence of cultural variations in cognitive styles, conceptions of the self, the view of choice, notions of fairness, and visual perception, among many other areas. Moreover, if, as a clinician, you become culturally encapsulated, that is, insensitive to cultural variations, minimize evidence contrary to your assumptions, and judge from your self-reference criteria (Wrenn, 1985), you can collide with cultural icebergs.

If you focus on individuals' superficial culture without examining their deep culture, you can engage in cultural stereotyping. To illustrate, Levy (2010, p. 255) discussed that generalized statements (i.e., those that fit almost everyone in a particular category), such as those listed below, nurture cultural stereotypes:

- White Americans favor members of their own ethnic group.
- Hispanics/Latinos[1] can be very passionate.
- Italians enjoy food.
- African Americans are sensitive to certain words.
- Christians attempt to forgive.
- Jewish people yearn to survive.
- Minorities just want their rights.
- Senior citizens don't want to be ignored.
- Men care about success.
- Women resent being taken for granted.
- People with disabilities resent being seen as inferior.

Furthermore, when you are unaware of your own cultural assumptions, you run the risk of behaving in an ethnocentric manner—in other words, believing that your worldview is inherently superior and desirable to those of others (Leininger, 1978). Ethnocentrism compromises clinical practice because the definitions of *health, illness, healing, functionality,* and *dysfunctionality* are culturally embedded. For example, if a multicultural client (e.g., the Latina who is assertive at work) expresses tolerance of the limitations of significant others during psychotherapy, individualistically oriented

[1] Hereinafter, I use the inclusive term *Latino* to designate "Hispanic/Latino."

19

clinicians may misinterpret such tolerance as poor judgment instead of viewing it as a culturally accepted norm. What's more, if one is solely exposed to monocultural groups, one can encounter difficulties identifying his or her distinctive cultural characteristics.

Because the foundation of ethnocentrism is unawareness, becoming aware of cultural icebergs is a crucial step in the development of multicultural awareness. As people examine their cultural assumptions, stereotypes, and biases, they challenge their ethnocentrism. For instance, you can examine the dominant cultural assumptions in the United States and compare them with your own. Such an examination can prove useful because, regardless of one's socioeconomic class, if one is a White American, he or she may tend to endorse cultural values that reflect only his or her ethnic background (Katz, 1985). Along these lines, Steward and Bennett (1991) argued that due to its White, Anglo Saxon, Protestant founding fathers, the dominant, White U.S. culture includes the following values:

- individualism;
- action-oriented accomplishment;
- democratic majority-rule decision-making system (when White people are in power; hierarchical decision-making when White people are not in power);
- communication that depends on standard English (which tends to be abstract) as opposed to an associate language (which tends to be linked to a shared context for enhanced meaning) such as nonstandard English;
- official communication that relies more on written forms than on oral expression;
- future-oriented time perception;
- religious system based mainly on Judeo-Christian values and customs;
- patriarchal nuclear family system; and
- emphasis on White male European history.

In addition, monocultural assumptions have shaped the dominant society. To illustrate, N. J. Adler (1998) argued that monocultural assumptions prevalent in the United States include (a) homogeneity, or the belief in the melting pot; (b) similarity, or the assumption that "you are just like me"; (c) parochialism, or the myth that "my way is the only way"; and (d) ethnocentrism, or the assumption that "my way is the best way." In contrast, a multicultural perspective includes (a) heterogeneity; (b) similarity and difference; (c) equifinity, or the belief that there are multiple ways of living one's life and, thus, that there are culturally parallel solutions; and (d) cultural contingency, or the belief that there are diverse and equally good ways to reach the same goal and that the best way is contingent on the cultural context.

Clinicians may have been trained to become aware of the monocultural assumptions in the mainstream society. However, they may be less conscious of the assumptions prevalent in their professional cultural iceberg. Clinical practice is a cultural activity replete of dominant cultural assumptions. Some of these monocultural assumptions include the psychological definitions of intimacy, relationships, motivation, activity, assertiveness, and agency, to mention a few.

Indeed, agency is a vivid example of the cultural differences in assumptions. Stephens, Hamedani, Markus, Bergsicker, and Eloul (2009) studied the perspectives on agency of observers and survivors regarding the people who "chose" to leave ("leavers") and those who stayed ("stayers") in New Orleans after Hurricane Katrina. These researchers found that observers evaluated leavers' behavior in positive terms as exhibiting agency—that is, they described the leavers as being independent and in control, in contrast to the stayers, whom the observers assessed negatively as being passive and lacking agency. Moreover, when the researchers interviewed the survivors, the leavers described their own behavior with an emphasis on independence, choice, and control, in contrast to the stayers, who emphasized interdependence, strength, and faith. Stephen and coworkers concluded that observers perceived agency as a White, middle-class concept consistent with an individualistic orientation and an ability to proactively influence the environment. Conversely, the stayers did not have the "choice" of leaving (because of a lack of significant others in other states, plus no socioeconomic resources for leaving) and, thus, described their agency in terms of a collectivistic orientation with a focus on interdependence, displaying strength against adversity, and having faith as a coping mechanism.

When you recognize your theoretical/professional assumptions, you can challenge ethnocentrism. To facilitate this process, consider the following cultural assumptions embedded in the dominant psychological assumptions (Pedersen, 2000; Weaver, 1998):

- Everyone is responsible for his or her actions.
- Everyone has a choice in every situation.
- Everyone is autonomous.
- Everyone has his or her own identity.
- Many clinicians assume that they are free of cultural bias.
- Individualism is presumed to be more appropriate than collectivism.
- Community support systems are not normally considered relevant in the clinical formulation of individuals' health.
- Ethnocultural ancestry and historical roots of individuals' backgrounds have minimal relevance in clinical treatment.
- Geopolitical issues bear no influence in clinical treatment.

Furthermore, contrast these assumptions with those of multicultural caring clinicians:

- Culture is complex and dynamic.
- Reality is constructed and embedded in context.
- Every encounter is multicultural.
- Clinicians' cultural competence is relevant to all clients.
- Clinicians' understanding of nonverbal communication and behaviors is crucial to healing.
- A Western worldview has dominated mainstream psychotherapy.
- Clinicians engage in cultural self-assessment.
- Healing is holistic and involves multiple perspectives.
- Healing entails empowering individuals and groups.

If you are unaware of your cultural assumptions, you risk ignoring the effects of diversity variables on individuals' help-seeking behavior and their adherence to treatment. To prevent these problems, you should avoid diagnosing multicultural clients' normative behaviors as resistance, deficit, and/or deviance (Young, 1990). Moreover, you should try to challenge your professional ethnocentrism by engaging in a critical examination of the established psychotherapeutic models and assumptions (such as the ones listed above). In fact, developing multicultural awareness is the beginning step in the journey toward cultural competence.

CULTURAL COMPETENCE: BECOMING A BETTER CLINICIAN

Cultural competence offers a compass to navigate the multicultural waters, and thus prevents colliding with cultural icebergs. Cultural competence applies to everyone because it enhances clients' treatment engagement, adherence, and completion. Research has shown that clients are more satisfied with their clinician not necessarily when they are ethnically matched but when they perceive the practitioner to be culturally competent, compassionate, and able to understand the client's worldview (Knipscheer & Kleber, 2004).

Cultural competence requires clinicians to be able to move from one cultural perspective to another (S. R. Lopez, 1997). In other words, cultural competence entails the awareness, attitude, knowledge, and skills that allow clinicians to understand, appreciate, and work with culturally diverse individuals (Betancourt, Green, Carrillo, & Ananch-Firempong, 2003). *Awareness* involves an ongoing self-reflection about one's worldview and cultural identity. Awareness also helps clinicians to recognize the presence of cultural icebergs as well as to identify their reactions to culturally different clients. *Attitude* involves developing sensitivity, respect, humility, empathy, and awareness of clients' contextual issues (Betancourt, 2003). Yet, an important aspect of attitude is the recognition that beliefs do not always coincide with behavior. For example, cognitive psychology studies have shown that individuals who in self-report measures appear nonprejudiced generally have negative attitudes toward African Americans (Dovidio, & Gaertner, 1998) and perhaps toward other people of color. Therefore, these individuals may engage in unintentional racist behavior even though they think that they are not prejudiced. *Knowledge* helps clinicians to understand how cultural, sociopolitical, and historical influences shape individuals' worldviews and related health behaviors (Betancourt, Green, Carrillo, & Ananch-Firempong, 2003). As a behavioral aspect of cultural competence, *skill* involves being able to effectively communicate and interact, as well as to negotiate differences and similarities in multicultural situations. In addition, multicultural skills require that clinicians adapt their clinical work to the cultural contexts of their clients. Moreover, Whaley and Davis (2007) emphasized the need for the internalization of the cultural competence process into one's clinical repertoire, to regularly apply it to multicultural individuals. Furthermore, cultural competence is more than the sum of its parts—awareness, attitude, knowledge, and skill. It is the integrative application of the interrelated cultural competence components into clinical assessment and treatment (Hansen, Pepitone-Arreola-Rockwell, & Greene, 2000).

Cultural competence is at the heart of multicultural care. Becoming culturally competent is a developmental process in which multicultural awareness is an initial stage. You can enhance your cultural awareness when you do the following (Comas-Díaz & Caldwell-Colbert, 2006; St. Onge, 2009):

- acknowledge that differences are always present—because every encounter is multicultural, recognize the existence of cultural differences;
- locate your own cultures—examine your cultural contexts and use the cultural iceberg metaphor to understand your cultures;
- engage in cultural self-assessment;
- develop intimacy with the culturally different "other"—in other words, increase contact with culturally diverse individuals of similar social status;
- see the dominant culture as one of many—when one aspect of a person's identity is part of a privileged group, he or she may not see it as a culture (e.g., like being White, male, or heterosexual);
- discover the influence of geography—physical location and geopolitical factors contextualize individuals' experience; for example, being a Latino immigrant in Arizona is different from being a Latino immigrant in Washington, DC, or being gay in San Francisco is different from being gay in Salt Lake City;
- look for divergent cultural norms—examine clients' cultural norms that conflict with your own, and assess your ability to work within the specific situation, or make appropriate referrals;

- examine intersecting identities—be mindful of how different components of identity relate to each other, for instance, an African American, lesbian, disabled woman frequently faces four types of interacting discrimination; and
- consider race a major identity issue in the United States.

This last point is central to cultural competence. Racism and colorism (i.e., a preference for light-color skin) pressure individuals to identify along color lines in the United States. Although many visible immigrants may self-identify by ethnicity and/or nationality (not along racial lines), as they acculturate, they tend to succumb to the White, Black, Brown, Yellow, or Red classification pressure. In my experience, compared with their immigrant parents of color, first-generation individuals tend to endorse a racial cultural identity. Chapter 4 presents a detailed discussion on cultural and racial identity development.

In brief, a journey into cultural competence can help you to

- conduct cultural self- assessments,
- enhance your multicultural awareness,
- navigate safely around cultural icebergs,
- learn about different worldviews,
- examine your attitudes toward self and other,
- acquire and incorporate cultural knowledge into your interventions and interactions,
- increase your multicultural clinical skills, and
- become a better clinician.

MULTICULTURAL SENSITIVITY STAGES

An essential component of cultural competence is the development of multicultural sensitivity. APA Multicultural Guideline 2 (APA, 2003) exhorts psychologists to recognize the importance of multicultural sensitivity, responsiveness, and knowledge, and to enhance their understanding about culturally different individuals. After examining your cultural iceberg, you can explore the developmental stage of multicultural sensitivity. This examination offers a baseline for cultural self-assessment. Bennet (2004) proposed the multicultural sensitivity development model as a useful structure to explore one's journey toward multicultural awareness and competence. Although Bennet's model describes a progression from one stage to the next, in reality, this model is a nonlinear development in which clinicians can find themselves in different stages, depending on the clinical context. Borkan and Neher (1991) adapted Bennet's model to a clinical setting and identified the stages of multicultural sensitivity developmental model as follows.

Ethnocentric stages:

1. *Fear.* Clinicians may fear working with a particular culturally diverse group, be mistrustful of differences, or both. The aim in this stage is to learn to decrease or eliminate fear by obtaining cultural knowledge.

2. *Denial.* Clinicians in this stage may exhibit cultural blindness and, thus, ignore and even deny cultural differences ("We are all humans"). Research findings revealed that cultural blindness is associated with lower levels of empathy (Burkard & Knox, 2004). The developmental task in this stage is to recognize the existence of cultural differences.

3. *Defense.* Clinicians in this stage tend to recognize the existence of cultural differences but feel threatened and, thus, defend against them. Defense mechanisms include dualistic negative stereotyping—that is, clinicians may feel their culture to be superior and denigrate other cultures. Conversely, they may denigrate their own culture as a result of identifying with another group's culture ("I wish I could give up my own culture and be one of these people"). The developmental task in this stage is to alleviate polarization.

4. *Minimization.* Reductionism and universalism characterize this stage. For example, a reductionism response emphasizes psychopathology and dysfunctionality while neglecting the effects of culture on mental health and on wellbeing. Clinicians who view their own culture as universal behave according to the minimization stage. They recognize cultural differences but minimize them, believing that similarities compensate for any difference. Similarity is assumed rather than known

("The other is just like me"). Cultural self-awareness can help clinicians to move into ethnorelative developmental stages.

Ethnorelative stages:

5. *Relativism.* Clinicians in the stage recognize, accept, and value cultural differences without judging those differences as positive or negative. They accept other cultures as complex and valid alternative representatives of realities. Cultural exploration and the acceptance of cultural differences build the foundation for empathy.

6. *Empathy.* Clinicians in this stage adapt to cultural differences and are able to shift in and out of alternative worldviews. As they embrace pluralism, they exhibit empathy—the ability to shift perspectives or capability to walk "in their multicultural clients' moccasins."

7. *Integration.* In the integration stage, clinicians expand their experience of self and other to include multicultural perspectives. They are able to engage in ethical decisions through a contextual assessment of critical cultural, individual and collective factors.

EXAMINING YOUR OWN CULTURAL COMPETENCE

After you place yourself in the multicultural sensitivity developmental continuum, you can use questionnaires to examine your cultural competence and obtain a baseline. Several of the cultural competence questionnaires are based on the work of Mason (1995), who developed the Cultural Competence Self-Assessment Questionnaire (CCSAQ). This instrument is a process tool. There are no poor performances with this questionnaire because cultural competence is a development. The CCSAQ assesses the areas of (a) knowledge of communities served, (b) personal involvement, (c) resources and linkages, (d) agency staffing, (e) service delivery and practice, (f) organizational policy and procedures, and (g) reaching out to communities. There are two versions of the CCSAQ, one for service providers and the other for administrative staff or human services organizations. I discuss in more detail the assessment of cultural competence in health and mental health organizations in Chapter 9.

Readers can assess their cultural competence baseline by completing the CCSAQ (available at http://www.rtc.pdx.edu/PDF/CCSAQ.pdf) before completing reading this book. Afterward, you can take this book's accompanying online course and complete its postassessment test. A list of cultural competence assessment tools can be accessed at http://www. transculturalcare.net/assessment-tools.htm.

Readers who are not interested in paper and pencil questionnaires can use a simple and practical tool to assess their cultural competence baseline. You can ask yourself the right questions. The Awareness, Skill, Knowledge, Encounters, and Desire (ASKED) method (Campinha-Bacote, 2002) is a simple mnemonic device to help you assess your multicultural literacy and competence. You can use the ASKED method in your ongoing cultural self-assessment by asking yourself the following questions

- Awareness: Am I aware of my biases?
- Skill: Do I know how to conduct an effective multicultural assessment?
- Knowledge: Do I know about culture-specific information, ethnopsy-chopharmacology, and biocultural ecology?
- Encounters: How many face-to-face encounters and interactions have I had with multicultural individuals?
- Desire: Do I want to become culturally competent?

CLINICAL ILLUSTRATION

As you explore the ASKED questions, you can enhance your multicultural awareness. With an improved culturally responsive perspective, let us take a second look at the clinical vignette presented at the beginning of this chapter. Of course, one can use diverse theoretical orientations to examine Sonia's vignette. However, an alternative scenario, in which Dr. Jenkins exhibits multicultural awareness, could yield different results from the first clinical scenario. To facilitate the illustration, I identify Dr. Jenkins's use of multicultural clinical strategies in parentheses.

Sonia: I'll castrate him.

Dr. Jenkins: You're quite upset.

Sonia: Of course I am. Dale has been abusing me and I don't know what to do.

Dr. Jenkins: Can you tell me more?

Sonia: [*Opens her purse.*] Do you have a light?

Dr. Jenkins: Sorry, I don't allow smoking in here. Do you want a glass of water instead?

(Empathic limit setting and acknowledgment of Sonia's anxiety)

Sonia: No, thanks. Can I have a tissue? [*Dr. Jenkins offers Sonia a box of tissues. Sonia takes a tissue and blows her nose on it*]. We've been married for 3 years, and he started the abuse right after the honeymoon.

Dr. Jenkins: Does your family know? (Using familism or the collectivistic value of family relations to explore Sonia's support system; see the discussion of familism in Chapter 4)

Sonia: Yes, but they told me to stay with Dale and pray. [*Eyes suddenly well up.*]

Dr. Jenkins: What is that like for you?

Sonia: I pray at times.

Dr. Jenkins: How does it make you feel? (Exploration of religious/spiritual orientation to assess violence potential)

Sonia: OK, generally. But it's of little use with my family.

Dr. Jenkins: How come?

Sonia: I don't think they care that much about me.

Dr. Jenkins: Can you tell me more?

Sonia: I don't want to talk about it now.

Dr. Jenkins: That's fine. Do you have children? (Taking Sonia's response at face value, engaging in sociocentric oriented assessment)

Sonia: Yes. A 2-year-old daughter.

Dr. Jenkins: Do you have a picture of her with you? (Use of a collectivistic interpersonal cultural approach)

Sonia: [*Opens her purse and pulls out from her wallet a picture of a girl wearing long black braids and a beaming smile.*] My daughter, Lluvia. [*Hands the picture to Dr. Jenkins.*]

Dr. Jenkins: That's an unusual name. What does it mean? (Showing interest in Sonia's culture) [*Returns Lluvia's picture to Sonia.*]

Sonia: Rain. [*Kisses the picture, places it back in her purse, and stops crying.*] Mami suggested the name Lluvia because rain comes from *el cielo.* In Spanish, the word *cielo* means both sky and heaven.

Dr. Jenkins: Is your mother concerned about Lluvia's well-being if you leave Dale? (Exploration of Latino traditional gender roles)

Sonia: That's what she says. She's old-fashioned and doesn't understand domestic abuse. [*Pulls another tissue from the box.*]

Sonia: Sometimes I think she blames me.

Dr. Jenkins: Umm . . .

Sonia: It's her religion. I'm so angry . . .

Dr. Jenkins: Do you really want to castrate Dale?

Sonia: No, he's already castrated. [*Blows her nose into the tissue.*] Real *machos* don't abuse their wives.

Dr. Jenkins: What do you mean?

Sonia: They protect their family. [*Leans forward in her chair.*] Can you help me protect myself?

This alternative scenario depicts Dr. Jenkins's helping to avoid a cultural misunderstanding. Dr. Jenkins's multicultural awareness fostered her exploration of Sonia's violence potential in a culturally and gender-sensitive manner and, thus, prevented a therapeutic impasse.

CONCLUSION

Increasing cultural self-awareness helps clinicians to understand themselves and others. An ongoing reflexive practice in the form of a cultural self-assessment facilitates the cultivation of multicultural awareness. When one commits to developing cultural competence, one engages in a lifelong process to become a better clinician.

MULTICULTURAL CLINICAL STRATEGIES

- Assess your multicultural sensitivity along a cultural competence developmental continuum.
- Avoid assumptions: If you need to assume, then assume difference until similarity is proven.
- Recognize that clinicians' cultural competence is relevant to all clients.
- Become aware of your own worldview.
- Be open to multiple worldviews.
- Commit to an ongoing cultural self-assessment.
- Be aware that clinical practice is a cultural activity.
- Consider every clinical encounter as a multicultural interaction.
- Examine and challenge your ethnocentrism: Read cross-cultural literature, especially memoirs of culturally diverse individuals, watch foreign films and films by and about people of color, and aim to learn a foreign language and to travel to other countries or to culturally different areas in the United States.
- Examine your cultural bias against individuals similar to and different from you.
- Increase contact with culturally diverse individuals of similar social status.
- Identify the presence of cultural icebergs.
- Recognize intragroup variations but avoid ethnocultural and racial stereotyping.
- Become aware of your values that are inconsistent with those of culturally diverse clients.
- Elicit information in a sociocentric fashion (e.g., family-centered context).

(continued)

(*continued*)

- Use the acronym ASKED as a method to assess cultural competence.
- Remember that multicultural clients prefer clinicians who are culturally competent, not necessarily ethnically matched.
- Recognize the culture-sensitive aspects of the ethics in being a multicultural caring clinician.

2

Engagement: Telling Stories

The one who tells the stories rules the world.

—Hopi proverb

Steve: I'm here because my doctor told me to.

Dr. Perez: Can you tell me more?

Steve: Yes, doctor! My internist said that I needed to see you.

Dr. Perez: Why do you think she asked you to see me?

Steve: Yes, doctor!

Dr. Perez: Let me ask you in a different way. How do you understand why she asked you to come here?

Steve: Maybe 'cause my heart hurts.

Dr. Perez: Can you tell me how your heart started to hurt?

Steve: I'm not sure.

Dr. Perez: Dr. Simpson mentioned in her referral note that you are originally from the Philippines.

Steve: Yes, doctor. I have been in this country for 3 years.

Dr. Perez: How has that been for you?

Steve: My family is still in Manila, and I have not seen them since I came here.

Dr. Perez: That must be difficult for you. How's your heart handling this?

Steve: It hurts.

Dr. Perez: What happened to you?

Steve: My daughter Agraciada was in a car accident a month ago in Manila.

How do you feel about this clinical situation? How would you have handled this initial session with Steve? How do you feel about clients who use somatic metaphors to describe their presenting complaints?

You can foster clients' engagement in treatment when you invite them to tell their story of distress. However, culture shapes the stories clients tell and modulates the voice they use in storytelling. In this chapter, I discuss the importance of the initial engagement and listening to multicultural clients. I present the explanatory model of distress as a culturally relevant instrument to elicit clients' health beliefs. Moreover, I highlight the relevance of listening to clients' perspectives with a "multicultural ear." To achieve this goal, I recommend using narrative approaches consistent with the oral traditions of many multicultural individuals. I conclude the chapter by suggesting that clinicians envision the initial session as a clinical consultation.

INITIAL CONTACT

Before narrating their stories of distress, multicultural clients expect their clinician to earn credibility and trust. *Credibility* refers to the client's perception of the clinician as a trustworthy and effective helper (S. Sue & Zane, 1987). Although most multicultural clients recognize professionals' clinical expertise, they are aware that such expertise does not necessarily translate into cultural competence. Cultural, historical, and sociopolitical circumstances influence clients' perception of their clinicians' credibility. In addition to credibility, many multicultural clients expect clinicians to "give" during clinical engagement (S. Sue & Zane, 1987). The concept of *giving* refers to the client's perception that something was gained from the clinical encounter. Examples of giving include acknowledging and, at times, addressing nontherapy issues (Thomas & Dansby, 1985). To illustrate, I frequently give to my clients by helping them to self-regulate with mind–body techniques during the beginning phase of treatment. Moreover, clinicians can earn credibility by demonstrating multicultural responsiveness while paying attention to context.

Many multicultural individuals use contextual information to assess the clinician's credibility and cultural responsiveness. Such assessment begins with the initial contact. Certainly, most clients see the initial contact as a window into treatment. For many multicultural individuals, however, the first contact becomes a two-way mirror. While the clinician is busy assessing the client, the client is assessing the clinician's multicultural awareness. Surely, many multicultural individuals decide to continue treatment on the basis of their first clinical interaction. To illustrate, an initial contact displays the surface of a clinician's cultural–professional iceberg. Just as people "read" others when they visit their houses, clients can infer information from examining the clinician's professional environment. In other words, they read how you describe your practice, where it is located, how your office is decorated, your presence (or absence) in the Internet, and other signs as potential expressions of your multicultural awareness.

I learned this lesson while practicing in cosmopolitan Washington, DC, with a multicultural clientele that comprises people of color; people from other countries; people who are gay, lesbian, or bisexual; and immigrants. I furnished my office with objects representing different cultural influences. In addition, my office is equipped with a bathroom that accommodates people in wheelchairs. As a "welcoming mat," my office reception area has multicultural reading materials. (However, you don't need to decorate your office as a local branch of the United Nations to show your multicultural sensitivity. Definitely, it is important to express your personal taste in your office decor.) Many of my clients comment on the office decor during the initial session.

A *cultural holding environment* goes beyond the surface of a clinician's office cultural iceberg. It includes how clients interpret the clinician's visible characteristics. To see an image of a client's initial impression of one's role as a clinician, refer to the ADDRESSING mirror (see Table 2.1 and the list in the next section; Hays, 2008).

CULTURAL SELF-ASSESSMENT: ADRESSING COMPLEXITIES

ADDRESSING who one is and who one's client is enhances multicultural communication. Everyone has a culture; in addition, everyone belongs to several subcultures, including those related to age, ethnicity, gender, sexual orientation, race, socioeconomic class, religion and spirituality, national origin, socioeconomic status, language preference, ideology, geographic region, neighborhood, physical ability or disability, and national origin, among others. These areas can be examined using the ADDRESSING model. Hays (2001) developed this concept as a mnemonic guide to examine the effect of culture and diversity variables on individuals as follows, where the first letters of each item spell "ADDRESSING":

- Age and generational influences;
- Developmental disabilities;
- Disabilities acquired later in life, such as neurological disorders, dementia, and so on;
- Religion and spirituality;
- Ethnic and racial identity;
- Socioeconomic status;
- Sexual orientation;
- Indigenous heritage;
- National origin; and
- Gender.

Clinicians can use Hays's ADDRESSING approach as a cultural self-assessment tool and a mnemonic reminder to examine the pervasive effects of culture on their own lives as well as on their clients' lives.

Table 2.1
Multicultural Engagement Instruments

Instrument	Explanation	Authors
ADDRESSING	Age and generational influences	Hays (2001)
	Developmental disabilities	
	Disabilities acquired later in life	
	Religion and spirituality	
	Ethnic and racial identity	
	Socioeconomic status	
	Sexual orientation	
	Indigenous heritage	
	National origin	
	Gender	
Explanatory model	What do you call your problem (or sorrow, illness)?	Kleinman (1980)
	What do you think your illness does to you?	
	How severe is your illness?	
	Will it have a short or long course?	
	What do you fear?	
	Why do you think this illness has occurred?	
	How do you think the illness should be treated?	
	How do want me to help you?	
	Who or what do you turn to for help?	
	Who should be involved in the decision making?	
BATHE	Background: What is going on in your life?	Lieberman & Stuart (1999)
	Affect: How do you feel about what is going on? What is your mood?	
	Trouble: What do you think is the most troubling about how you are feeling?	
	Handling: How are you handling the problems you are having?	

(*continued*)

Table 2.1
Multicultural Engagement Instruments (*Continued*)

Instrument	Explanation	Authors
	Empathy: This must be very difficult for you.	
LEARN	Listen with sympathy and understanding to the client's perspective of the problem.	Berlin & Fowles (1983)
	Explain your perceptions of the problem.	
	Acknowledge and discuss differences and similarities.	
	Recommend treatment.	
	Negotiate agreement.	
ETHNIC	Explanation: How do you explain your problem?	Levin et al. (2000)
	Treatment: What treatment(s) have you tried?	
	Healers: Have you asked advice from folk healers, alternative medicine practitioners, spiritual guides, or other helpers?	
	Negotiation: Negotiate mutually acceptable options.	
	Intervention: Agree with your client on an intervention.	
	Collaboration: Collaborate with client, and when relevant, include the support system, healers.	
BELIEF	Belief about health and well-being: What caused your illness or problem?	Dobbie et al. (2003)
	Explanation: Why did it happen at this time?	
	Learn: Help me to understand your belief.	
	Impact: What is the impact of this illness or problem on your life?	
	Empathy: This must be very difficult for you.	
	Feelings: How are you feeling about it?	

CLINICAL ILLUSTRATION

Let us look at Dr. Cassidy's reflection in the ADDRESSING mirror:

- Age and generational influences: 44 years old.
- Developmental disabilities: None.
- Disabilities acquired later in life: None.
- Religion and spirituality: Raised Catholic, now practicing a syncretism of Buddhism and Christianity.
- Ethnic and racial identity: Irish American.
- Socioeconomic status: Raised middle class, currently upper class.
- Sexual orientation: Heterosexual, married with two children, ages 18 (daughter) and 16 (son).
- Indigenous heritage: None.
- National origin: United States.
- Gender: Male.

During the completion of his ADDRESSING, Dr. Cassidy realized that socioeconomic class and social mobility had a major effect on him. As a case in point, he was the first member of his family to become a doctor. In addition to being a cultural self-assessment method, the ADDRESSING tool can be used to examine clients' diversity areas and contrast them with yours as the clinician. Let us follow Dr. Cassidy during an initial treatment session in which he examined his client's ADDRESSING.

A 44-year-old African American man, John, went to see Dr. Cassidy, an Irish American psychologist. When John saw a Redskins coffee mug on Dr. Cassidy's desk, he exclaimed, "Go Redskins!" Both men talked about their favorite football team's latest game. After exchanging some social pleasantries, John commented on a photo on Dr. Cassidy's desk: "Lovely family." Dr. Cassidy felt comfortable enough with the emerging rapport to explore John's ADDRESSING areas.

- Age and generational influences: John reported that he was 44 years old and added, "Proud to be of President Barack Obama's generation."
- Developmental disabilities: None.
- Disabilities acquired later in life: Not assessed.

- Religion and spirituality: "None." John's tone of voice changed—it became louder and strident. After a few moments he said, "I was raised Southern Baptist."
- Ethnic and racial identity: African American.
- Socioeconomic status:

John: Is this important to my treatment?

Dr. Cassidy: I would like to understand you better. But you don't need to answer if you don't feel like it.

John: I'm middle class by virtue of my employment and my engineering degree.

- Sexual orientation: John turned his head toward Dr. Cassidy's family photo and said, "I'm gay." Noticing a change in John's body language, Dr. Cassidy asked, "How do you feel about your sexual orientation?"

John: That's a complicated story—my father was a Baptist minister. [*Moves backward in his chair.*] I no longer go to church.

Dr. Cassidy: How do you feel about it?

John: I'm Black and gay. It's not like your son.

Dr. Cassidy: What do you mean?

John: I can tell by your family photo that your son is gay.

Clients' responses to the ADDRESSING tool can reveal sensitive areas and, thus, can be of therapeutic value. For example, Dr. Cassidy took mental note of John's change in voice tone as he answered the religion question. He then explored this issue during subsequent sessions. During this initial contact, John identified the conflict between his sexual orientation, the religion he was raised in, and his strained relationship with his minister father. Moreover, Dr. Cassidy exercised his clinical judgment when he faced John's apparent discomfort around the question about socioeconomic class. Dr. Cassidy's reaction—"I would like to understand you better. But you don't need to answer if you don't feel like it"—seemed to convey cultural sensitivity and respect. Perhaps Dr. Cassidy's awareness of his own socioeconomic mobility (raised in the middle class and belonging to the upper class) after completing his own ADDRESSING helped him to be more sensitive to John's feelings about socioeconomic class issues.

However, a major issue that this vignette illustrates is that most multicultural clients attempt to discern their clinicians' cultural awareness by reading their office environment. Whether Dr. Cassidy's son was gay or not, John's statement provided a therapeutic opportunity. Dr. Cassidy used this opportunity and invited John to elaborate on what it was like to be a Black gay man raised Southern Baptist with a father who was a minister. Later in the session, the issue of client–clinician differences surfaced, and Dr. Cassidy asked John how he felt about their cultural–racial/ethnic and sexual orientation differences. "I'm glad you asked," John said. Their subsequent discussion on cultural differences facilitated the emergence of a therapeutic alliance.

I recommend that you raise the issue of visible cultural differences between you and your client at the beginning stages of treatment. The following questions can help in this process: How do you feel about our cultural differences? How do you feel about my being Asian American? White? Black? Iranian? Some clients will reply that they are fine, or that the differences do not matter. However, by raising the issue of cultural, racial, and ethnic differences, a clinician exhibits multicultural awareness and, thus, identifies the elephant sitting in the middle of the clinical hour. Likewise, I recommend that clinicians raise the issue of cultural similarities (How do you feel about our cultural similarities?). This practice recognizes that culture matters and enhances your multicultural credibility.

It is not necessary to ask all of the ADDRESSING questions (Hays, 2008); instead, use your clinical judgment, and consider the relevance of these dimensions in your clients' lives. Examining the ADDRESSING areas conveys interest in your clients' lives. Such interest enhances the development of multicultural communication.

MULTICULTURAL COMMUNICATION: CONVERSING WITH STRANGERS

Clinicians witness the healing effect of being understood. This feeling eases the isolation of clients' distress and helps to restore their sense of connectedness that they need in order to feel whole (Suchman, Markakis, Beckman, & Frankel, 1997).

Improving one's ability to communicate with multicultural clients is central to one's journey toward cultural competence. As clients look for clues to decipher clinicians' multicultural awareness and sensitivity, they pay particular attention to the clinician's language and communication style. Indeed, cultural and communication misunderstandings frequently lead to misdiagnosis and clients' premature treatment termination (Satcher, 2001).

Communication barriers with culturally diverse clients are frequently unconscious and may include

- lack of multicultural awareness;
- fear, discomfort, and disgust;
- racism and xenophobia;
- ethnocentrism;
- stereotyping;
- language barriers; and
- differences in perceptions and expectations.

Enhancing your ability to communicate effectively with clients is essential to becoming a multicultural caring clinician. Without a doubt, proficiency in cross-cultural communication is a useful skill in your voyage towards cultural competence. As a clinician, you already have the foundation for engaging in effective communication. Succinctly put, you can rely on your clinical training, active listening skills, empathy, and clinical judgment. To complement these skills, I suggest that you approach your culturally different client as you would approach a stranger. As I have noted, communication conceals deep and unconscious elements.

High- and Low-Context Communication

According to E. T. Hall (1976) communication styles can be divided into high and low context, in other words, how much people rely on context rather than words in conversations. *High-context communication* refers to the use of contextual references where many things are left unsaid because the culture does the explanation. Although low-context communication is vested in the explicit code, high-context messages are less coded, explicit, and transmitted. For example, members from collectivistic cultures tend to communicate in an implicit and indirect manner, rely substantially on nonverbal communication, and pay significant attention to context (Armstrong & Swartzman, 2001). By contrast, clients from individualistic cultures prefer to communicate in a direct, explicit, and specific manner, paying less attention to context. Although the collectivistic voice is high in context—that is, messages adhere to a rich web of cultural nuances and meaning—the individualistic voice is characterized by a low context, in which communication tends to rely on the literal meaning of words (E. T. Hall, 1976).

Of course, individuals can use both high- and low-context communication styles. However, when presented with an unfamiliar situation, many culturally diverse individuals tend to communicate in a high-context manner. Some people of color will raise cultural issues such as racial, ethnic, gender, socioeconomic, ideological, and political concerns during treatment, as a high-context means of evaluating the clinician's cultural credibility. To illustrate, many Latino clients engage in *plática* (small talk) to check out their therapist. A social lubricant, *plática* is a light conversation used prior to the discussion of serious issues (Comas-Díaz, 2006a). As such, this high-context communication *plática* helps to address potential conflicts, desensitize painful reactions, and offer a safety net for delving into deeper issues in therapy. Latinos are not the only clients who may engage in small talk during treatment. Therefore, you may know that even during small talk, communication style may vary cross-culturally. For example, during informal conversations, individuals from Northern European countries may tend to give facts, as opposed to collectivistic members, who may ask about one's family (Axtell, 1985).

Self-Assessment: High- and Low-Context Communication

You can ask yourself the following questions about your communication style:

- Do I prefer to convey indirect (high-context) or direct (low-context) verbal messages?

- Do I use a significant amount of nonverbal elements during conversations (high context)?
- Do I see conversation as an art form of engagement (high context)?
- Do I prefer verbal over nonverbal communication (low context)?
- When do I use high-context communication? When do I use low-context communication?

Understanding Specific Cultural Contexts

In addition to understanding whether a client uses a high- or low-context communication style, multicultural caring clinicians strive to understand the client's specific cultural context. For example, the meaning of the same Spanish word varies across diverse Latino groups. Moreover, if a Japanese client says "*Hai, Hai*" (literally meaning "yes, yes") when you are speaking to him or her, it just means that she is listening to you—not necessarily that she is in agreement with what you are saying (Tseng & Streltzer, 2004). Remember Steve's answer ("Yes, doctor!") to Dr. Perez's questions at the beginning of this chapter? According to Tseng and Streltzer (2004), "Yes, doctor!" denotes a sign of respect toward—not necessarily agreement with—the doctor among many Filipino clients. In a similar vein, it took me a while to realize that when some of my Southeast Asian Indian clients moved their head side to side to side as I spoke, this gesture did not mean that they were disagreeing with my statement, but quite the opposite. Indeed, the significance of nonverbal language is culturally encased. To illustrate, the hand gesture of making a circle with the thumb and index fingers means "OK" in the United States, whereas in Brazil it is a lewd gesture (Axtell, 1985).

Definitely, culture shapes the expression of emotions. For instance, many African Americans (Parham, White, & Ajamu, 1999) and Latinos associate the emotional and affective expressions in interpersonal relationships with sincerity and honesty. Moreover, numerous Latinos kiss each other when greeting and departing. We tend to recognize the communication iceberg when clients speak with an accent, are bilingual, or are multilingual. As a nation of immigrants, accents are ingrained in the collective unconsciousness of the United States. However, clients' accents can trigger unconscious reactions in their clinicians. A cultural self-assessment can help you examine the deep contents of the communication iceberg.

Language

Unfortunately, the English-only movement tends to devalue bilingualism and multilingualism (Comas-Díaz & Padilla, 1992). Likewise, the clinical literature has neglected language issues in clinical practice (Claus, 1998). For example, monolingual clinicians may misunderstand their bilingual and multilingual clients' experiences (Santiago Rivera & Altarriba, 2002), missing the multiple layers of meaning that language and bilingualism provide to people's lives (Javier, 2007). Along these lines, Javier (1995) recommended that clinicians working with bilingual clients integrate both languages into their clinical interventions. Indeed, American Psychological Association (APA) Multicultural Guideline 5 (APA, 2003) urges psychologists to respect clients' language preferences and ensure accurate translation of documents by providing informed consent about the language in which assessment, therapy, and other procedures will be conducted.

Moreover, we cannot assume that we understand multicultural clients who are fluent in English. Speaking the same language is not equal to being able to communicate effectively. When in doubt, ask. Even though clients may speak English fluently, clinicians may want to adhere to cross-cultural communication principles, particularly during the beginning phases of treatment. Some of the cross-cultural communication principles (Gudykunst & Kim, 1995) relevant to clinical practice include the following:

- Choose language that conveys denotative meanings; thus, avoid idioms and slang words.
- Do not rely on unconscious and stereotypic scripts of communication.
- When in doubt, ask for confirmation of understanding.
- Observe nonverbal signs, particularly changes in body language.
- Look for silent forms of communication (e.g., facial expressions, paralanguage, hand gestures, voice tone, use of space).

- Pay attention to your client's communication style (low or high context).
- Listen with a multicultural ear.

Self-Assessment: Communication and Language

Clinicians can ask themselves the following questions regarding communication and language:

- What is my communication style (high or low context, or a combination of these two)?
- How do I feel about my native language?
- Do I speak other languages besides my native language? Do I have an accent?
- Do I speak in a dialect?
- What does my accent convey to my clients? How do I feel about accents? British? Spanish? German, French, Mandarin, and so on? How do I feel about the diverse U.S. English accents? How do I feel about Black English, or Ebonics? What about Southern, Midwestern, New York, Italian American, and other accents? How do I feel about Spanglish?
- How do I feel about the English-only position?

TELL ME A STORY: WHAT HAPPENED TO YOU?

Multicultural clients need to be understood in their own language. To illustrate, many culturally diverse individuals express their distress through a cognitive emotional narrative style. Narrative approaches are a preferred way to construct meaning, particularly among people who feel disempowered (K. Anderson & Jack, 1991). Indeed, many people of color communicate through storytelling. Consequently, as the Hopi proverb at the beginning of this chapter indicates, when we ask our clients to tell their stories, we help them to "rule their world." Because many oppressed individuals carry a sense of voicelessness, storytelling can be an affirmative and empowering healing tool (Semmler & Williams, 2000). When you listen to your clients' stories of distress, you exchange narratives and thus increase the possibility for a successful negotiation of these two stories.

Inviting multicultural clients to tell their cultural story is a culturally respectful way of assessment (McGill, 1992; E. R. Shapiro, 1998). When you listen to your client's story, you allow the emerging information to shape your clinical intervention. Moreover, you can elicit clients' narratives through the use of explanatory models of distress.

EXPLANATORY MODEL OF DISTRESS

The explanatory model of distress is a structured approach that examines individuals' experience and feelings of being sick and vulnerable, as well as their expectations of caretakers, and enlists their support systems in the healing process (Kleinman, 1980, 1988). As an anthropological tool, the explanatory model is an effective and culturally validated method (Lloyd et al., 1998) that elicits clients' expectations and perspectives on their illness (Kleinman, 1980).

You can introduce the explanatory model by stating that everyone experiences illness and distress and has expectations of treatment according to their beliefs. Next, you can invite your clients to share their story by asking, "What happened to you?" In listening to your client's story, you can ask the following questions (Kleinman, 1980):

- What do you call your problem (or sorrow, illness)?
- What do you think your illness does to you?
- How severe is your illness? Will it have a short or long course?
- What do you fear?
- Why do you think this illness has occurred?
- How do you think the illness should be treated?
- How do you want me to help you?
- Who or what do you turn to for help?
- Who should be involved in the decision making?

Besides providing clients with the experience of being heard and understood, the explanatory model facilitates the emergence of the therapeutic alliance. Consider Maya's (a mixed-race American woman) first session with me (a Latina [Puerto Rican] woman). After exchanging social pleasantries, the formal aspect of the session began:

Lillian: What happened to you? (Invitation to tell her story)

Maya: I don't know where to begin.

Lillian: Can you start with what brought you here? (What do you call your problem [or sorrow, illness]?)

Maya: Well, that will be masochism. I'm tired of letting others abuse me.

Lillian: Can you tell me more?

Maya: I guess I choose abusive relationships . . . that's what my friend Annie told me.

Lillian: Annie seems to be a caring friend.

Maya: Yes, she's my best girlfriend.

Lillian: What does masochism mean to you? (What do you think your illness does to you?)

Maya: I don't understand your question. [*Leans back in her seat and is quiet for a few minutes.*] Masochism hurts me.

Lillian: If you were to give a voice to your masochism, what would it say? (What do you think your problem does?)

Maya: Oh, well—That it's part of me. [*Maya started to cry, and Lillian handed her a box of Kleenex. After following Maya's nonverbal clues Lillian continued.*]

Lillian: From your perspective, does masochism have a function in your life?

Maya: That's a strange question. [*Blows her nose on the tissue.*] Honestly, I think about this in a different way.

Lillian: How?

Maya: Well, I always wondered if I let others hurt me so I can't get close to them.

Lillian: Can you tell me more?

Maya: I don't know. [*Puts the box of Kleenex on the table.*] I want to be with people, but not to get too close, I guess.

Lillian: That's interesting. Do you mind if I ask you a related question?

Maya: Go ahead.

Lillian: What will happen if you continue to let others hurt you? (What do you think the natural course of your illness is?)

Maya: I'll die.

Lillian: How?

Maya: What do you mean? [*Opens her eyes wide.*]

Lillian: How do you feel about death? (Exploration of suicidal potential)

Maya: I see where you're going. [*Possibly picking up on Lillian's nonverbal communication.*] No, I will never kill myself.

Lillian: What do you fear?

Maya: That I will end up alone.

Lillian: It sounds like loneliness may be your worst fear.

Maya: [*Nods.*]

Lillian: Why do you think the masochism happened? (Why do you think this problem has occurred?)

Maya: I don't know. But . . .

Lillian: But?

Maya: Sometimes I suspect that I protect myself against being alone.

Lillian: You protect against loneliness by—

Maya: Yeah, by hooking up with people who will hurt me. [*Starts to cry again, and there is a moment of silence. Picks up a box of Kleenex that is laying on the table next to her.*] Please ask me something.

Lillian: Is that how the masochism started?

Maya: Maybe . . . Yes.

Lillian: Does the masochism keep you connected—

Maya: Yes. And at the same time, I don't get too close to others.

Lillian: Do you have a sense of how to address the problem? (How do you think the sickness should be treated?)

Maya: No. That's why I'm here. [*Looks straight into Lillian's eyes.*] What do you think?

Lillian: I do have some observations, but before discussing them, I would like to ask you if you have any idea of how to manage your masochism.

Maya: Now that you put it this way . . . Maybe it's karmic.

Lillian: What does *karmic* mean to you?

Maya: You know, the effect of past lives.

Lillian: What does it say about you?

Maya: That I need to learn from my previous incarnations.

Lillian: How can I help you? (How do you want me to help you?)

Maya: Can you clean karma?

Lillian: I don't know, but maybe I can help you break the cycle of masochism and—

Maya: That's cleaning karma.

Lillian: I would like to hear more about karma, but for now, is there someone else that needs to be involved in your healing? (Who do you turn to for help? Who should be involved in the decision making?)

Maya: Funny you ask.

Lillian: Why?

Maya: I trust my psychic. She told me to see a therapist.

Lillian: How do you feel about seeing a Latina therapist?

Maya: I'm not sure yet. But I don't feel you're judging me.

For many culturally diverse individuals, the explanatory model often reveals Western as well as non-Western cultural beliefs. Indeed, individuals' responses to the explanatory model questions may not necessarily be coherent because they can simultaneously hold diverse and even contradictory beliefs (Callan & Littlewood, 1998). As an illustration, Maya disclosed her belief in karma but also indicated a dynamic understanding of her ambivalence toward intimate relationships.

When you elicit your clients' exploratory model of distress, you actively engage them in their treatment. In summary, the explanatory model of distress helps clinicians to

- enhance the capacity to listen to the client with a multicultural ear;
- acknowledge clients' subjective truth informed by culture, experience, language, history, politics, power dynamics, alternative healing sources, and other essential factors in their worldviews;
- allow clients to express their concerns, fears, and beliefs; and
- invite clients' active participation in their treatment.

BATHE, LEARN, ETHNIC, AND BELIEF

Several mnemonic tools are available to help clinicians assess clients' explanatory models of distress. Use your clinical judgment to choose the tool that works best for you and your client.

Background, Affect, Trouble, Handling, and Empathy, or BATHE, is a mnemonic method that facilitates multicultural communication during the initial contact (Lieberman & Stuart, 1999). It is particularly useful for clinical consultations and short-term psychotherapies. You can elicit a client's perspective by asking the following questions from the BATHE method.

- Background: What is going on in your life? (What happened to you?) This type of questioning elicits the context of the presenting problem.
- Affect: How are you feeling? How do you feel about what is going on? What is your mood?
- Trouble: What do you think is the most troubling about how you are feeling? (Assessment of the symbolic meaning of the distress or problem.)

- Handling: How are you handling the problems you are having? (Assessment of client's coping mechanisms.)
- Empathy: This must be very difficult for you. (As a clinician, you know that empathy helps clients to engage in emotional reprocessing. Empathy contributes to fostering multicultural clients' self-healing by creating a space for personal involvement and openness to the psychotherapeutic process.)

Clinicians can enhance the clinical engagement process by following the LEARN method. Soliciting clients' stories of distress enhances multicultural communication and facilitates the emergence of a therapeutic alliance. LEARN (Berlin & Fowkes, 1983), a simple mnemonic tool, stands for

- Listen with sympathy and understanding to the client's perspective of the problem.
- Explain your perceptions of the problem (In other words, share your story of treatment).
- Acknowledge and discuss differences and similarities.
- Recommend treatment.
- Negotiate agreement.

Another simple mnemonic tool, ETHNIC, stands for Explanation, Treatment, Healers, Negotiation, Intervention, and Collaboration (Levin, Like, & Gottleib, 2000). Clinicians using the ETHNIC model assess the following:

- Explanation: Elicit clients' explanation of their problem.
- Treatment: Explore clients' approaches to solve the problem.
- Healers: Examine the use of folk healers, alternative medicine practitioners, spiritual guides, and or others helpers.
- Negotiation: Negotiate mutually acceptable options that incorporate the client's beliefs.
- Intervention: Agree with the client on an intervention.
- Collaboration: Collaborate with the client, and when relevant, include the support system, healers.

Still another practical mnemonic device for the explanatory model of distress is BELIEF. This mnemonic tool stands for Beliefs, Explanation, Learn, Impact, Empathy, and Feelings (Dobbie, Medrano, Tysinger, & Olney, 2003):

- Belief about health and well-being: What caused your illness or problem?
- Explanation: Why did it happen at this time?
- Learn: Help me to understand your belief.
- Impact: What is the impact of this illness or problem on your life?
- Empathy: This must be very difficult for you.
- Feelings: How are you feeling about it?

Table 2.1 summarizes the above instruments, along with others discussed in this chapter to facilitate engagement.

ENGAGEMENT AS CONSULTATION

In my experience, many multicultural individuals perceive clinical practice as a consultation. That is, they may not expect to adhere to the clinician's prescribed length of treatment. Although multicultural clients tend to complete treatment when working with culturally competent clinicians, in fact, a significant number of people of color attend only one or two therapy sessions (S. Sue & Zane, 1987). You may find yourself engaging in single-session therapy (Talmon, 1991). However, the story is more complex. For example, I have seen several multicultural individuals, couples, and families in a single consultation session, who years later return to complete their treatment. Moreover, many of my clients who attend only one session refer their relatives, friends, and coworkers to me later on. Several of my colleagues also share this experience.

Consequently, how you treat the initial session is crucial for engaging multicultural clients. I suggest that after exchanging stories (clients' explanatory model of distress, plus your narratives of diagnosis and treatment) you conceptualize the initial session as a consultation. During this consultation, try to avoid asking culturally incongruent questions such as "How do you see yourself compared with other people?" or directive questions such as "Are you angry with your mother?" (Paniagua, 1994). Alternatively, clinicians can ask "What do friends, family, or others say about your symptoms?" (Levin et al., 2000). Along these lines, you can use open-ended questions and give to your clients to foster rapport. As I indicated previously, *giving* refers to clients' perception that they receive immediate benefits from the therapeutic encounter (S. Sue & Zane, 1987). These benefits can be in the form of anxiety reduction, depression relief, cognitive clarity, normalization of affect, reassurance, hope and faith, skills acquisition, a coping perspective, or goal setting. As an illustration of giving, I use mind–body techniques, such as deep muscle relaxation, healing light exercise, butterfly hug, safe place exercise (E. R. Shapiro, 1994), and guided imagery during the engagement phase of treatment.

You can elicit your client's life story during the consultation; using photographs can aid in this process. Recall Sonia's second vignette from Chapter 1, in which Dr. Jenkins asked Sonia to show her a photo of her daughter, Lluvia. Using photos for storytelling enhances self-esteem among multicultural individuals, particularly among people of color (Falicov, 1998). This strategy is effective in addressing clients' issues of skin color and race. Clinicians can invite clients to tell their life stories by asking questions such as (Remen, 1989):

- What would you like to tell me about your life?
- What stories are you telling yourself?
- What matters to you about your current situation?
- What do you need?
- What or whom are you calling on for strength?
- The fact that you have gone through this—what does that say about you? What does it mean?
- What is important to you?
- What is of ultimate concern to you?

Yet another useful tool during consultations is *instant autobiography*. This method refers to the compressed re-narration of the client's life story focusing on a central issue. Some clients choose to focus on their identity, translocation, relationships, or other related topics in their narration. For example, the clinical vignette at the beginning of this chapter revealed that Steve's central issues were his heartache caused by having his family in Manila (because of his immigration), his 3 years in the United States without seeing his family, his daughter's accident (crisis), and his sense of hopelessness. Moreover, some clients choose to focus on the role the distress, problem, symptom, or all three, plays during an instant autobiography (Omer, 1993). For instance, Sonia, the client from Chapter 1, seemed to focus on her story of domestic abuse as a central issue in her narrative. Indeed, abuse and trauma are topics that tend to emerge in the lives of many multicultural individuals with oppressive experiences.

I use a consultation technique with clients who may be ambivalent about mental health treatment. I offer them a three-session consultation (psychotherapy) format. This approach helps me to listen to clients' explanatory models of distress, elicit their instant psychobiographical stories, offer a holding environment for the reduction of symptoms, and when necessary, provide psychoeducation. After completing treatment in the three-session format, many of my clients schedule future mental health checkups.

CONCLUSION

The engagement phase is crucial in multicultural care. Multicultural clients expect clinicians to be culturally credible and to earn their trust as a prerequisite for engagement. To achieve this goal, you can give to your clients, work toward a culturally holding environment, and elicit their stories of distress. Remember to use cross-cultural communication principles while listening to clients' stories and while narrating your diagnosis and treatment stories.

MULTICULTURAL CLINICAL STRATEGIES

- Aim to achieve cultural credibility and trust.
- Promote and cultivate a culturally holding environment in your practice.

(continued)

(*continued*)

- Consider adding magazines, brochures, and other printed materials reflective of a culturally diverse clientele to your reception area.
- Examine your reflection in the ADDRESSING mirror and compare it with your clients'.
- Initiate the exploration of cultural differences and similarities during the initial interview. Ask questions such as, "How do you feel about our cultural difference? How do you feel about my being _____?"
- Become aware of diverse styles of communication (high- and low-context communication).
- Conduct a cultural self-assessment exploring your own communication style and language use.
- Ask culturally inquisitive questions.
- Aim to enhance your cross-cultural communication skills.
- Learn to interpret verbal and nonverbal behaviors in a culturally relevant way.
- Consider learning or at least becoming familiar with a foreign language.
- When in doubt, ask.
- Identify the first clinical session as a consultation and explain the nature of a consultation to the client.
- If appropriate, adjust your style to a more interactive one during the engagement phase.
- Elicit your clients' story: Examine their explanatory model of distress.
- When appropriate, invite clients to tell their life story.
- Use the BATHE, LEARN, ETHNIC, and BELIEF methods to elicit clients' explanatory models.

3

Multicultural Assessment: Understanding Lives in Context

I am I plus my circumstances.

—Jose Ortega y Gasset (1961)

Paolo: You think you understand, but you don't. [*Turns his body away from his wife and continues speaking.*] You're not Italian.

Karen: You always say that when you don't agree with me. [*Her face reddens.*]

Lillian: Can you tell us more?

Karen: I know that Paolo and I have cultural differences. [*Takes a tissue and continues.*] But I mean something else. [*Places the tissue on her lap.*] I'm talking about our problems as a couple.

Paolo: What? [*Leans forward in his chair.*]

Karen: [*Slapping the arm of her chair with every word she utters.*] You – don't – have – time – for – us. We're always with your family.

Paolo: I don't get it. [*Lowers his voice.*] My family is your family.

Karen: I married you, not the Verdis.

Paolo: You're wrong. [*Voice echoes throughout the office.*] You married the Verdis. The whole clan.

How do you feel about Paolo and Karen's couples' session? What are the issues Lillian must deal with? How would you approach Paolo and Karen if they were your clients? Is there a cultural conflict? If so, what do you think it is?

This clinical vignette illustrates a cultural difference regarding family boundaries. Karen, a White American woman whose ancestry is British, seems to perceive the couple as a separate unit. Conversely, Paolo—an Italian American—sees the couple as part of his family of origin. This difference demonstrates the contrast between individualistic and collectivist worldviews.

As readers may remember from Chapter 1, the essential difference between the individualistic and the sociocentric perspective is the relative importance people assign to context. In other words, Paolo's sociocentric view of marriage as part of his extended family contrasts with Karen's individualistic perception.

Regardless of a clinician's worldview orientation, he or she can benefit from paying attention to clients' multiple contexts. To achieve this goal, you can complement the explanatory model of distress (see Chapter 2) with a process-oriented clinical assessment. In this chapter, I discuss multicultural assessment. Although there is some overlap between the previous chapter and this one, I emphasized initial engagement and cross-cultural communication in Chapter 2, whereas here I emphasize gathering and analyzing information for assessment and treatment. Nonetheless, the tools presented in this chapter will yield information useful for engagement, and the tools used in engagement will strengthen assessment.

MULTICULTURAL ASSESSMENT: A PROCESS-ORIENTED APPROACH

A multicultural clinical assessment is a process-oriented approach that examines the multiple contexts in people's lives. This clinical process can be used for both evaluation and treatment. Engaging in a multicultural assessment conveys genuine interest in a client and thus fosters a culturally holding environment. Of course, not all of the contexts may be relevant to a client's current circumstances. As with any multicultural strategy, remember to rely on clinical judgment when conducting a multicultural assessment. I recommend that you ask your clients to have a physical examination. Because many multicultural individuals are referred to mental health treatment by their internist, your clients may have already undergone a physical evaluation. Such an examination is helpful in identifying physical conditions, such as thyroid malfunctioning, that may mimic mental health problems. Moreover, you will be exploring your clients' health status in a holistic multicultural assessment.

Individuals' circumstances may be explored throughout the evaluation and treatment phases. Indeed, some culturally different clients require an extended time to share their stories (Mollica & Lavalle, 1988) and for clinicians to earn clients' trust and demonstrate cultural credibility. The use of a multicultural assessment demonstrates cultural integrity on the part of the clinician and enhances the emergence of a therapeutic alliance.

Exhibit 3.1 lists overlapping areas that you may want to consider when using a multicultural assessment. This is not an exhaustive list. Moreover, many contextual areas relevant to assessment are not mutually exclusive. Some of the diversity variables acquire more prominence than others for certain individuals. For example, although gender may be a pivotal variable for most women, the ethnic/racial–gender interaction achieves centrality in the lives of many women of color. Clinicians can elicit the contextual information throughout several evaluation sessions as well as during the treatment phase.

MULTICULTURAL ASSESSMENT DOMAINS

The multicultural assessment examines the contextual areas through four domains: ethnocultural heritage, journey, self-adjustment, and relations (Jacobsen, 1988). In the following sections, I discuss the four domains separately.

Exhibit 3.1

Multicultural Clinical Assessment Areas

Ability and Disability Status

- Cultural beliefs around disability
- Family beliefs, attitudes

Acculturation

- Assimilation
- Biculturalism
- Culture shock stages
- Transculturation

Age

- Age cohort
- Cultural meaning of age
- Interaction of age with gender, ethnicity, race, class, and other variables

Biocultural

- Health status
- Medical history
- Illnesses, genetic predisposition to illness
- Nutrition, common foods, vitamins, herbs
- Physical activity
- Substance use or abuse
- Traditional healing practices

Development

- Cultural meaning of developmental stages: infancy, childhood, adolescence, menarche, adulthood, menopause, old age

Exhibit 3.1

Multicultural Clinical Assessment Areas (*Continued*)

Discrimination

- Anti-immigration movement, classism, racism, heterosexism, ageism, ableism, sizeism, colorism, xenophobia
- Historical and contemporary oppression
- Microaggressions

Education

- Education level
- Occupation, avocation
- Professional status

Ethnicity

- Ethnic identity and identification
- Ethnocultural heritage
- History of (im)migration and generations from (im)migration
- Acculturation and transculturation
- Languages spoken by client, family of origin, and current family

Family

- Adoption and foster parenting
- Family of origin and multigenerational history
- Family life-cycle development and stages
- Family structure (patriarchal, matriarchal, egalitarian; nuclear, extended; traditional; reconstituted)
- Non–blood-related extended family members, such as *padrino, madrina* (godparents), *doula* (person who mothers the mother by providing specialized maternal infant care, including emotional and practical support)

(continued)

Exhibit 3.1

Multicultural Clinical Assessment Areas (*Continued*)

- Gender and family roles (hierarchies, responsibilities) (What are the cultural specifications for being a mother, father, grandparent, etc.?)

Folk Beliefs

- Culture-bound syndromes
- Anger management and cultural expressions of anger (i.e., *amok, mal de pelea,* and *hwa-byung;* see Chapter 8 for a discussion of culture-bound syndromes)

Health-Related Folk Beliefs

- Use of folk healers, complementary and alternative medicine

Gender

- Cultural roles of male, female; interaction of gender, ethnicity, and race

Geographic Location

- Presence and impact of ethnic group members vary according to locale (e.g., Mexican Americans in California, Polish and Polish Americans in Chicago)

Geopolitics and History

- Ethnic group's politicohistory
- Ethnic group's relationship with dominant group (including wars and political conflict)
- Ethnic group's relationship with other ethnic groups
- Historical era
- Sociohistory
- Political ideology
- Wars (including civil war)

Exhibit 3.1

Multicultural Clinical Assessment Areas (*Continued*)

Health and Mental Health Beliefs

- Attitudes around mental health or illness
- Attitudes toward, and expectations for, mental health treatment
- Beliefs, customs, and attitudes surrounding death
- Meaning of pain and suffering

Immigration and Migration

- Age of immigration
- Asylum experience
- Culture shock stages
- International living experiences
- Refugee experience
- Type of immigration (voluntary, involuntary)
- Ulysses syndrome

Language

- Accent
- Bilingualism, multilingualism, dialects
- Languages spoken at home
- Language fluency
- Nonstandard English
- Speech difficulties (e.g., stammering)

Lifestyle

- Health-maintenance behaviors, exercise, vitamin and herb supplements
- Recreation, avocations (e.g., mountain climbing), and hobbies
- Risk-taking behaviors; sensation seeking
- Special roles

(*continued*)

Exhibit 3.1

Multicultural Clinical Assessment Areas (*Continued*)

Marital Status

- Marriages (heterosexual, same sex, common law liaisons, sexual partnerships)
- Divorce, singlehood, separation, widowhood, political widowhood

National Origin

- Legal status (alien, resident, naturalized, native born)
- Citizenship (single, dual)

Oppression

- Ableism
- Ageism
- Elitism
- Functional and dysfunctional reactions
- Heterosexism
- Homophobia
- Institutional
- Internalized oppression
- Racism
- Religious (e.g., anti-Semitism, anti-Islam, anti-Catholicism, cult)
- Sexism
- Sizeism (discrimination due to body size)

Pets

- Past and current pets
- Reaction to pet's death

Physical Appearance

- Attractiveness (self and other, cultural group and mainstream group perception)

Exhibit 3.1

Multicultural Clinical Assessment Areas (*Continued*)

- Minority status may increase as individuals deviate from the White European American phenotype
- Distinctive physical characteristics (e.g., birthmarks, tattoos)
- Hair texture
- Size and body type

Politics and Ideology

- Political groups
- Ideology

Race

- Interaction of race, gender, age, sexual orientation, class
- Phenotypical characteristics
- Skin color, hair texture, facial features
- Racial history (individual and collective)
- Racial socialization

Religion and Spirituality

- Folk beliefs
- Religions raised and practicing
- Spiritual beliefs
- Effect of religion or spirituality on health and well-being
- Ecstatic experiences, paranormal experiences
- Psychospiritual journey
- Relationship with the divine

Sexual Orientation

- Asexual, heterosexual, gay/lesbian, bisexual, transgender
- Internalized oppression

(continued)

Exhibit 3.1

Multicultural Clinical Assessment Areas (*Continued*)

Sexuality

- History, including partners, and other pertinent information
- Reproductive history (abortion, miscarriages, stillborn, offspring)

Socioeconomic Class

- Current socioeconomic status (SES)
- SES of family of origin
- Changes in socioeconomic class
- Financial health
- Financial history (Great Depression, culture of poverty)

Strengths

- Cultural resilience
- Cultural strengths
- Talents, gifts, special abilities

Stress

- Types of stress (acculturative, racial or ethnic, financial, ecological—inner-city living)
- Life stressors
- Stress management

Trauma

- Abuse (bullying, emotional, domestic, physical, verbal)
- Collective
- Combat trauma
- Cultural or historical
- Individual (crime, accident, insidious, natural catastrophes)

Exhibit 3.1

Multicultural Clinical Assessment Areas (*Continued*)

- Gender (sexual, incest, battered spouse syndrome, forced pros-titution, sexual abduction, trafficking, tortuous inducement of abortion of pregnant imprisoned females)
- Ethnoracial (prejudice, discrimination, microagression, victim-ization, scapegoating, hate crime)
- Political (e.g., refugee trauma, repression, persecution, torture)
- Racial terrorism
- Survivor syndrome

Work and Employment

- Attitude toward work
- Employment and unemployment history
- Impostor syndrome
- Glass ceiling experiences
- Promotions, demotions, etc.

Ethnocultural Heritage

Exploration of clients' ethnocultural heritage elicits ancestry, history, genetics, biology, and sociopolitical legacy. More specifically, clinicians obtain contextual information on clients' maternal and paternal cultures of origin, religions, social class, gender and family roles, languages, and other variables. As you examine your clients' multiple contexts, make sure to consider the larger historical and sociopolitical factors that inform their lives. In addition to eliciting collective narratives, you can assess genera-tional experiences such as disconnection; dislocation; and trauma, includ-ing sociopolitical trauma, such as a group history of slavery, colonization, the Holocaust, and others. Moreover, you can inquire about history of *collective formative events.* These may include natural disasters, political violence, terrorism, and social cataclysms, such as the Great Depression, that tend to lead to an enduring and distinguishing membership affiliation

(Elder, 1979). Such affiliation engenders feelings of shared participation in social experiences that create firm bonds, distinguishing persons who have endured these events from those who have not. For example, a bonding experience for many baby boomers is the Vietnam War. Likewise, clinicians can explore experiences with collective oppression and trauma. For instance, whereas many women feel connected by experiences of sexism, many people of color feel bonded by experiences of racism, and many women of color are "branded" by sexist racism. Moreover, having lived through collective bonding events tends to shape responses to subsequent events. These bonding experiences can lead to sympathetic trauma or feeling secondhand (vicarious) trauma if one witnesses a trauma inflicted upon a person of one's cultural group. To illustrate, many African Americans experienced traumatic responses to the televised incident in which White policemen were beating African American Rodney King (Shorter-Gooden, 1996). Their sympathetic trauma was akin to a realization that "it could happen to me." This type of indirect trauma goes beyond psychological identification and empathy for the pain of others and relates to the fact that one's membership in an ethnic group predisposes him or her to potentially become a victim of a hate crime.

It is important to explore the presence of historical and contemporary cultural trauma. *Cultural trauma* refers to the victimization that individuals and groups may experience because of their culture, including their ethnicity, race, gender, sexual orientation, class, religion, or political ideology, and their interaction with other diversity characteristics. These events can have long-standing effects on individuals and groups. For example, individuals with a history of colonization may experience postcolonization stress disorder (PCSD). PCSD results from a historical and generational accumulation of oppression, the struggle with racism, cultural imperialism, and the imposition of mainstream culture as dominant and superior (Comas-Díaz, 2000; Duran & Duran, 1995). As a form of posttraumatic stress disorder, however, PCSD is an entity unto itself. Contemporary exposure to racism, xenophobia, homophobia, hate crimes, and other forms of oppression causes cultural trauma. Moreover, many individuals experience cultural trauma individually, collectively, vicariously, intergenerationally, or all of these ways. The following vignette illustrates the usefulness of exploring clients' ethnocultural heritage.

An upper-middle-class married woman, Laura sought treatment for anxiety after Sister Mary, her spiritual advisor, suggested psychotherapy to her. Laura's symptoms included sweaty palms, heart palpitations, nervousness, and dizziness during social interactions with her husband's colleagues. As an attorney, Laura did not experience dysfunctional symptoms in her professional role. Her husband, John, was a White philanthropist who could trace his ancestral origins back to the Mayflower. Laura's clinician, Dr. Cross, was a psychologist with cross-cultural experience (he spent a year in Sicily as an American field student) and a White American man of British ancestry. After completing a clinical assessment, Dr. Cross decided to conduct a multicultural assessment to further explore the source of Laura's anxiety. In exploring Laura's ethnocultural heritage, he found out that her mother, Clara, was a Mexican sculptor who grew up in a working class neighborhood in Arizona, where she suffered severe ethnic and gender discrimination. Laura's father, Don, a lawyer who is a White American and whose ancestry is British, met Clara at an art exhibition. In discussing her maternal ethnocultural heritage, Laura realized that she felt like an impostor and harbored fears of being "found out" as half Mexican. Consequently, she was able to identify the dread of being rejected by her husband's social and business circle as the source of her anxiety. Laura was a tall, blonde, fair-skinned woman who many believed "did not look stereotypically Mexican." Even though Laura did not report being the victim of direct ethnic prejudice, her mother's stories about being called a "wetback" (a pejorative term used to designate Mexicans without a legal residence status) were vivid in her mind and in her nightmares. It appeared that Laura was experiencing an intergenerational trauma (Danieli, 1998) arising from her mother's exposure to racism and xenophobia in Arizona. The succession of traumatic events and oppression that members of a cultural group endure, *historical trauma* has intergenerational effects (Evans-Campbell, 2008). Unfortunately, the intergenerational trauma continues to affect subsequent generations because when the cultural trauma is not resolved, it becomes internalized.

Sociopolitical Timelines

To explore the effects of history and cultural trauma on clients, clinicians can chart a sociopolitical timeline. This process helps individuals to connect their history to the present and to envision a future.

You can complement the examination of the effects of sociopolitical and historical factors through the exploration of your client's sociopolitical timeline. A timeline helps to identify your client's personal, family and historical events.

Laura's sociopolitical timeline is as follows:

- April 25, 1846: Mexican American War begins
- January 1848: Peace agreement and Treaty of Guadalupe Hidalgo
- 1950: Clara, Laura's mother is born
- 1955: Clara immigrated to the United States
- 1964: Civil Rights Act
- 1960s: Chicano movement
- 1970s: Women's movement
- 1975: Laura's parents are married
- 1980: Laura is born
- 2008: Barack Obama, the first person of color (mixed race, White and Black African), is elected president of the United States
- April 28, 2010: Arizona anti-immigration law (see Arizona State Senate, 2010)

Biocultural and Ecological Contexts

The meaning of pain and suffering has cross-cultural variations. Consequently, when you delineate your client's ethnocultural heritage, you can explore *biocultural* variables—the physical factors grounded in a cultural context. For a more detailed discussion of ethnopsychopharmacology, or the physiological, ethnic, and gender differences in drug metabolism, see Chapter 7. When you adopt a physical health mode during the first stage of the assessment, you can examine your client's health and illness belief systems. For instance, a belief in mind–body–spirit unity is relevant to an understanding of culture-bound syndromes as coping skills, particularly anger management. To illustrate, *mal de pelaa* among Latinos and *hwa-byung* among Koreans are syndromes related to anger management within a culturally specific context (American Psychiatric Association, 2000). I discuss culture-bound syndromes in Chapter 8.

When you promote health as a holistic construct, you help to cement a multicultural therapeutic alliance. Assessing biological functioning is congruent with culturally diverse clients who are familiar with the U.S. medical or public health model. Moreover, you can explore your clients' biocultural genetic predispositions to illnesses. As an illustration, one in four Ashkenazi Jews carries a genetic predisposition to develop Tay-Sachs disease, Canavan disease, Niemann-Pick disease, Gaucher disease, familial dysautonomia, Bloom syndrome, Fanconi anemia, cystic fibrosis, and mucolipidosis IV (see Jewish Virtual Library, 2011). Likewise, lower rates of Alzheimer's dementia are present in African Americans, Japanese (with autopsy confirmation), and Cree Indians than in White populations (Sakauye, 1996). As a clinical implication of these findings, if a Japanese American presents with Alzheimer's-related symptoms, clinicians may want to explore the existence of other types of disorders, such as multi-infarct dementia.

Exploring a client's biocultural background can provide useful information. For example, Laura reported that her maternal uncle had died of diabetes-related complications. After learning about Laura's maternal Mexican ancestry, Dr. Cross inquired about Laura's propensity to develop diabetes. A physical exam revealed that Laura had a prediabetic condition.

Similarly, clinicians can gather information following a wellness perspective. Many sociocentric individuals view wellness as a balance among the physical, emotional, relational, cognitive, ecological, and spiritual dimensions. Therefore, you can examine clients' lifestyle through questions about nutrition (special foods), physical activity, ability or disability status, use of alternative medicine, intake of vitamins and herbs, relaxation practices, spiritual practices, use or abuse of substances, and others. In addition, you can explore clients' ecological contexts, such as living in the northern latitude and being susceptible to seasonal affective disorder, as well as being exposed to higher than normal lithium soil quantities in the U.S. Southwest. Along these lines, you can examine your clients' environmental circumstances. For example, Caspi, Taylor, Moffitt, and Plomin (2000) found that lower income neighborhoods are associated with children's development of behavioral problems. Living in high-density areas forces inner-city individuals to endorse specific survival adaptations—behaviors that become dysfunctional when living in low-crime areas. Although one's clients may not reside in a lower income neighborhood, they may be vicariously affected by having significant others who do.

Multigenerational Genograms

You can diagram clients' ethnocultural heritage with the use of *multigenerational genograms* (McGoldrick, Gerson, & Petry, 2008; McGoldrick, Gerson, & Shellenberger, 1999). Similar to family trees, genograms present family relationships, issues, and concerns in a multigenerational format. A multigenerational genogram recognizes the centrality of a collective identity, highlighting the connections with intergenerational and historical linkages. It is important to earn a client's trust and credibility before attempting to do a genogram.

When you diagram a genogram, you can use symbols to organize and understand a client's family history and dynamics from a nuclear to an extended genealogical perspective (McGoldrick et al., 1999, 2008). A multigenerational genogram goes back at least three generations and helps you to map a client's patterns and dynamics in a collective context (McGoldrick et al., 1999). See Genopro (n.d.), for basic genogram symbols; see also McGoldrick et al. (1999, 2008).

Cultural Genograms

Genograms are particularly useful when you compare your own geneology with your client's. As a clinical tool, a genogram helps one examine clinician–client similarities and differences. As part of your clinical training or personal therapy, you may have already completed your own genogram. However, when working with multicultural clients, you should diagram your own cultural genogram. Note that clinicians should make sure that they have earned enough cultural credibility before introducing this multicultural tool.

Cultural genograms place individuals within their collective contexts, including but not limited to genealogical, biological, developmental, historical, political, economical, sociological, ethnic, and racial influences (Hardy & Laszloffy, 1995). In short, cultural genograms emphasize the role of context in the lives of individuals. Hardy and Laszloffy (1995) advanced the concept of the cultural genogram as an extended genealogical tool to map contextual relationships among heritage, affiliation, history, collective trauma, ecology, place, community, racial socialization, experiences with oppression, ingroup dynamics, outgroup dynamics, relationship with dominant society, relationship with members of other racial ethnic groups, politics, identity, immigration, translocation, adaptation, acculturation, transculturation, ethnic/racial identity development, and many other contextual factors. In particular, cultural genograms examine the management of cultural differences and similarities. Because of the emphasis on ethnocultural heritage, it is important to go at least five generations back when completing a cultural genogram. In addition to the regular information obtained through a genogram, cultural genograms (Comas-Díaz, 2011b; Hardy & Laszloffy, 1995) chart culture-specific information such as

- activities of daily life;
- birth, marriage, death, and developmental milestone rituals;
- meaning of cultural similarities and difference;
- meaning of leisure;
- ethnocultural heritage;
- cultural translocation;
- cultural adaptation, acculturation, and transculturation;
- dual consciousness, biculturalism, and multiculturalism;
- communication style;
- cultural–racial/ethnic identity development;
- soul wounds;
- historical and contemporary trauma;
- racial socialization;
- gender racial socialization;
- experience with oppression and privilege;
- internalized oppression and privilege;

- orientation to time;
- sense of agency;
- ingroup/outgroup member dynamics;
- relations with dominant society members;
- spirituality and faith;
- geopolitics, ecological influences; and
- psychopolitical influences.

Clinicians should not expect to complete a cultural genogram in a single session. Allow yourself enough time to let clients' cultural genealogical stories emerge. Both an assessment and a treatment instrument, a cultural genogram promotes clients' self-healing because it allows them to reconnect with their cultural heritage. Use your clinical judgment when conducting a cultural genogram with your multicultural clients. Information on cultural genograms is in Hardy and Laszloffy (1995).

Clinicians should complete their own cultural genogram. Figure 3.1 shows an example. The client in this cultural genogram, Marcia, is discussed in Chapter 7.

Journey

As you examine your clients' ethnocultural legacies, you lay down the foundation for unearthing their journey. To elicit such a journey, you can assess your clients' translocations, family sagas, and trauma histories. Psychology of place elucidates the relevance of the journey because one's location affects one's sense of attachment, familiarity, and identity (Fullilove, 1996). In assessing your clients' translocation story you can explore their family, clan, tribe, and when pertinent, national history. Such narrative sharpens the understanding of the role of cultural, historical, and geopolitical contexts on individuals and groups. The family saga includes the ancestral, cultural, and personal stories that reveal the cultural schema. When you elicit the family saga, you explore the circumstances that led your clients or their multigenerational families, or both, through cultural translocation. A *cultural translocation* refers to a geographical, developmental, psychological, socioeconomic, sociopolitical, and historical transition. Although most

Marcia's Cultural Genogram

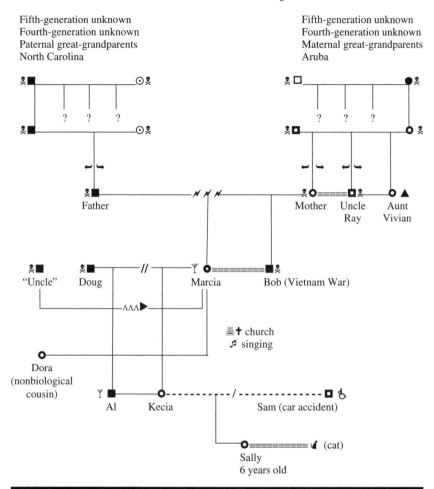

Fifth-generation unknown
Fourth-generation unknown
Paternal great-grandparents
North Carolina

Fifth-generation unknown
Fourth-generation unknown
Maternal great-grandparents
Aruba

Father

Mother   Uncle   Aunt
         Ray   Vivian

"Uncle"   Doug   Marcia   Bob (Vietnam War)

church
singing

Dora
(nonbiological
cousin)   Al   Kecia   Sam (car accident)

Sally
6 years old

Figure 3.1

Example of a cultural genogram. Please note that "Red slaves" are people who were kidnapped from Goajira (Venezuela) and forced into slavery (see Regional Office for Culture in Latin America and the Caribbean, n.d.). The genogram information here follows the genogram formulation by McGoldrick and colleagues (1999, 2008; standard genogram symbols can be viewed at http://courses.wcupa.edu/ttreadwe/courses/02courses/standardsymbols.htm). The essential differences between a genogram and a cultural genogram are that the latter goes back at least five generations, emphasizes ethnoracial identity, acknowledges the sociopolitical and historical contexts, and recognizes sociocentric cultural values. Here, some genogram symbols were modified to reflect racial-ethnic identification and collectivistic cultural values, and "universal" symbols were added to simplify the diagram.   (*continued*)

LEGEND

Cultural symbols
● Marcia
○ Mixed-race woman or girl
■ African American man or boy
◨ Mixed-race man or boy
☐ Venezuelan Red slave
⊙ Native American woman or girl
⚥ Deceased
↤|↦ Person has lived in 2 cultures
♿ Physical disability
▲ Family secret
⌂✝ Christian Church
⚡⚡ Conflict
♪ Music
🍷 Alcohol abuse
🐈 🐕 Pet (cat, dog)
Color (Marcia used the following colors)
○ Orange - self-designation
○ Gold - daughter Kecia
☐ Blue - son Al
○ Pink - granddaughter Sally
⊙ Reddish brown - paternal Cherokee great-grandmother
◨ Red - maternal great-grandfather Red slave Venezuelan
Emotional relationship symbols
_____ Good
____⚡⚡⚡____ Basically good, some powerful arguments
⚡⚡⚡⚡⚡ Conflicted
====== Close or Enmeshed

Relationship

Married

Cohabiting

Common law marriage

Divorced

Separated

Sexual abuse

Figure 3.1 (Continued)

people go through transitions while leaving the parental home, committing to a romantic relationship, getting or changing jobs, becoming parents (or not), getting divorced, coping with losses, and other relational experiences, a *cultural journey* refers to a significant transition that bears profound effects.

A classic example of a cultural journey is immigration. Many culturally diverse individuals have a collective or personal history of immigration, or both. Certainly, immigration entails a cultural adjustment (P. S. Adler, 1975) that can engender a developmental milestone (Akhtar, 1995). Indeed, immigration changes individuals' sense of affiliation because the old ways of connecting may no longer be efficient, requiring the person's creation of new ways of relating (Akhtar, 1995, 1999; Espin, 1987). Imagine visiting a foreign country and not speaking the national language. This temporal experience may be similar to interacting with the nation's superficial culture iceberg. In contrast, a multicultural client's immigration entails coping with the mainstream's deep culture iceberg.

To have a complete picture of a client's journey, you need to explore the type of translocation (voluntary or forced, during war or peace) involved. In addition, you can examine whether your client had a refugee experience (Marsella, Bornemann, & Orley, 1994) or whether the immigration was legal or undocumented. Moreover, you can explore whether the translocation was recent or generations ago. The thoughts and feelings regarding the transition also provide a blueprint for understanding your clients' adaptation to the host environment. For instance, many migrants have a family saga of escaping from starvation or political repression, a search for adventure, or being members of a displaced elite who escaped their country of origin. Yet, for others, as in the case of many African Americans, their family saga translocation is one of historical slavery and oppression. Likewise, you can explore the posttranslocation circumstances. For example, you can examine whether family members stayed together and whether they have a sense of family unity. Moreover, you can inquire about the relationship of the family with their ethnocultural group and examine how they have fared emotionally, socially, and financially.

Clinicians can assist clients' articulation of identity by exploring their family saga. This process promotes healing because cultural, family, ancestral, and personal storytelling are powerful multicultural therapeutic tools (Deveaux, 1995). Moreover, as you go about gathering family and ancestral stories, you can activate and facilitate clients' family saga inquiry when you ask about the perspectives of others. To illustrate, for many indigenous people and people of color, ancestry is important for both individual and collective identity, and because ancestors can represent spiritual guides who aid in times of crises. Similarly, many clients perceive their land or environment as a significant dimension in their life.

Separation from significant others, culture, place, or all three, can lead to disconnection. A particular form of disconnection, *translocation*—moving from one environment (physical, emotional, cultural) to another—involves an implicit dislocation, loss, uprootness, separation, and grief. The psychology of place and displacement advanced by Fullilove (1996) helps to explain the effects of translocation. Fullilove asserted that individuals require a "good enough environment," which they are linked to through attachment, familiarity, and identity. Displacement threatens these psychological processes, resulting in disorientation, cultural fatigue, adjustment, dislocation, and even trauma.

Another area to explore during the saga stage is the presence of historical, cultural, and individual trauma. For example, a significant number of immigrant children relocate without their parents because the adults immigrate first to send money to their families back home (Suárez-Orozco & Suárez-Orozco, 2001). In addition to coping with grief, many immigrant children struggle with feelings of parental abandonment and rejection. Therefore, examining the age and context of immigration is crucial to assessment. For instance, several kinds of immigrants, particularly refugees, may have experienced trauma in the form of political repression and torture; witnessing violence, sexual, and domestic abuse; forced prostitution; and many other types of oppression. Of course, not all trauma stories are related to translocation; nonetheless, these are problems encountered in dislocation. However, I recommend that clinicians use clinical judgment and ascertain the existence of trauma. Although the adaptation to a new environment is mediated by various factors, including the cultural similarities between the original culture and the host culture, many immigrants and culturally diverse people experience a range of trauma-related symptoms. These symptoms may include guilt and survivor's guilt regarding relationships left behind either in their countries of origin or in the ethnic communities. For instance, the development of new relationships in the host country or dominant society at times may be experienced as a betrayal of those who live in their original communities (Espin, 1987).

Regardless of the nature of a client's journey, a cultural translocation evokes a sense of displacement that can result in loss, dislocation, acculturation, and adjustment difficulties. Adjusting to the mainstream society and functioning in two different cultures can be stressful and distressing. Unlike most mainstream clients, culturally diverse individuals' lives tend to have cumulative effects that are shaped by life stressors. For instance, as a regular move may reenact an immigrant's original translocation, it may lead a refugee to relive dislocation related traumatic experiences.

Mapping the Journey: Culturagram

You can map your clients' journey by examining their cultural transitions and identifying the multigenerational family translocations, their interaction with developmental stages, and the family sociocultural evolution in a changing society (Ho, 1987). Moreover, you can uncover the translocation effects at the personal, family, and communal levels. As you collect demographic, psychological, social and cultural data, you assess clients' transitional position and family cultural homeostasis. Examining clients' translocations helps to affirm their ethnic and gender identity through the use of cultural heritage, photographs, folklore, art, literature, and music.

Besides examining the family and individual transition, I suggest that clinicians inquire about other societal and global transitions, such as wars, sociopolitical, and economic events (e.g., the Great Depression, Black Monday, September 11,the election of Barack Obama as the first president of color of the United States) and explore their interaction with clients' lives. A culturagram maps a client's (and his or her family's) journey or cultural translocation (Congress, 1994, 2002). This tool helps clinicians to examine in more detail issues such as reasons for relocation; type and nature of journey (immigration, migration, refugee, international sojourn); age at immigration (younger immigrants tend to adapt faster than older individuals); legal status; languages spoken both at home and in the community; length of time in the community; health beliefs; impact of crisis events; holidays and special events; adherence to cultural, spiritual, and religious organizations; values about education and work; and values regarding family structure, power, hierarchy, rules, subsystems, and boundaries, among others. A main function of the culturagram is to contextualize clients' translocation and illuminate the journey's implications for their lives (Congress, 1994, 2002). As with all multicultural clinical tools, use clinical judgment to infuse a richer interpretation into the culturagram. Figure 3.2 shows an example. The client in this culturagram, Marcia, is discussed in Chapter 7.

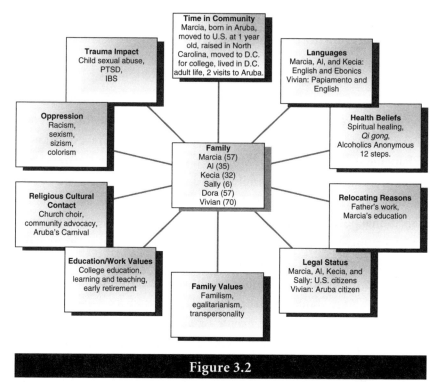

Figure 3.2

Example of a culturagram. PTSD = posttraumatic stress disorder; IBS = irritable bowel syndrome.

As you examine your clients' journey, you can assess their cognitive and emotional perception of their family's cultural identity in the host society since the translocation. For example, you can explore the family's reaction to the journey, including the diverse rates of acculturation of family members. In other words, you explore the place carved by the family after the transition. In addition, you can assess clients' cognitive and emotional perception of their family saga. Certainly, clients' internalization of their cultural journey provides a blueprint of their entry into the world. In other words, a client's adjustment to the journey may be different from that of her or his family members.

Cultural Self-Assessment: Mapping Clinicians' Journeys

Clinicians can use culturagrams to chart their own cultural locations and to examine similarities and differences vis-à-vis their clients' journeys. If you do not have a personal history of immigration, map your ancestors' journey saga. Native Americans (or descendants of the Hispano population that has always lived in what is now the Southwest United States) can map their ancestors' journey of being emigrants in their own land.

Self-Adjustment

A significant cultural translocation such as immigration can act as a psychological individuation (Akthar, 1995). Therefore, you can examine your clients' self-adjustment to their journey. *Self-adjustment* relates to clients' own perceived adaptation to the context, situation, or host culture as individuals and is distinct from their family's adjustment. Regardless of their worldview, culturally diverse people tend to experience an individual adaptation (separate from that of their family, peers, or both) to cultural translocation. For instance, a client may have what Achotegui (2004) termed *Ulysses syndrome,* a type of depression with somatic reactions that some immigrants living away from loved ones may experience as part of their cultural adjustment. For example, Steve, the Filipino man referred to Dr. Perez in Chapter 2, seems to illustrate a case of Ulysses syndrome.

In assessing a client's adaptation, you can review the client's interactions with members of his or her own ethnocultural group, as well as with members of other cultural groups. When you explore the self-adjustment domain, you can examine the client's connection and his or her disconnection story. Exploring the disconnection story could be useful in identifying areas in which the individual feels separate from the family, peers, and perhaps the rest of the world.

You can assess clients' acculturation level, which is part of their self-adjustment. How individuals adapt to cultural translocation can take diverse forms, ranging from assimilation, acculturation, biculturalism, and transculturation.

Brief Clinical Assessment of Acculturation

Freddy Paniagua (1994, p. 11) described the use of a brief acculturation scale that is useful in clinical settings. This acculturation scale—based on the work of Burnam and colleagues (1987); Cuellar, and colleagues (1980); as well as Suinn and his associates, (1987)—can help you to assess three acculturation variables: generation, language, and social activity. According to this scale, Laura's score is consistent with high acculturation.

Acculturative Stress

In assessing a client's acculturation levels, remember to explore his or her acculturative stress. Generational acculturation conflicts frequently involve parents wanting to preserve traditional cultural beliefs in their children and the stress their offspring experience as they are pressured by the dominant culture and thus feel alienated from their parents. Moreover, racial, gender, and personal characteristics intervene in an individual's reaction to acculturative stress. For example, Latinos with the darkest skin tend to be less acculturated than those with lighter skins (L. A. Vázquez, Garcia-Vasquez, Bauman, & Sierra, 1997). Furthermore, acculturative stress can bear intergenerational effects. For example, Laura, the fair-skinned, half-Mexican woman from the clinical vignette in this chapter, experienced intergenerational trauma due to her mother's exposure to racism and xenophobia.

As you explore your clients' self-adjustment, you can assess their strengths. More specifically, you can help clients to analyze the functionality of their behaviors—including coping skills—in diverse contexts. An important aspect of assessing clients' strengths is to pay attention to their adaptive functioning. For example, many individuals develop cultural resilience in connection to their collective survival and as a response to historical and cultural trauma. *Cultural resilience* refers to the host of strengths, values, and practices that promote coping mechanisms and adaptive reactions to traumatic oppression (Elsass, 1992). It fosters resourcefulness, flexibility, and creativity. Along these lines, you can ask clients about their talents, gifts, special abilities, avocations, artistic expressions, and other strengths. Research has documented, for example, that exposure to multicultural experiences is associated with increased creativity (Leung, Maddux, Galinksy, & Chiu, 2008). Moreover, you can use clients' strengths in clinical interventions.

When you explore your clients' self-adjustment, you help them to contrast their cultural identity with that of their family, group, and community. Generational acculturation conflicts between parents and offspring further nurture clients' self-adjustment and cultural identity development. I expand the discussion of the development of cultural identity in Chapter 4.

Relations

The examination of relationships is essential to multicultural assessment because affiliation is at the center of a sociocentric individual's life. A relational perspective grounds clients to place and time. The domain of *relations* refers to all relationships—with family, loved ones, confidants, ancestors, and others. Moreover, the American Indian concept of "all my relations" includes individuals' relationships (or lack of) with spirituality or higher power(s). You may want to include pets (and in some cases, animal spirit guides or totems) among clients' significant others. Indeed, relationships with animals or pets are significant for many people. For clients who experienced cultural translocation, an animal or a pet can be a transitional object from one culture to another. As you examine your client's relationships with their pets, consider what resources are available for pet bereavement.

The relations domain pays special attention to the self and other relationship. When appropriate, and with the client's consent, you can invite family members and significant others to participate in the multicultural assessment.

Multicultural Interpersonal Inventory

To further assess the relationship domain, I suggest that clinicians use a multicultural interpersonal inventory based on interpersonal psychotherapy (Klerman, Weissman, Rounsanville, & Chevron, 1984). This tool examines individuals' relationships in a cultural context. Let us explore Laura's interpersonal inventory.

Dr. Cross: Who or what are you close to?

Laura: Besides my husband, John, there is Nana Blanca, the woman who helped Mami raise me. There's also Sister Mary, my spiritual advisor, and Pat. But I am mostly close to Pat.

Dr. Cross: Who's Pat?

Laura: My best friend. We grew up in the same neighborhood, went to school and college together.

Dr. Cross: When you are with Pat, how do you feel?

Laura: Great. She's my confidant.

Dr. Cross: What do you treasure most in your relationship with Pat?

Laura: Her loyalty. By the way, she gave me Coco.

Dr. Cross: Who's Coco?

Laura: My beautiful poodle.

Dr. Cross: That's nice of Pat. If you could change one thing about your relationship with Pat, what would it be?

Laura: Let me think. This is hard. Maybe that she is too supportive and does not give me criticism.

Dr. Cross: Have you ever asked Pat to give you critical feedback?

Laura: Ah-ha.

Dr. Cross: What happened?

Laura: She couldn't do it.

Dr. Cross: How's that for you?

Laura: Well, she is loyal, that's one of the reasons I love her.

An interpersonal inventory can provide rich clinical information. Clinicians can diagram clients' multicultural interpersonal inventory following a genogram format. Figure 3.3 illustrates Laura's multicultural

Laura's Multicultural Interpersonal Inventory

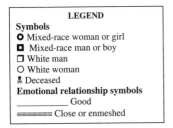

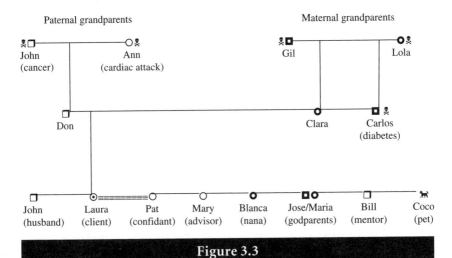

Figure 3.3

This inventory (based on Klerman et al., 1984) was diagrammed following an adaptation of the genogram formulation by McGoldrick and colleagues (1999, 2008). Additionally, the cultural genogram model was used to inform the interpersonal inventory (see Figure 3.1 for an example of a cultural genogram). As a result, some of the genogram's symbols were modified to reflect racial-ethnic identification and collectivistic values and symbols were added to represent specific meanings.

interpersonal inventory. I based this inventory on Klerman et al.'s (1984) interpersonal psychotherapy, McGoldrick et al.'s (1999, 2008) genogram formulation, and Hardy and Laszloffy's (1995) cultural genogram model (see Figure 3.1 for an example of a cultural genogram). I also created some unique genogram symbols to reflect racial–ethnic identification and collectivistic values.

Therapeutic Relationship

Most theoretical and clinical orientations recognize the therapeutic relationship as a core factor in clinical practice. The development of an effective therapeutic relationship is of utmost relevance in becoming a multicultural caring clinician. When you examine your clients' relations, you can obtain a blueprint of their expectations regarding their clinician. Above and beyond obtaining a wealth of information that is crucial for therapeutic interventions, a multicultural assessment frequently opens new channels for the recognition of self in the culturally different other.

Feel free to conduct your own multicultural assessment to determine specific areas of real and or potential overlap with your clients. I discuss the multicultural therapeutic relationship in more detail in Chapter 5.

CONCLUSION

Clinicians are aware of the complexities in human life. Examining the multiple and interactive contexts of individuals' lives is culturally competent clinical care. A multicultural clinical assessment is a process-oriented method of examining people's lives in context. As part of the assessment, clinicians can use multicultural clinical tools such as cultural genograms, sociopolitical timelines, culturagrams, multicultural relationship inventories, and psychospiritual assessments (I discuss this tool in Chapter 4). People's lives evolve out of multiple contexts and circumstances. The multicultural assessment recognizes the complexities in human life.

MULTICULTURAL CLINICAL STRATEGIES

- Use a process-oriented clinical assessment.
- Examine clients' multiple contexts and cohort experiences.
- Conduct a cultural genogram.
- Diagram a culturagram.
- Conduct a multicultural interpersonal inventory.
- Identify clients as partners in assessment and treatment.
- Capitalize on clients' strengths and mitigate weaknesses.
- Complete one's own multicultural assessment and determine specific areas of real or potential overlap with the client's.

4

Cultural Analysis: Looking Through a Multicultural Lens

It is because my roots are so strong that I can fly.

—Mira Nair (2006)

Tom: That Ni—r was a jerk.

Dr. Winston [*Scrutinizes Tom's face and sees a smiling White face*]: What do you mean by the *N* word?

Tom: A spade's a spade.

Dr. Winston: [*Leans back into his chair.*] Can we examine your racist remarks?

Tom: Racist remarks? I've been seeing you for 3 weeks.

Dr. Winston: What do you mean?

Tom: Can't you see I'm mixed race? We Blacks call each other Ni—r.

Would you have approached the encounter differently than Dr. Winston did? If so, how? Did you assume Dr. Winston was White, Asian American, Latino, Native American, or mixed race? Can you name a mixed-race client in your practice and examine how your racial assumptions influenced your clinical work? Are you aware of your clients' cultural identity? Are you aware of your own cultural identity?

The above clinical encounter illustrates the impact of the client's cultural identity on the healing relationship. Dr. Winston hit a cultural iceberg because he was unaware of Tom's mixed racial identity. Instead, he assumed that Tom was White. An awareness of cultural identity models helps to examine the effect of Tom's comment on the clinical relationship. The development of a cultural identity is based on multiple interacting factors, not solely on skin color. For instance, the development of a mixed-race cultural identity is complex. At times, some individuals feel a pressure to identify with one race, at the exclusion of their mixed racial ancestry. At other times, mixed-race individuals may affirm a cultural identity according to the specific context. A mixed-race man, Tom chose to racially identify as Black during the clinical interaction with Dr. Winston. Tom's clinical vignette provides a dramatic example of the role of cultural and racial identity on the therapeutic relationship.

In this chapter, I present the use of cultural analysis in multicultural care. I discuss how this approach can help you see your client's reality through their cultural perspective—in other words, how you can enter the life of your multicultural clients. I compare cultural analysis to looking through a multicultural lens. A cultural analysis can facilitate the understanding of one's clients' culturally situated reality in both assessment and treatment. Following the discussion of cultural analysis, I illustrate its application through the examination of cultural–racial identity. I then discuss three collectivistic values, namely, familism, contextualism, and syncretistic spirituality. Finally, I conclude by considering how cultural analysis can be incorporated into the ethics of clinical practice.

CULTURAL ANALYSIS AND FORMULATION

When you use a cultural analysis in your practice, you become aware of the effects of culture on treatment. A *cultural analysis* is an ethnographic approach that helps to uncover the cultural knowledge clients use to organize their behaviors in order to interpret their experiences (Spradley,

1990). Succinctly put, a cultural analysis helps to guide clinical treatment by offering a multicultural lens. An example of a cultural analysis is the American Psychiatric Association's (1994, 2000) cultural formulation. This clinical tool is a process-oriented assessment and treatment method that helps clinicians place clients' realities in a cultural context. When you apply a cultural formulation, you examine your clients' cultural identity, elicit their cultural explanations for individual illnesses, explore cultural factors related to the psychosocial environment and levels of functioning, identify cultural elements of the clinician–client relationship, and finally, consider the overall cultural assessment for diagnosis and treatment (see Chapter 2 for tools to elicit this information).

When you use a cultural formulation, you examine your client's cultural identity. This concept refers to individuals' self-construal of identity over time and includes ethnicity, race, gender, age, ability or disability, religion and spirituality, acculturation or biculturality, sexual orientation, socioeconomic status, and political orientation, among other variables (P. Weinreich & Saunderson, 2003). Next, you explore clients' explanatory model of their illness (see Chapter 2), including treatment preferences and use of complementary, alternative, and folk medicine. Following the client's explanatory models, you examine the cultural factors related to the psychosocial environment, including stressors, as well as emotional, family, spiritual, and instrumental support. Subsequently, you explore the cultural factors related to the clinician–client relationship. In this component of the cultural formulation, you examine the cultural elements of transference and countertransference, as well as your cultural identity and cultural competence. I discuss these issues in more detail in Chapter 5. The last element of the formulation integrates the cultural data into a process-oriented assessment and treatment plan. In Chapter 3, I illustrate the use of a process-oriented assessment.

Clinicians can examine the components of a cultural formulation through a multicultural care framework as follows:

- cultural identity (cultural identity development theories),
- cultural explanations for individual illnesses (explanatory model of distress),

- cultural factors related to the psychosocial environment and levels of functioning,
- cultural elements of the clinician–client relationship (multicultural therapeutic relationship), and
- overall cultural assessment for diagnosis and treatment (multicultural assessment).

Remember Tom's vignette from the beginning of this chapter? Let us apply a cultural formulation to Tom's clinical presentation.

Presenting Complaint

Tom, a 40-year-old married man, was referred by his internist to a psychologist, due to moderate symptoms of anxiety. A comprehensive physical exam revealed that Tom was in good health.

Cultural Identity

Tom, a mixed-race (White mother and Black father) man who "looks" White, self-identified as Black during a previous session with Dr. Winston. Tom and his wife, Antonia, a former Italian model, have no children. Tom stated that they are devoted to their two Abyssinian cats, Isis and Ramses.

Cultural Explanations for Illness

Tom's responses to the explanatory model of distress revealed that he attributed his symptoms to his line of work. A professional photographer, Tom traveled frequently to shoot fashion shows. He told Dr. Winston that during a business trip to South Africa, a *sangoma* (folk healer) told him that an ex-lover put a *rootwork*, or hex, on him (see Chapter 8, for a discussion of the culture-bound syndrome *rootwork*). According to Tom, the folk healer found the root of the hex and removed it. When Dr. Winston explored Tom's interpretation of the sangoma's diagnosis, he found that Tom agreed with the folk healer's explanation. Tom stated that he believed in the negative effects of jealousy and envy. Tom identified his ex-girlfriend,

Gail, an African American, as the person who placed the hex on him. He explained: "Gail became enraged when I married Antonia."

Cultural Factors Related to the Psychosocial Environment and Levels of Functioning

Tom stated that his mixed-race cultural identity helped him to work in a cosmopolitan professional arena. He identified his ability to relate to models from diverse cultural backgrounds as an asset to his career. However, Tom disclosed that he was using marijuana to cope with his anxiety. He reported that marijuana use was rampant in his line of work. He revealed that he found solace in his spirituality, a mix of Christianity and Afrocentric beliefs. A believer in alternative medicine, Tom mentioned that he used melatonin for jet lag and to modulate his sleep. Moreover, he believed that his cats Isis and Ramses protected him from his ex-girlfriend Gail's future rootwork. The sangoma informed him that when one is the target of a hex, one's pets, particularly cats, mitigate the hex's effect.

Cultural Elements of the Clinician–Client Relationship

Tom seemed to like Dr. Winston and expressed feeling comfortable with him. When Dr. Winston asked him how he felt about their racial and cultural differences, Tom replied, "I trusted you enough to use the *N* word with you." Exploring the incident further, Tom said, "Perhaps I was unconsciously testing you to see if you were racist."

Overall Cultural Assessment for Diagnosis and Treatment

Dr. Winston completed Tom's multicultural assessment. During the completion of his cultural genogram, Tom revealed that his mother died of breast cancer at age 40. In discussing his family's history, Tom agreed with Dr. Winston that his mother's death at age 40 and Tom's recent 40th birthday triggered his anxiety. As a result, Dr. Winston decided to treat Tom with a combined cognitive–behavioral therapy for anxiety and an interpersonal psychotherapy approach. Dr. Winston asked Tom to stop his use of marijuana as a condition for treatment. Tom did not agree to stop using cannabis. Dr. Winston engaged in a collaborative dialogue with Tom. As a result, Tom agreed to reduce his cannabis use.

Even though the cultural formulation is an initial step to promote clinical cultural competence (Lewis-Fernández & Díaz, 2002), unfortunately, this format is limited in its scope. Based on a medical model, the cultural formulation emphasizes individual pathology rather than strengths. However, clinicians can bridge this gap by using a cultural analysis to elicit clients' strengths. In other words, use of a cultural analysis enhances clients' culturally sanctioned coping mechanisms and helps them learn new ways to prevent or manage problems (Tseng, 2001).

Indeed, clinicians can adopt a cultural studies perspective (Sardar & Van Loon, 2004) and integrate findings from disciplines such as the social sciences, humanities, arts, and others into a cultural analysis. For example, Lo and Fung (2003) suggested a cultural analysis based on an object-relation treatment model. These authors emphasized the cultural aspects of self, relationships, and treatment. The self-domain in this analysis relates to cultural influences on the psychological aspects of identity. The relations domain captures the cultural influence on clients' relationships with significant others, groups, spirituality, and environment. Finally, the treatment domain examines healing elements influenced by culture, such as communication, problem–solution models, and the therapeutic relationship. I now discuss cultural identity as an example of a cultural analysis.

CULTURAL IDENTITY

A cultural–racial identity develops out of individuals' interaction with an oppressive society. It involves racial, ethnic, national, gender, religious, sexual orientation identification, or some combination thereof. Many people of color in the United States, particularly African Americans, receive racial socialization as part of their cultural identity development. Racial and ethnic socialization involves the process parents use to transmit to their children messages about the role race and ethnicity play in their lives, including racial dynamics, expectations of discrimination and racism, intergroup relations, and racial and ethnic pride (Hughes et al., 2006). Because all people have a cultural identity, you can explore your client's cultural identity and its interaction with your own.

Cultural Identity Development

The formation of cultural identity can provide a lens into an individual's worldview. Being a member of an oppressed minority group influences the development of identity. For example, visible people of color's identity development involves both personal identity and racial/ethnic group identity. As an illustration, a Latina may have a positive personal identity but harbor a negative orientation toward her ethnic group as a whole (M. Vasquez & Comas-Díaz, 2007).

Cultural identity developmental theories are grounded in the societal power differential between minority and majority group members. In other words, these theories describe relationships among people of color, women, people who are members of a sexual minority group, among other minorities, and the majority group members. For many people of color, the development of their cultural identity depends on their visibility as an ethnic person and racial "other." The degree of minority status is relative to ethnic individuals' skin color, hair texture ("good" versus "bad" hair), eye shape, phenotype, and body type. In other words, ethnic minority status increases as the person's physique deviates from the White American standard. The concept of double consciousness may have historically contributed to the development of ethnic minority identity theories. W. E. B. Du Bois (1903/1996) introduced the term *double consciousness* to designate African Americans' feelings of contradiction between their sociocultural values and the experience of being Black in the United States. Double consciousness encompasses African Americans' conflict between the social ideals of the United States (which they share) and their experience of exclusion and racism, resulting in overlapping forms of identification. Fanon (1967) expanded the double consciousness concept in his psychology of the colonized.

Cultural–racial identity models propose that members of minority groups move through diverse developmental stage processes in terms of valuing their cultural identity. To illustrate, members of minority groups tend to initially value the dominant group and devalue their own group; then they value their own group while devaluing the dominant group; and finally, they evolve to integrate and value both groups (Atkinson, Morten, & Sue, 1998; W. E. Cross, 1991). Specifically, people of color's cultural identity development may include the following stages: (a) *conformity*, in which individuals internalize racism and choose values, lifestyles, and role models from the dominant group; (b) *dissonance*, in which individuals begin to question and suspect the mainstream cultural values; (c) *resistance-immersion*, in which individuals endorse minority-held views and reject the dominant culture's values; (d) *introspection*, in which individuals establish their racial ethnic identity without adhering to all cultural standards, beginning to question how certain values fit with their personal identity; and (e) *synergism*, in which individuals experience a sense of self-fulfillment toward their racial, ethnic, and cultural identity without having to categorically accept their minority group's values. For people of color, an essential milestone in cultural identity development is overcoming internalized racism.

The evolution of a cultural identity is an active, dynamic, and lifelong process. It can change according to context, as well as cycling when the person copes with new challenges and developmental milestones. Cultural identity development involves decision making and context specificity. Tom, the mixed-race client in the vignette at the beginning of this chapter, illustrated this point when he chose to identify as Black.

The cultural identity development of mixed-race individuals follows a different course from that of monoracial individuals (Gillem, Cohn, & Throne, 2001). The process culminates in an integrated mixed-race identity ranging from (a) personal identity, (b) choice of group categorization, (c) enmeshment or denial, (d) appreciation, to (e) integration (Poston, 1990). Root (1990, 1992, 2004) proposed an ecological model of identity development for mixed-race individuals. She acknowledged the creation of identity in a context, including the complex variables such as family, community, generation, geographic region, racial conflict history, gender, and personality. For instance, Root grounded gender in personal identity, identified the role of regional history of race relations, highlighted inter-group and intragroup discrimination as well as internalized racism, and finally, asserted the mediating effect of class on discrimination.

Multicultural identity models influenced the emergence of gay and lesbian identity developmental theories. Gay and lesbian identity stages frequently entail (a) *confusion,* in which individuals question their sexual orientation; (b) *comparison,* in which individuals accept the possibility that they may be members of a sexual minority; (c) *tolerance,* characterized by the person's acceptance that he or she is gay or lesbian; (d) *acceptance,* in which there are increased contacts with other gay men and lesbians; (e) *pride,* in which the person prefers to be a gay man or a lesbian; and finally, (f) *synthesis,* in which the person contacts allies and supportive heterosexuals and is reconciled with his or her own sexual orientation (Cass, 1979).

For most lesbian, gay, bisexual, and transgender (LGBT) individuals, the coming-out process is a significant milestone in their cultural identity development, as well as in their lives. Many have to contend with homophobia (societal and internalized), heterosexism, religious condemnation, and family-of-origin conflicts. Sexual minority clients have recognized that having a clinician who helps them achieve a positive identity is one of the most valuable gains in psychotherapy (Page, 2007). However, for some bisexual individuals, the development of a positive identity may be challenging because of negative stereotypes that result in mistrust, invalidation, and rejection (Rust, 2002). Furthermore, for sexual minorities of color, the cultural identity developmental process may be complicated by the negotiation of diverse, and at times, conflicting, identities (race, ethnic sexual orientation, and religious affiliation). Many of my LGBT clients of color agonize over the coming-out process and have conflict with their White partners over coming out to their families of origin. The American Psychological Association (APA, 2000, 2011) developed its *Guidelines for Psychotherapy With Lesbian, Gay, and Bisexual Clients* to address the areas of (a) attitudes toward homosexuality and bisexuality, (b) relationships and families, (c) issues of diversity, and (d) education.

Other cultural identity development theories include women's feminist identity development. Feminist identity proponents stipulate that females struggle with their reactions to their experiences with sexist discrimination and that this process concludes with the emergence of a feminist identity. A feminist identity develops through the following stages: (a) passive acceptance, (b) revelation, (c) embeddedness–emanation, (d) synthesis, and (e) active commitment (Downing & Roush, 1985).

One does not have to be a person of color to have a cultural identity. Helms (1990a) proposed a White American identity developmental theory in which members are familiar with their Whiteness and journey through several stages, ranging from contact, disintegration, reintegration, pseudoindependence, immersion–emersion, to autonomy. In the contact stage, according to Helms, individuals are oblivious to their own cultural–racial identity. Moreover, they tend to be unaware of the concept of oppression and believe that the system is fair and impartial regarding race and ethnicity. In the disintegration stage, individuals experience disorientation resulting from racial and ethical dilemmas, choosing between their own racial group and principles of humanity. In this stage, White individuals acknowledge that prejudice and discrimination exist. Those individuals in the reintegration tend to blame the victim and believe in reverse discrimination. In the pseudoindependence stage, individuals accept racial and ethnic minority group members at a conceptual level and become interested in understanding differences. The final stage, autonomy, finds White individuals becoming knowledgeable about cultural, racial, and ethnic similarities and differences to accept, respect, and appreciate both minority and majority group members. White American identity development concludes with individuals' understanding the role of White privilege in a dominant European American society.

Immigrant and Crossroads Identity

Globalization, international travel, and the current transnational era facilitate exposure to diverse cultures. This contact can influence how people see themselves and others. Immigrant, international, and transnational individuals may develop a specific cultural identity according to the context they find themselves in. For example, in their study of immigrants' adaptation to a Canadian context, Lalonde, Taylor, and Moghaddam (1992) found that visible immigrants self-identified according to their experiences with discrimination. In other words, visible immigrants, such as Haitians, chose the immigrant identity as a reaction to racial and ethnic discrimination, in contrast to Southeast Indians, whose cultural self-identification was associated with educational level, age at immigration, and Canadian citizenship status, instead of their experience with ethnic discrimination.

Some individuals develop a crossroads identity. Anzaldua (1987) advanced this concept in her discussion of *transfrontera,* or borderlands, reality. According to Anzaldua, individuals dwelling at the border of intersecting cultures develop a *crossroads identity*—a hybrid, flexible, context-specific, and creative sense of self. This survival mechanism (Moya, 2001) allows individuals to enact different identities according to the context they are immersed in. A form of syncretistic consciousness (C. Sandoval, 1998), a crossroads identity fosters individuals' participation in transculturation—the production a new culture out of a cross-cultural encounter (De Granda, 1968). Migrants and immigrant individuals who maintain contact with their country of origin tend to develop this form of identity. For instance, my crossroads identity developed from my transculturation background. This experience began when I was born in Chicago to Puerto Rican migrant parents, moved to Puerto Rico at age 6, and left the island in my early 20s to return to the United States. My interest in traveling continues to nourish my transculturation experience. Likewise, many international clients develop a crossroads identity due their transnational experience and global lifestyle. A crossroads cultural identity is an example of nonstage fluid development models.

In summary, you may want to become familiar with other cultural identity developmental models, including studies on Asian, African American, White, Mexican, Mestizo, Native American, biracial, and multicultural identity models (see D. W. Sue & Sue 2008), in addition to nonstage fluid identity development theories.

Clinical Implications of Cultural Identity

Cultural identity development theories provide a lens for understanding how people of color process and perceive themselves and their circumstances. In other words, the developmental stages affect people's beliefs, emotions, behaviors, attitudes, and interpersonal style (Brewer & Brown, 1998). Moreover, the cultural identity stages reflect how people of color relate to members of the dominant society, as well as to members of their own ethnocultural group, and members of other minority groups. These developmental stages influence how individuals present to treatment and even how they select their clinician. As an example, clients of color whose cultural identity development is at the denial stage may prefer a clinician from the dominant group as opposed to a clinician from their own cultural group. In contrast, clients endorsing a reintegration cultural identity may prefer a clinician from their own ethnic or racial group. Furthermore, clients' cultural identity influences how they define problems and their treatment expectations as well as their expectations from their clinician.

Indeed, the racial identity developmental theories affect how clients of color process, as well as how they present to, treatment and even how they select their practitioner. For example, clients of color in the denial cultural identity phase may use racial projection to work through intrapsychic issues when in therapy with a White clinician. For instance, Holmes (1992) observed that an African American client could experience the clinician's Whiteness as a representation of an idealized, never attained object. As I mentioned previously, a crucial milestone for minorities in their cultural identity development is overcoming internalized oppression. You can help your clients to achieve this goal when you engage in a cultural analysis. This process entails a systemic analysis of the interaction of cultural, historical and sociopolitical factors into your understanding of clients' individual, family, and community contexts.

A cultural analysis helps you to expand your clinical lens because cultural identity theories are limited and merely reflect an aspect of clients' complex behaviors. As discussed earlier, many international and recent immigrants culturally identify with their nationality or country of origin.

Moreover, research findings on clinician and client ethnic racial matching seem complex. For example, the research literature suggests that clients working with clinicians of similar ethnic backgrounds and languages tend to remain in treatment longer than those clients whose practitioners are not ethnically or linguistically matched (S. Sue, 1998). Along these lines, empirical studies revealed that clients in similar clinician–client dyads participate more in their care than do those in race-dissimilar dyads (Cooper-Patrick et al., 1999). However, research results on clinician–client ethnic matching (Karlsson, 2005) are contradictory. Some clients are concerned about confidentiality and tend to prefer a clinician who is not a member of their ethnocultural group. However, clinicians should not get lost in an identity labyrinth; instead, they should use a cultural analysis as a guiding thread. Indeed, research suggests that clients stay longer in treatment when they considered their clinician to be culturally competent, compassionate, and understanding of their sociocentric worldview regardless of ethnocultural match (Knipscheer & Kleber, 2004).

MULTICULTURAL SOCIOCENTRIC WORLDVIEW: RELATIONSHIPS, CONTEXT, AND SPIRIT

APA Multicultural Guideline 1 (APA, 2003) encourages psychologists to understand clients' worldview (see Chapter 1) to appreciate how culture affects clinical practice. To illustrate, if you endorse an individualistic orientation, you may tend to view yourself independently from others. Indeed, your worldview may differ from your socioecentric client, who frequently associates her identity with her relationship with significant others. A cultural analysis helps you to examine the influence of worldviews on clinical process. As you become aware of the differences between your worldview and your client's, you can enhance treatment collaboration.

Next, I discuss three multicultural worldview values. These sociocentric values, or *collectivist* values (see Chapter 1), ground individuals to their relationships with significant others (*familism*), to their context (*contextualism*), and to spirit (*syncretistic spirituality*).

Familism

As I discussed before, sociocentric members tend to endorse connectedness and prefer relational values that emphasize interdependence (Shweder & Bourne, 1982). A classic multicultural value, familism highlights the centrality of family bonds in people's lives. This cultural value is an inclusive concept that extends family relations beyond bloodlines and designates as family members those individuals who have a significant role in the person's life. In addition, familism involves filial responsibility and specific views toward family roles, including older family members and authority figures. Of course, there are differences in how ethnic groups endorse familism. For example, a systematic review of the literature found ethnic differences among African American, Latino, and Chinese American caregivers of dementia patients in the domains of familism, filial responsibility, and views toward older people, among other factors (Nápoles, Chadiha, Eversley, & Moreno-John, 2010).

Kurtz (1992) provided an interesting cross-cultural illustration of familism. He argued that the inclusion of the Hindu child in a group of multiple mothers who share caretaking and have responsibilities and authority to make demands on the child is an example of a non–Western development of self and object relations. According to Kurtz, the psychological impact of such a group (and a child's passage from an exclusive relationship with the birth mother to multiple mothers) often leads to experiences of psychological growth different from "normative" or individualistic Western ones. As an example, some of these individualistic experiences include the separateness from, and unreliability of, the birth mother; the negotiation of the passage from entitled narcissism to healthy self-regard; the development of the Oedipus (or Electra) complex; and gender identification without multiple parental figures. Kurtz emphasized that these normative experiences do not necessarily occur in the Hindu sociocentric society, where the boundaries between self and other, and between nuclear and extended family, differ from those in individualistic societies. Let us consider the role of familism in the following vignette.

Remember Paolo and Karen from Chapter 3? They expressed difficulties in managing the boundaries between the couple and Paolo's family of origin, particularly Karen's relationship with her in-laws—the Verdi clan. From a familism orientation, Paolo perceived Karen as a member of his family of origin. As a sociocentric value, familism endorses helping relatives, including providing financial assistance during crises. Both Paolo and Karen were successful lawyers who enjoyed a comfortable lifestyle. However, whereas Karen's family of origin was middle class, Paolo's family of origin was working class. In fact, Paolo was the only member of his family to complete a graduate degree and to hold a stable job. As a result, money management was a major stress for his family, the Verdi clan. Whenever his siblings were unemployed, Paolo lent them money, free of interest. Although his siblings returned the borrowed money most of the time, Karen (who saw herself as a generous person) expressed discomfort with Paolo's practice of "lending money to relatives." On the contrary, Paolo was "happy to help," because "it was the right thing to do." Whereas Karen interpreted Paolo's behavior as "co-dependent," Paolo saw it as a financial obligation toward his relatives. Needless to say, this cultural difference created marital problems between Paolo and Karen.

Differing views regarding financial resources are a common problem for intercultural couples. Falicov (2001) discussed the cultural meaning of money, highlighting the cultural differences between Roman Catholic, working class Latinos and White, middle class Protestant Anglo Americans. She discussed the differences between sociocentric and individualistic views on financial resources. Falicov identified these differences in terms of obligations toward self or others; religious beliefs; locus of control; spending on gifts; cultural balance of work, leisure, and family; and others. I agree with Falicov's observations because I frequently encounter this issue in my couples therapy practice. For example, I helped Paolo and Karen to negotiate their differences in this area by culturally empathizing with each other. I suggested therapeutic mirroring. Specifically, I used a Buddhist psychology exercise in which each person identified the partner's struggles, challenges, and gifts (Kornfield, 2008). This meditative exercise helped Paolo and Karen to appreciate their differences. In addition, I suggested watching movies depicting sociocentric and individualist cultural values. After Paolo and Karen learned to empathize with each other's perspectives, we worked on a cultural mediation for their differences. Out of this process, Karen proposed that Paolo's lending money be redefined as gifts. This reframing allowed Karen to perceive Paolo's behavior as helping his family devoid of her interpretation about lending money to relatives.

I have noticed young clients who, regardless of their ethnicity, tend to endorse a chosen familism as they behave toward selected individuals outside their nuclear and extended family roles with familism ties. In other words, young individuals exposed to an increasingly multicultural world (with friends of diverse colors) seem to choose a preferred family with concomitant familism conduct. In most cases, their chosen family is their peers.

Cultural Self-Assessment: Familism

Do you have clients who espouse familism? Do you endorse familism? Does your life partner or best friend endorse familism?

Contextualism

Contextualism refers to the importance that people attribute to context. This sociocentric concept relates to the propensity to describe oneself and others using more contextual references and fewer dispositional references (Choi, Nisbett, & Norenzayan, 1999). In brief, persons who contextualize tend to be more context bound, compared with individualistic persons, who are more inclined to guide their behavior by reference to their internal set of independent characteristics (Kühnen, Hannover, & Schubert, 2001). Such a difference in worldview orientation seems to have physical implications, according to Hedden, Ketay, Aron, Markus, and Gabrieli (2008), who found that context-dependent or independent orientation can influence brain functioning. These researchers studied the cultural influences in neural substrates of attentional control using functional magnetic resonance. They assessed performance on simple visual spatial tasks in which participants made absolute judgments (context independent—ignoring visual context) or relative judgments (context dependent—taking visual context into account). They found that activation in frontal and parietal brain regions (associated with attention control) was greater during culturally nonpreferred judgments than during culturally preferred judgments. On the basis of these results, the researchers concluded that there was a difference in the neural substrates of attentional control of individuals who behave in a context-dependent way, compared with participants who behave in a context independent manner.

Regardless of frontal and parietal brain activation, in my experience, many multicultural clients behave according to the specific context. In other words, they behave relative to context. Indeed, individuals who negotiate multiple cultural realities tend to engage in context-relative behaviors. I see context relativity as the ability to shift from context dependence to context independence according to what a specific situation requires. *Context relativity* refers to the experience of living at the border of different cultures and developing what Anzaldua (1987) called a *crossroads identity* (see the section on cultural identity in this chapter). I expand the concept of crossroads identity and call it *multicultural brain*: A multicultural brain involves the capacity to simultaneously hold multiple beliefs, shift from one viewpoint to another, integrate several cultural perspectives, and develop a syncretistic consciousness (Comas-Díaz, 2008). Such a syncretistic consciousness (C. Sandoval, 1998) promotes context specificity, allowing individuals to enact different behaviors and identities according to the context they are immersed in. Moreover, cultural code-switching is prevalent among individuals with a multicultural brain. *Code switching* is a sociolinguistic concept that denotes a facility to switch from formal to informal speech and vice versa (U. Weinreich, 1953). Hong, Morriss, Chiu, and Benet-Martínez (2000) expanded this concept to describe a cultural frame-switching in which multicultural individuals possess more than one cultural meaning system and can shift between these frames in response to cultural cues in the environment. Cultural code-switching is a flexible adaptation to the multiple social realities a person of color encounters (La Fromboise, Trimble, & Mohatt, 1990).

Multicultural individuals who engage in code switching adapt to the majority culture by communicating in a particular way in the dominant society, as opposed to the way they communicate in their ethnocultural community. The use of "Spanglish" is an example of multicultural individuals' code-switching behavior. Consequently, a crossroads identity, or multicultural brain, can be analogous to a bilingual, bicultural mental framework. Notably, research has suggested that bilingual, bicultural individuals may express different aspects of themselves according to the language they speak. To illustrate, Luna, Ringberg, and Peracchio (2008) found that bilingual, bicultural individuals incorporate two cultures, have distinct sets of culture-specific concepts, and develop mental frameworks that activate different aspects of their identities.

Cultural Self-Assessment: Contextualism

Are you context dependent, context independent, or context relative? Are you aware of your clients' orientation to context? Do you engage in cultural code-switching?

Spirit: A Syncretistic Spirituality

In their application of a cultural analysis to clinical practice, Lo and Fung (2003) recommended the study of clients' spiritual orientation. Different from religion, *spirituality* is an overarching concept that emphasizes the transpersonal and transcendental dimensions in life (Walsh, 1999). Spirituality provides a sense of connection to self, others, community, history, and context—an important function in the lives of many people of color. Spirituality is personal construct imbued with cultural meaning that facilitates integration, development, and transformation among ethnic minorities (Ho, 1987). For instance, many people of color, such as African Americans (Boyd-Franklin, 2003; Parks, 2007), Asian Americans (D. W. Sue & Sue, 2008), American Indians or Native Americans (P. G. Allen, 1992), and Latinos (Comas-Díaz, 2006b), recognize the presence of spirit in their life. Indeed, many are keenly aware of their spiritual ancestry and connect it to a collective survival. For example, analysis of clinical interviews revealed that many African American clients make frequent references to spirit and faith during treatment (Cunningham, Foster, & Warner, 2010). Likewise, many Latinos use spiritual language and invocations during interpersonal interactions (Comas-Díaz, 2006b). Moreover, a significant number of Asian Americans observe traditional Eastern philosophical approaches at home, whereas they exhibit a Western cultural practice in the workplace (Tan & Dong, 2000). In fact, many immigrants of color find "home" in the host country through their participation in a religious or spiritual ethnic community. Furthermore, immigrants and people of color use spirituality to cope with cultural adjustment, racism, sexism, elitism, and xenophobia.

Spirituality can act as a collective unconsciousness that links visible people of color who share a history of oppression (Comas-Díaz, in press). Many people of color use spirituality to cope with illness and, thus, tend to view suffering as a vehicle for spiritual transformation (Comas-Díaz, 2006b). They frequently interpret problems and obstacles as trials, where the goal is to fulfill one's life mission. A case in point, spirituality is a coping mechanism that helps people of all colors to mitigate their despair and to make meaning out of adversity (Cervantes & Parham, 2005). As a result, a syncretistic spirituality has evolved among individuals who struggle with soul wounds (Comas-Díaz, in press). Because of their history of slavery, about 85% of African Americans describe themselves as fairly religious or very religious and cite prayer as a most common coping strategy (Satcher, 2001). To empower themselves, many African Americans interact with spiritual forces through worship, visions, dreams, and trance (Wimberly, 1991). Likewise, with its strong Eastern philosophical roots, Asian American spirituality emphasizes consciousness, liberation, and enlightenment (Tan & Dong, 2000). Similarly, many Latinos endorse a syncretism of folk healing beliefs, such as *curanderísmo, Santería, espiritismo,* among others, with Christianity (Comas-Díaz, 2006b). I describe these folk healing systems in Chapter 8.

Spirituality is a way of life among most Native Americans (Weahkee, 2008). Many Native Americans adhere to the spiritual concept of "all my relations" ("we are all related"). They believe that the all-my-relations concept goes beyond family and significant others to include sacred relations with all sentient and nonsentient beings. Individuals who endorse Native American spirituality aspire to individual and collective transformation (Trujillo, 2000). Native American spirituality recognizes the sacredness in daily life. As a vivid example, many people of color acknowledge a metaphysical dimension in life (D. W. Sue & Sue, 2008). The belief in the interconnection of mind, body, spirit, and environment often results in a significant number of multicultural individuals' adherence to transpersonality.

Transpersonality

Most sociocentric individuals accept as true a transpersonal existence alongside the individual, collective, and cosmos level. Likewise, simultaneous body, mind, and polis levels of existence (Kakar, 1982) permeate the spiritual beliefs of many people of color. Historically, many Western clinicians have perceived clients' belief in transpersonality as a sign of deficiency, pathology, or regression. Currently, however, an increasing number of mental health professionals view transpersonality as a process of development (Scotton, 1996). In brief, the belief in transpersonality acknowledges the role of supernatural factors in people's lives (Keller, 2002). Those individuals subscribing to transpersonality endorse a co-agency, one that fosters the interpenetration of cosmic forces into their lives (Comas-Díaz, 2006b). Therefore, *transpersonality* refers to the sharing of a personal sense of mastery with external powers. These external forces can be spiritual, natural, supernatural, or cosmic entities. These entities influence humans through meditation, contemplation, personal reflection, prayer, and other spiritual activities (Cohen, 1998). For example, many people of color believe that they can continue their relationship with the dead through dreams, visions, and other supernatural avenues (Council of National Psychological Associations, 2003). Along these lines, they believe that such relationships influence and guide them. Of course, belief in the existence of spirits is not limited to people of color—many cultures recognize the presence of spirits in human life.

Although the professional literature is beginning to acknowledge the role of spirituality in health and well-being, the relationship between psychology and spirituality is still in its infancy. Regardless of where you are in the psychology–spirituality dialogue, you can foster your cultural competence when you become aware of the role of syncretistic spirituality in your clients' lives. An accessible clinical avenue to this approach is the interpretation of dreams.

Dream Work

Dreams play a major role in the lives of multicultural individuals. Like ancient Egyptians and Greeks, many multicultural persons consider dreams a psychospiritual expression of a supernatural communication. I tend to use a combined Jungian and cultural perspective when interpreting the dreams of multicultural clients. Regardless of your theoretical orientation, you may want to consider adding dream interpretation to your multicultural care practice. Remember to examine your client's cultural context when you interpret dreams. To illustrate, many of my African American clients believe that dreams are a window into the future. Consider Rose, a 50-year-old divorced woman who received a call from Eliza, her best friend and colleague. Rose and Eliza had been best friends since their student years at a historically Black college. During the phone conversation, Eliza related a dream in which Rose had suffered an accident during a business trip. In the dream, Eliza was packing Rose's belongings at the hotel. Eliza interpreted the dream as a warning for Rose to be careful during her next travel. Two weeks later, Rose's sister called Eliza. Crying, she said that Rose had died earlier that day in an airplane accident. She asked Eliza to help her collect Rose's belongings left at a hotel. During our next therapy session, Eliza expressed survivor's guilt. She disclosed that she was supposed to accompany Rose on the business trip, but because of her dream, she decided not to go. My acceptance of Eliza's cultural dream interpretation opened up a space for her to work through her survivor's guilt and grief.

As a general guide, I suggest that clinicians incorporate a Jungian, psychodynamic, and cultural interpretation into dream analysis. When working with dreams, consider culture and personality as interdependent, do not overemphasize pathology, and be actively involved as a participant observer in an interpersonal process (Maduro, 1982). Of course, you can always resort to your clients as experts in the cultural meaning of symbols manifested in their dreams. Discussing and interpreting dreams is a culturally congruent way to invite multicultural clients to disclose their spiritual beliefs.

As a journey toward wholeness, spirituality can expand clients' consciousness, strengthen their internal center, clarify their life purpose, transform their personal demons, and deepen their connection to themselves (Brussat & Brussat, 1996). Moreover, a syncretistic spirituality teaches oppressed individuals that a psychospiritual journey is a transformative development that infuses meaning into life. You can witness your clients' psychospiritual journeys by listening to their sacred stories.

Psychospiritual Journey

You can invite your clients to share their spiritual or existential journey. This exploration depends on several factors, including the client's availability to discuss these issues, the phase of treatment, and the therapeutic relationship. When you elicit clients' sacred stories, remember to listen with cultural respect. A significant number of individuals report communicating with a higher power through paranormal experiences such as visions, hearing voices, or feeling the presence of the spirit. Therefore, sorting out these experiences and distinguishing them from psychotic symptoms is a challenge for any clinician. However, paranormal experiences may be culturally congruent and do not necessarily represent psychopathology (Pierre, 2010). Use clinical judgment to differentiate between a thought disorder with a religious content, and sacred stories depicting a psychospiritual journey. A goal in eliciting sacred stories is to promote clients' empowerment. An important aspect of this process is inquiry about ancestors and spiritual guides (Fleming, 1992).

You can explore your clients' psychospiritual journey using clinical judgment and asking questions (McGoldrick, Gerson, & Petry, 2008; Remen, 1989; Walsh, 2011), such as

- What would you like to tell me about your life?
- Who are you in connection to your ancestors?
- Do you honor your ancestors to maintain their memory alive?
- Why do you think you were born to your parents?
- What life lessons did your parents provide you?
- What insights did your mother's life story offer you?
- What insights did your father's life offer you?
- How do you integrate these insights into your life?
- The fact that you have gone through your current problem, what does that say about you? What does it mean?
- What are your sources of hope?
- What or whom are you calling on for strength?
- What is of ultimate concern to you?
- What is your purpose in life?
- What does life ask of you?
- What aspects of your life are positive and/or satisfactory to you?
- What aspects of your life are negative and/or unsatisfactory to you?
- Do you have an existential life project?
- If so, what is your existential project?
- When do you feel most alive? Less alive?
- What do you consider is your greatest achievement?
- What are your gifts (blessings)?
- What are your burdens?
- If you could change one thing in your life, what would it be?
- What relationships remain unhealed in your life, and how could you begin healing them?
- How satisfied are with your life?
- Have you lived your life with wisdom?
- Do you believe in a higher power, in G–d?
- If yes, what is your relationship with this higher power?
- Have you had spiritual experiences with relatives or significant others who have died?
- Have you had experiences with spirits, ghosts, saints, angels, demons, or other forms of non-incarnated entities?
- Do you have spiritual guides?

- Do you engage in spiritual or psycho spiritual practices (e.g., meditation, rituals, dream-work)?
- Have you had premonitions, visions, prophetic dreams, or second sight?
- Knowing we will all die, what is truly important in life?
- If you were to die tomorrow, what would you regret not having done?
- Do you conceptualize death as a final, transpersonal, or transcendental experience?

Clinical Vignette

At times you can see the surface of a client's spiritual iceberg in his or her story of distress. In responding to these questions, Maya, my client from Chapter 2, disclosed that she believed in karma in her responses to the explanatory model of distress. This revelation provided an opportunity to explore Maya's existential issues through a psychospiritual assessment.

Lillian: Who are you in connection to your ancestors?

Maya: I'm in a long line of service to humanity.

Lillian: Why do you think you were born to your parents?

Maya: To learn life lessons . . . and to teach.

Lillian: What life lessons did your parents provide you?

Maya: They taught me to serve others with humility and compassion.

Lillian: How do you integrate these insights into your life?

Maya: Not sure. I think they made me aware of a conflict between my ego and my service.

Lillian: The fact that you have gone through your current problem, what does that say about you?

Maya: I don't understand.

Lillian: What do you think your problems mean?

Maya: Perhaps that I need to tame my ego.

Lillian: What or whom are you calling on for strength?

Maya: That's easy, I have guidance from my ancestors, and from her.

Lillian: Who?

Maya: She's our mother, the Queen of Heaven. I see her in my dreams.

Lillian: What aspects of your life are positive and/or satisfactory to you?

Maya: I don't see things that way. Aspects are both positive and negative. It all depends on the balance.

Lillian: That's interesting. Perhaps we can discuss this more lately. But for now, when do you feel most alive?

Maya: I feel alive when I'm fulfilling my sacred duty.

Lillian: What are your gifts (blessings)?

Maya: Life's a blessing.

Lillian: What are your burdens?

Maya: Not being able to fulfill my higher purpose.

Lillian: If you could change one thing in your life, what would it be?

Maya: That's why I am here, to work these things out.

Lillian: Do you believe in a higher power, in G–d?

Maya: I told you I believe in Her.

Lillian: Do you have an existential life project?

Maya: I do—it's to reconnect with my true nature.

Lillian: What is your true nature?

Maya: I used to be a Goddess priestess in a previous reincarnation.

Lillian: What is your concept of reincarnation?

Maya: That will take a long time.

Lillian: I'm all ears . . .

Maya: How much time do we have?

Lillian: Oh. [*Checks the clock.*] We may need to wait until the next session.

Maya's vignette illustrates how a psychospiritual assessment can be helpful in multicultural care. Her belief in reincarnation seemed to help her cope with her collective soul wound. Moreover, her affirmation of having been a priestess of the goddess helped to enhance her self-esteem. The assessment of the psychospiritual journey is a fluid process ranging from assessment to treatment. Certainly, you can continue to elicit your clients' responses to these questions through several sessions.

Cultural Self-Assessment: Spirituality

Do you profess spiritual beliefs? Do you engage in spiritual practices? Do you meditate, practice yoga, pray? How do you feel about individuals who endorse religious and spiritual beliefs different from yours? How do you feel about individuals who share your religious and spiritual beliefs? How do you feel about transpersonality? Do you adhere to syncretism? What is your view regarding dreams? Do you interpret your clients' dreams? Have you experienced a psychospiritual journey? Did you complete your own psychospiritual assessment?

INCORPORATING A CULTURAL ANALYSIS INTO ETHICS

As you become a better clinician, you will need to incorporate a cultural analysis into your professional ethics. Just as you critically examine the Western-based treatment paradigm, you need to culturally analyze your ethical behavior with multicultural clients. For example, what would you do if your client invites you to give a lecture at her children's school? Certainly, you would have to adhere to your professional code of ethics. For instance, as a psychologist, I follow the APA Ethics Code (APA, 2010). However, when you see multicultural clients you need to consider the context, use clinical judgment, and exercise cultural sensitivity. Ignoring these issues can lead to cultural malpractice or to overlooking, discounting, and/or neglecting cultural aspects in treating multicultural clients (C. I. Hall, 1997).

Gallardo, Parham, Johnson, and Carter (2009) contended that to avoid cultural malpractice, clinicians need to reconsider their conceptualizations of culture and cultural responsive practice, to struggle with conflicts in mainstream training that may promote culturally incongruent treatments, and to consider the ethical implications of their practices on multicultural clients (Gallardo et al., 2009). Along these lines, Fisher (2009) described multicultural ethical competence as clinicians' responsiveness to clients and awareness of their own boundaries, competences, and obligations. She added that multicultural ethical competence requires flexibility and sensitivity to context, role responsibilities, and stakeholder expectations unique to each clinical encounter. Specifically, Fisher advocated for the application of ethical contextualism to multicultural practice. According to Fisher, *ethical contextualism* assumes that moral principles such as respect for human dignity, justice, and freedom (among others) are universally valued cross-culturally, but the expression of an ethical problem and the correct actions to resolve it can be unique to the cultural context.

Moreover, ethical contextualism calls for clinicians' application of their ethics code as a means of understanding ethical meanings around diverse contexts without prioritizing specific principles or values over the moral frameworks of others (Fisher, 2009). Furthermore, it requires clinicians to look at the extent to which these values and behaviors function to achieve human goods (Fisher, 2009). For the purposes of this chapter, I discuss several examples of ethical areas that require cultural consideration. As illustrations, I select the areas of gift giving, practice in a "small" multicultural community, clinician self-disclosure, extratherapy behavior, and touch.

Gifts

Most clinicians accept nominal gifts and consider the event to be a social convention (Bonitz, 2008). Professional training teaches practitioners to use their clinical judgment and ascertain their client's meaning at gift giving. In other words, does one's client's gift giving represent an acting-out transference, a manifestation of unconscious symbolic desires, such as a need to please the clinician or to become intimate with the clinician outside the therapy (Kritzberg, 1980), an attempt to manipulate, or other types of motivation? In addition to the examination of client's motivation to give a gift, the clinician needs to become aware of the status of his or her therapeutic relationship (Herlihy & Corey, 1997).

Gift giving may acquire different meanings when working with multicultural clients. Certainly, the meaning of gift giving varies according to cultural context. For example, among many Native Americans, gift giving is an important aspect of interpersonal relations. It is a collectivistic dynamic that solidifies gratitude within an interdependent context. Following this reasoning, if an Asian client presents a clinician with a small gift, it may be a cultural expression of gratitude and a response to an act of kindness (S. Sue & Zane, 1987). Likewise, many Latinos may offer a clinician a small gift as a token of their appreciation and as well as an expression of familism or the tendency to value family relations over individual interests. Moreover, some Latinos experience difficulties in receiving or accepting psychological help unless they can give something in return (Simoni & Perez 1995). The Code of Ethics of the American Counseling Association (ACA, 2005) states that some cultures designate gift giving as signs of gratitude and respect. Within this context, the ACA recommends to therapists whose clients offer them gifts to consider the therapeutic relationship, the gifts' monetary value, the client's motivation for giving the gift, and their own motivation for accepting or refusing the gift. In my multicultural practice, I tend to accept nominal gifts from clients when they present me with a memento at the end of treatment. These gifts usually consist of inexpensive souvenirs, books, consumables, flowers, handmade items, and other tokens of appreciation. I accept gifts of modest financial value and decline those of significant monetary value. Within this context, I aim to be culturally sensitive about accepting and declining gifts from clients.

Practicing in a Small Multicultural Community

There are benefits and challenges in delivering clinical services in a small community (Schank, Helbok, Haldeman, & Gallardo, 2010). Regardless of its size, the multicultural community is "small." This means that multicultural individuals may see each other at common locales, such as cultural activities, ethnic grocery stores, religious events, political rallies, and others. Thus, when you work with multicultural clients, you may need to assume that you practice in a small community. For example, many multicultural clients may refer their spouses, relatives, colleagues, friends, and other significant others to their clinician. Of course, you may want to address these requests within your theoretical orientation as well as level of comfort. You may even consider attending to these referrals by working with couples, family, group, network therapy modalities, or a combination of these. Regardless of your decision, remember that these kinds of requests frequently reflect clients' perception of you as a culturally credible clinician.

Activities Outside of Therapy

If your multicultural clients perceive you as a member of their extended family, then you may receive invitations to activities outside of therapy. Most of these invitations will be around significant events or milestones in a client's life. For example, clients may invite their clinicians to weddings, funerals, *quiceañeara* (sweet 15) parties, baptisms, graduations, celebrations of their creative work (e.g., readings of their books, gallery exhibitions of their art), and other significant events. Again, temper your response to these invitations with clinical judgment, professional style, theoretical orientation, and cultural sensitivity. Personally, I tend to decline these invitations in a culturally sensitive manner. To illustrate, my client Luis, a Latino school principal, invited me to speak at his school during a Latino pride month event. I responded that I was honored by his invitation, declined it in a culturally appropriate manner, and offered him the names of colleagues as potential speakers. However, several of my multicultural colleagues may behave in a different manner. If you are presented with these kinds of requests, I suggest that you use your clinical–cultural judgment as well as your personal–professional preference in your analysis on a case-by-case basis.

Clinician Self-Disclosure

Selective self-disclosure is a clinical intervention used by many trauma therapists. These clinicians carefully choose to disclose something about themselves when they believe the disclosure would be therapeutically helpful for their clients (Mandell, 1998). Likewise, feminist clinicians use selective self-disclosure as a modeling and empowerment strategy with their clients. Regardless of your theoretical orientation, clients of color may ask you personal questions, such as, Where are you from? How old are you? Where did you go to school? Are you married? Do you have children? How old are your children? Are you gay or straight? Clients may use these types of questions to contextualize the clinician, check him or her out, and/or cultivate the therapeutic alliance (see a detailed discussion of this issue in Chapter 2). Some of these inquiries may vary according to the ethnic and gender interaction clinician and client match. For example, multicultural heterosexual women tend to ask their female clinicians about marital and motherhood status more than their male clinicians. I use clinical–cultural judgment to carefully select when and what questions I answer. Addressing these issues requires a balanced act of self-disclosure. Certainly, clients can find a lot of their clinicians' personal information by doing an Internet search on the clinician's name.

Touch

Touch is a controversial ethical topic in mental health practice. On the one hand, it can offer healing within a psychotherapeutic context (Durana, 1998); on the other hand, it can provide the potential for harmful effects on, and sexual abuse of, the client (Stake & Oliver, 1991). Certainly, some multicultural individuals have a holistic expectation of treatment, in which touch is an element of healing (Bonitz, 2008). In her review of the literature on touch and psychotherapy, Bonitz (2008) cited clinical examples of cross-cultural variations in the use of touch in psychotherapy. A Latina clinician, according to Bonitz's review, reported that not touching her Latino clients would be culturally incongruent. Following this analysis, many Latinos express affection by kissing and hugging (Falicov, 1998). Some Latino clients may kiss their clinician on the cheek at the beginning of a session (salutation) and at the end of the session (farewell; Comas-Díaz, 2006b). These clients observe gender protocol—usually females initiate the greetings and farewell. Moreover, Bonitz's review revealed that some Europeans (Germans and Swiss) expect to shake hands with their clinician at the beginning and end of each session. I certainly relate to this clinical observation because many of my international clients engage in this greeting and departing practice. As a rule, culture-sensitive touch in psychotherapy is practiced for the client's therapeutic needs—it is not sexual or used to satisfy clinician's needs. As with other aspects of ethics, I suggest that clinicians use clinical judgment combined with a critical analysis and cultural sensitivity. Multicultural clients' holistic expectations are not limited to touch in treatment. In particular, many clients of color expect their healing experience to be anchored in a holistic foundation, as I discuss in Chapter 8.

CONCLUSION

A cultural analysis helps you to frame the clinical formulation in the client's context. When you see through a multicultural lens, you can "enter" the client's reality. Indeed, when you conduct a cultural analysis, you enhance your view of a client's cultural identity and worldview. Many multicultural individuals share a sociocentric worldview infused by relational values, contextualism, and a syncretistic spirituality. When you see your clinical practice through a multicultural lens, you explore the ethnocultural factors in the therapeutic relationship. In addition, multicultural practice requires negotiation of ethical issues within a culturally responsive framework. I discuss the multicultural therapeutic relationship in more detail in the next chapter. Below is a list of key multicultural clinical strategies presented in this chapter.

MULTICULTURAL CLINICAL STRATEGIES

- Use intersectionality to examine the impact of diversity variables on cultural identity.
- Use a cultural analysis in clinical formulation and treatment.
- Identify clients' cultural identity development, as well as one's own.
- Examine clients' adherence to familism.
- For sociocentric individuals, being tolerant of the limitations of others does not always imply poor judgment.
- Bear in mind that spirituality is a central element in the lives of many people of color.
- Consider adopting a cultural interpretation into dream analysis.
- When appropriate, assess the client's psychospiritual journey.
- Consider conducting one's own psychospiritual assessment.
- Exercise ethical contextualism when working with multicultural clients.

5

Multicultural Therapeutic Relationship: Seeing Yourself in the Other

The challenge of being a human being is not only to be oneself,
but to become each one.

—Robert Desnos

Marcia: It was racism! The White woman dissed me. She assumed I was lying about my lost registration form. [*Stares at the Haitian painting, a colorful depiction of women walking on a sunny beach carrying fruit baskets on their heads, hanging on Lillian's office wall.*]

Lillian: How did that make you feel?

Marcia: What do you think? [*Says this in a loud voice and emphasizes "you," as she continues to stare at the picture.*]

Lillian: You mentioned that the woman told you she was assisting the lecturer first, and then you later.

Marcia: Yes, but she needs more therapy than I do. [*Does not move her eyes from the Haitian women's brightly colored clothes in the painting.*] If I was White, she would have registered me before the conference began. [*Keeps* *staring at the Haitian women.*] After I paid $55, the woman made me wait. I missed the first part of the lecture. [*Moves her eyes away from the Haitian women to Lillian's.*] Of course, when she found my name on the list, she was all apologies. She's a racist hypocrite.

Lillian: Are there alternative explanations?

Marcia: [*Eyes return to the painting; there is a long pause.*] Red makes me see blood.

Lillian: You sound angry.

Marcia: Of course I'm angry. It's easy for you to ask about alternative explanations. You're not Black.

How do you feel about this clinical encounter? What issues does the clinician (Lillian) need to deal with? Have you experienced similar situations? How do you handle clients' anger?

Marcia's vignette suggests that racial differences between the clinician and the client can affect the therapeutic relationship. As her clinician, I did not validate Marcia's presentation of an oppressive incident. My behavior resulted in a rupture in the therapeutic relationship.

The multicultural therapeutic encounter reflects the relationship between self and other. Moreover, the multicultural encounter can mirror Robert Desnos's challenge of being human as not only being ourselves but as becoming each other (see the opening quote in this chapter). I devote this chapter to the multicultural therapeutic relationship, an essential agent of change in multicultural care. First, I present the relationship between self and other as a backbone of multicultural care. Next, I discuss the management of the multicultural therapeutic relationship. I conclude the chapter with a presentation of cultural elements of transference and countertransference.

SELF AND OTHER

Research findings document the relevance of the therapeutic relationship in predicting psychotherapeutic change (Marmar, Horowitiz, Weiss, & Marziali, 1986; Norcross, 2002). Certainly, clinicians are aware of the centrality of the healing relationship in treatment. In addition, clinicians are aware that culture mediates the therapeutic relationship. If the healing relationship is the vehicle for therapeutic change, then culture is its steering wheel (Comas-Díaz, 2011a).

Clinical work with multicultural clients tests the therapeutic relationship by providing rewards and challenges. On the one hand, working with multicultural clients can enrich one's life because it offers excitement and a deeper connection. In addition, multicultural encounters provide an opportunity for personal growth (Montuori & Fahim, 2004). On the other hand, developing a therapeutic alliance can be challenging because the multicultural encounter frequently acquires unconscious dimensions. Definitely, the multicultural clinical hour is a fertile ground for projections because each encounter is full of conscious and/or unconscious messages about the client's and the clinician's cultural backgrounds. For these reasons, managing the relationship between self and other is the foundation of multicultural care. As people try to make sense of their social world, they tend to categorize individuals as ingroup or outgroup members. Consequently, membership in one group helps to shape conscious and unconscious perceptions about same group and outside group members (Allport, 1954).

Unfortunately, relating to the cultural other can cause frustration because clinicians often feel more comfortable with clients who are like them. Empirical data seem to substantiate this assertion, as people habitually use themselves as the referent in comparisons with others, judging on how familiar they are (Catrambone, Beike, & Niedenthal, 1996; Hart et al., 2000). Notably, researchers have identified where and when racial similarities and differences matter at a neural level. Scientists recorded activity in the fusiform face area (FFA) of the brain as African Americans or European Americans studied pictures of faces from different races (Golby, Gabrielli, Chiao, & Eberhardt, 2001). Interestingly, the researchers found that the FFA was more active when either group was learning and recognizing faces of their same race. Such biological self-reference appears to aid in the communication of emotions. Notwithstanding the universality of some nonverbal expressions of emotions (Ekman, Sorenson, & Friesen, 1969), Marsh et al. (2003) found cultural differences in the facial expression of emotion through the existence of nonverbal accents—subtle differences in the appearance of facial expressions of emotions. The investigators concluded that because people from their own race and culture look familiar while expressing emotions, they tend to develop favorable attitudes toward members of their own ethnoracial group. Consequently, nonverbal accents may explain attraction to individuals who are familiar (Byrne, 1997), as well as rejection of those who are different, and even the emergence of xenophobia (Warnecke, Masters, & Kempter, 1992). In sum, neurological and cultural findings attest to the tendency to recognize and affiliate with individuals of one's same culture or race, as well as to exclude individuals who are culturally and/or racially different from oneself.

People tend to be unaware of their racial bias. As I mentioned in Chapter 1, research has documented that White individuals who in self-report measures rated themselves as nonprejudiced often had generally negative attitudes toward African Americans (Dovidio & Gaertner, 1998). Known as *aversive racism*, this phenomenon involves dissociation between implicit and explicit stereotyping (Abelson, Dasgupta, Park, & Banji, 1998). Cognitive psychological studies have empirically showed that both liberal and conservative Whites discriminate against African Americans (and most likely against other people of color) in situations that do not implicate racial prejudice as a basis for their actions (Whaley, 1998). If a person is White and grew up as a member of a majority group, he or she may covertly harbor racist attitudes (Brown, 1997) and, thus, exhibit aversive racism. Certainly, clinicians' unexamined aversive racism, unconscious ageism, ethnocentrism, sexism, elitism, xenophobia, homophobia, and heterosexism, among other forms of bias, can profoundly affect the therapeutic relationship.

American Psychological Association (APA) Ethics Code, Principle E (APA, 2010b), Respect for People's Rights and Dignity, asks psychologists to try to eliminate the effects of the above-mentioned biases on their work. Likewise, APA Multicultural Guideline 1 (APA, 2003) encourages psychologists to explore their beliefs, values, and attitudes, including their own preferences toward their ingroup members and attitudes toward outgroup members. The client classifications of (a) young, attractive, verbal, intelligent, and successful (YAVIS) and (b) humble, old, unattractive, nonverbal, and dumb (HOUND; Schofield, 1964) constitute examples of stereotypic outgroup impression in clinical practice. According to this classification, the YAVIS person has been identified as an ideal client for exploratory and problem-solving talk psychotherapy. Conversely, the HOUND person has been perceived as more suitable for nonverbal and supportive psychotherapy. Multicultural people can be misperceived as HOUND clients on the basis of their clinicians' inability to understand them (Comas-Díaz, 2006b). It is interesting to note that another acronymic concept, Western, educated, industrialized, rich, and democratic (WEIRD) cultures (Henrich, Heine, & Norenzayan, 2010), has emerged to counterbalance the HOUND notion. Because psychologists and clinical researchers routinely use WEIRD individuals in their studies, and according to Henrich, Heine, and Norenzayan (2010), such findings do not represent the majority of the global population, they consequently tend to make broad and unsupported claims regarding human behavior.

My clinical practice is composed of WEIRD and minority, immigrant, non-White, ethnic (MINE) clients. Clinicians should examine their own ingroup and outgroup membership classifications or acronyms. However, remember to challenge your categorizations, because impressions are resistant to change once formed (Gilbert, 1998). When you become conscious of your reactions toward culturally different clients, you improve your ability to trust yourself as a healing instrument. For example, a clinician can become aware of the pervasive influence privilege has on the lives of White individuals. To illustrate, ingroup favoritism—with its informal networks that provide contacts, support, mentoring, rewards, and benefits to same group members—tends to exclude people of color in predominantly White work environments (Rhode & Williams, 2007). Consequently, if one is unaware of White ingroup favoritism, he or she may minimize its effects on one's racially different clients (Galinsky & Moskowitz, 2000). Conversely, as you understand the stigmatizing effects of being a member of an oppressed group, you foster your multicultural therapeutic alliance. If you are White, you can examine your internalized privilege through a cultural self-assessment.

WHITE PRIVILEGE: UNPACKING THE INVISIBLE KNAPSACK

A clinician can become aware of White privilege by unpacking what McIntosh (1988) called the "invisible knapsack." McIntosh equated White privilege to an invisible knapsack because unacknowledged systems give social power to White Americans and to men. She provided examples of how structural social privilege favors members of dominant groups as opposed to racial minorities. To illustrate, you unpack the invisible knapsack of White privilege when you realize that you can

1. go shopping alone most of the time, pretty well assured that you will not be followed or harassed;
2. turn on the television or read the front page of the newspaper and see European American people widely represented;
3. count on your skin color not to work against the perception of financial reliability whenever you use checks, credit cards, or cash;
4. be pretty sure of renting or purchasing housing in an area that you can afford and where you would want to live;
5. avoid the need to racially socialize your offspring to be aware for their own daily physical protection;
6. remain unaware of the language and customs of persons of color who constitute the world's majority without feeling any penalty for such oblivion;
7. exist with little fear about the consequences of ignoring the perspectives and powers of people of other races;
8. encounter a person of your own race if you ask to talk to the person in charge;
9. are confident that if a state trooper pulls you over, you haven't been racially profiled (singled out because of your race); and
10. take a job with an affirmative action employer without having your coworkers suspect that you got it because of your race.

Readers can review all of the examples of White privilege at http://seamonkey.ed.asu.edu/~mcisaac/emc598ge/Unpacking.html.

The discussion of White privilege can be clinically useful not only when working with White individuals but also when working with interracial couples and families. Such discussion can even be extremely useful when working with ethnic minority families. For example, when Pilar, a light-skin-colored Latina, realized that she benefited more from White privilege than Eduardo, her darker-skin-colored husband, she stopped accusing him of being oversensitive to "subtle" forms of racism. It is not surprising that Latinos with dark skin encounter more discrimination in school, problems with the police, and difficulties in employment than do their lighter skinned Latino siblings (L. A. Vázquez, Garcia-Vasquez, Bauman, & Sierra, 1997).

MICROAGGRESSIONS: RACISM, SEXISM, HETEROSEXISM, AND XENOPHOBIA

As in the examples of White privilege, racial differences acquire significance in the daily lives of visible people of color. To illustrate, many individuals are exposed to racial *microaggressions,* that is, the assaults that occur on a regular basis solely due to their race and/or ethnicity (Pierce, 1995). Examples of racial microaggressions include being ignored by clerks in favor of White customers, being mistaken as service personnel, being labeled as an "affirmative action person" (i.e., a beneficiary of racial favoritism), being racially profiled, and other indignities. In the vignette at the beginning of this chapter, Marcia experienced the incident with the White clerk as a microaggression ("She's a racist hypocrite"). My question to her—"Are there alternative explanations?"—although intended to foster a cognitive reframing, was racially insensitive and, as a result, threatened our therapeutic alliance.

Incidents of aversive racism tend to be difficult to identify because of their subtle nature. Given the vague nature of Marcia's microaggression experience, perhaps my response reflected the irritating question as to whether the microaggression really happened (Crocker & Major, 1989). As a female clinician of color who has experienced racial microaggressions, I may have defended against vicarious trauma. To examine this issue, I consulted with a colleague and conducted a cultural self-assessment. I realized that I needed to validate Marcia's experience of being a victim of a microaggression and balance this understanding with the need to empower Marcia.

D. W. Sue and colleagues (2007) expanded the microaggression concept to include *microassault,* or the explicit racial derogation through verbal or nonverbal attack (e.g., name calling, avoidant behavior) with the intention to hurt the victim; *microinsult,* or insensitive communications geared to demean a person's cultural heritage and identity; and *micro-invalidation,* or communication that excludes, negates, or nullifies a person's of color's thoughts, feelings, or experiential reality. Microaggressions can result in long-standing effects as they retraumatize individuals' soul wounds. Microaggressions alter victims' sense of trust ("You cannot be trusted"), competence ("You are inferior"), inclusion–exclusion ("You don't belong"), normality ("You are abnormal"), and visibility ("You are all the same"; D. W. Sue et al., 2007).

Members of minority groups are exposed to microaggressions. For example, women and girls may be told that they cannot be presidents of their nation. Gay men and lesbians may be told that they cannot be good parents, or Boy Scouts or Girl Scouts leaders. Moreover, racial micro-aggressions rob people of color of their individuality by putting pressure on them to represent the whole ethnoracial group. Examples of racial, gender, and sexual orientation microaggression include the following:

- attribution of being alien, foreign, undocumented, or all three (see in this chapter the section on ethnocultural transference and counter-transference; Asian Americans, Latinos, and other people phenotypically different from Whites are assumed to be foreign born);
- ascription of intelligence ("You are a credit to your race");
- assumption of inferiority ("You speak with an accent, you are dumb");
- assumption of heterosexuality (e.g., a clinician ignores her client's bisexuality);
- color blindness ("I don't see color, I see people" or "We are all the same under the skin");
- myth of meritocracy (verbal and nonverbal messages conveying that race and ethnicity play a minimal role in success in employment and in life); and
- sexist and heterosexist language (use of *he* when referring to all people, calling an assertive woman a "bitch," using the term *gay* to describe a socially ostracized student). (D. W. Sue & Sue, 2008)

Regrettably, racial microaggressions can also occur in clinical practice. These microaggressions range from the clinician's color blindness, denial, or minimization of individual racism; to believing in the myth of meritocracy; to pathologizing culturally diverse values and styles (D. W. Sue et al., 2007). Lamentably, if a clinician denies, minimizes, defends against, ignores, or has all of these reactions to his or her clients' references to racism, he or she may engage in racial microinvalidation (e.g., when I asked Marcia about alternative explanations to her perception of the White clerk). Most clinicians believe that they are unbiased. Unfortunately, unawareness of one's implicit biases can result in microaggression during the clinical hour. Clinicians should be vigilant against "colorblind" statements such as "We are all human beings," "We are all unique," and others. Although these statements may be intended to provide support, in reality they can result in clients feeling misunderstood, negated, and invalidated (D. W. Sue et. al, 2007). Furthermore, a clinician's use of language can reflect bias, as well as unawareness of the effect of oppression on one's clients. For example, if you use words such as *blind analysis*, you convey insensitivity toward visually impaired individuals and their significant others. Similarly, clinicians should remember to use the terms preferred by the ethnic and racial groups for their self-designation. For example, avoid using the term *Oriental* or *colored* to designate some ethnic minorities (D. W. Sue et al., 2007). For a more comprehensive discussion of how to avoid language bias, see the sixth edition of the *APA Publication Manual* (APA, 2010a).

Clinicians can enhance their understanding of microaggressions when they examine the symbolic representation of the therapeutic relationship in the context of the effects of historical and sociopolitical events on individuals' lives. Indeed, APA Multicultural Guideline 2 (APA, 2003) encourages practitioners to understand the effects of historical and contemporary cultural oppression on individuals and the effects of being minority group members. The heritage of cultural oppression and trauma among most Americans of color includes, among other geopolitical events, the American Indian Holocaust; African American slavery; the forced annexation of Mexican territories; the 1846–1848 Mexican–American War; the colonization of the Philippines, Guam, and Puerto Rico (as a result of the 1898 Spanish–American War); and concentration camps for Japanese Americans. Most of these events are related to the Manifest

Destiny doctrine—the 19th-century imperialistic policy advocating for the expansion of the United States across North America, annexing Texas, Oregon, and California, as well as the nation's extension into the Caribbean (Puerto Rico) and the Pacific (Philippines, Guam). In addition, the proponents of this doctrine used Manifest Destiny as a rationale for appropriating the lands of Native Americans (i.e., Trail of Tears) and other non-European individuals.

Recent historical events, such as the September 11, 2001 attacks, nurtured the current climate of xenophobia, and hate crimes toward many Americans of color on the basis of ethnicity and religion. In addition to Muslim Americans, many Latinos were attacked solely because they physically look Arab (Dudley-Grant, Comas-Díaz, Todd-Bazemore, & Hueston, 2004). In a similar vein, the passage of the 2010 anti-immigration laws in Arizona targeted individuals who "looked Latino," as police were allowed to detain anyone whom they believed may be in the state illegally (Arizona State Senate, 2010).

Unfortunately, reactions to these historical and sociopolitical incidents can find their way into the therapeutic relationship. Consequently, some clients of color develop a historical transference (Duran, 2006) and become overly sensitive to oppressed–oppressor dynamics during the clinical encounter. As a vivid example, John, the African American gay man I introduced in Chapter 2, revealed in a later session that he feared Dr. Cassidy would attempt to "change" his sexual orientation.

The history of cultural oppression can bear a psychological mark—a soul wound—caused by historical trauma, suffering, ungrieved losses, internalized oppression, disconnection from ethnic roots, learned helplessness, and anomie (Duran, 2006). Moreover, the legacy of medical mistreatment against Americans of color, known as *medical apartheid* (Washington, 2007), has aggravated this soul wound. Examples of medical apartheid include the Tuskegee project—in which African American men who had syphilis were given a placebo, whereas White men were treated with penicillin, despite the fact that a cure for syphilis was found during the course of the research (Washington, 2007). In addition, women of color underwent forced sterilizations (Garcia, 1982), and many patients of color experienced psychopharmacological mistreatment (Melfi,

Croghan, Hanna, & Robinson, 2000; Rey, 2006) and other forms of medical malpractice. More recently, Green et al. (2007) presented medical residents with a story depicting White and Black emergency room patients who had symptoms of a heart attack, and asked the physicians if they would prescribe the appropriate medication. The results showed that although medical residents reported no explicit preferences for Black or White patients, their responses to a test measuring their implicit racial preferences revealed that they held more negative perceptions toward Black patients.

As you become aware of the legacy of cultural trauma, you can experience frustration, overwhelming guilt, paralysis, fear of offending again, patronizing, overidentification, and becoming a strident and ineffectual spokesperson, among other types of reactions (Tamasese & Waldegrave, 1994). In extreme cases, clinicians can even develop a hostage countertransference (Kauffman, 1992, as cited in Neumann & Gamble, 1995) because they may feel silenced by a client's reality. Moreover, a client's story can induce a vicarious traumatization that promotes the erosion of the clinician's personal and cultural history (Neumann & Gamble, 1995).

The unawareness of your reactions to clients' historical and contemporary cultural oppression can trigger an empathic break in the therapeutic relationship. To illustrate, I return to the vignette at the beginning of this chapter. As I indicated before, Marcia perceived my inquiry regarding alternative explanations for the White woman's behavior as a racial microinvalidation. Needless to say, a racial microaggression of any type compromises the multicultural therapeutic alliance. My insensitivity regarding Marcia's societal position as a Black woman, the social distance between Blacks and Whites, and her history of personal and collective racial discrimination seemed to test our healing alliance. Indeed, the single most common problem (regardless of social class) underlying psychotherapy with African American women is racism-related distress (Landrine & Klonoff, 1996, 1997). Marcia's reaction was no exception: It reflected the pervasiveness of racism in the lives of many African American women. Moreover, my question about alternative explanations appeared to rekindle Marcia's cultural trauma. Below, I examine Marcia's situation through a cultural oppression lens.

Marcia: Of course I'm angry. It's easy for you to ask about alternative explanations. You're not Black.

Lillian: You're right, I'm not Black. How do you feel about working with a non-Black clinician?

Marcia: Now, I'm not sure. Initially I wanted to see a woman of color.

Lillian: I'm sorry I was insensitive about your experience with the White attendant.

Marcia: You must have some sensitivity—you're not White. [*Continues staring at the picture of the Haitian women in the office.*]

Lillian: Can we talk about your experiences with racism?

Marcia: You really want to hear it?

Lillian: Yes, I really want to hear it.

Marcia: [*Turns her body toward Lillian; there is a long pause before she replies.*] First, you cry.

Lillian: [*Hands Marcia a box of tissues.*]

Perhaps you, as a clinician, have experienced ruptures in the therapeutic alliance as indications of crucial moments in therapy. When you address and effectively work through a rupture, you can strengthen the multicultural therapeutic relationship and even model a constructive way of handling interpersonal conflict. You can facilitate these processes when you examine the power differences between you and your clients.

POWER DIFFERENTIAL ANALYSIS

A *power differential* mediates the relationship between self and other in which the person who is labeled as the "other" is the one with less power. Many multicultural clients experience power differentials with their clinician because of their ethnicity, socioeconomic class, immigration status, acculturation pressures, color, and language, among other differences. The multicultural clinical encounter frequently becomes a fishbowl that magnifies power differences. Likewise, the inherently unequal power dynamics within the client–clinician relationship may reinforce multicultural clients' societal powerlessness. You can learn to engage in a power differential analysis as part of your cultural self-assessment. A power differential analysis is a multicultural tool that helps you to examine the differences between your client's group's social status and yours. Going beyond the power differences inherent in the clinician–client dyad, a power differential analysis helps you learn about your position in relation to societal power, privilege, and oppression (Worell & Remer, 2003). As you compare your privilege and oppression areas with those of your client, you can identify and challenge internalized privilege and oppression. Succinctly put, a power differential analysis helps clinicians to enhance their cultural credibility.

As you conduct power differential analyses, be aware that all people occupy multiple positions, depending on specific contexts. For example, White European American women may have racial privilege but not gender privilege. Similarly, African American men have gender privilege but not racial privilege. Along these lines, location can change areas of power and oppression. As an illustration, while living in New England, my Spanish accent was a source of oppression; conversely, my accent became a privilege when I moved to cosmopolitan, multilingual Washington, DC.

I now analyze the power differential between my client Marcia and me. The areas that Marcia identified as sources of oppression include race and ethnicity (African American), color (dark skin color), gender (woman), gender–race combination (Black woman), body size (50 pounds overweight), mental health (history of family and domestic abuse, posttraumatic stress disorder [PTSD], anxiety, obsessive compulsive traits), history of substance abuse, physical health (diabetes, irritable bowel syndrome [IBS]), socioeconomic class (struggling middle class), employment status (retired government employee), age (Marcia considered her middle age as a negative status), marital status (divorced), family (deceased parents, adult daughter with substance abuse, adult son with manic depression), and interpersonal style ("I have a sharp tongue").

Marcia identified as privilege areas her education (college degree), religion (Methodist), sexual orientation (heterosexual), support system (Dora, her cousin; friends), voice (operatic voice, talented singer, church choir member), lifestyle (commitment to her own healing), intelligence ("My wit cuts both ways, but I'm happy my brain works very well"), spirituality ("I'm blessed; I'm God's child"), and language ("I'm bilingual— Standard English and Black English").

My oppression areas include ethnic minority status (Latina/Puerto Rican), gender (woman), ethnoracial–gender interaction (mixed-race Latina), skin color (non-White, high yellow), speech (Spanish accent in most of the United States), and physical health (repaired cleft palate).

My societal areas of privilege include skin color (high yellow—this characteristic can be both an area of oppression and privilege, depending on the context), age (middle age as a positive status for a female psychotherapist), education (PhD in clinical psychology), employment (full time in private practice), sexual orientation (heterosexual), marital status (married), socioeconomic status (raised working class, currently upper middle class because of educational level), body size (petite, average), language (multilingual), lifestyle (commitment to healing), and spirituality (syncretism).

As is evident in this power differential analysis, even though Marcia and I are both women of color, my client's status as a woman of color is different from mine. To illustrate, body size emerged as a significant issue during the power analysis. Although Marcia had lost 50 pounds in 2 years, she still experienced difficulties with her body image due to sizeism. Her physician (who referred Marcia to me) recommended that Marcia join an online support group for dealing with body image issues. Marcia joined Health at Every Size (the Association of Size Diversity and Health; go to http://www.groups.yahoo.com and search for "ASDAH" for more information), a group for health care practitioners. Moreover, the power analysis revealed how oppressed Marcia felt by the interaction of her race, gender, and body size. In particular, as clinicians, we need to be aware of how the interaction of racism with other types of oppression (sexism, classism, heterosexism, sizeism) affects people of color. As you complete power analyses, you can examine your ability to be vulnerable and powerful in interactions with your clients, and to be able to validate your clients' pain and anger without engaging in defensive, passive, guilt rid-den (Adams, 2000), and/or punitive behaviors. In short, power differential analysis can significantly enhance your cultural competence.

CULTURAL VARIATIONS IN THE CLINICIAN ROLE: HEALER, TEACHER, ELDER, RELATIVE, AND MORE

Do your multicultural clients see your clinician role the same way you do? APA Multicultural Guideline 5 (APA, 2003) encourages practitioners to understand the diverse cultural expectations people may have about the establishment and maintenance of the therapeutic relationship, as well as their expectations of their clinicians. The cultural variations in the clinician role extend beyond traditional clinical expectations (Portela, 1971). Multicultural clients often perceive their clinicians' clinical role, style, and persona through their cultural lens. In other words, they may identify the clinician's helper role as an authority figure, a member of their family, facilitator, mediator (i.e., they may expect the clinician to mediate their family intergenerational difficulties), or all of these roles. For instance, Latinos who endorse familism may relate to you as a member of their extended family. Accordingly, they will ask you personal questions in order to place you within a sociocentric matrix. Because many Latinos do not subscribe to asymmetrical reciprocity, they experience difficulties accepting your help unless they give you something in return (Simoni & Perez 1995). This means that many Latino clients may offer you a small token of their appreciation, demonstrate affection toward you in nonerotic ways, invite you to special family gatherings (Comas-Díaz, 2006b), or all of these. (See my discussion of the ethics of being a multicultural caring clinician in Chapter 4.) Likewise, some Asian clients may see you as a member of their family and expect you to adhere to hierarchical roles with reciprocal obligations (Shon & Ja, 1982). Moreover, when multicultural clients see their clinician as an authority figure, they tend to relate in a deferential, inhibited, ashamed, suspicious, and at times, hostile manner (Sakauye, 1996). As a result, if you subscribe to an egalitarian and nondirective approach, your clinical style may create dissonance with clients who expect you to be hierarchical and directive (Koss-Chioino & Vargas, 1992).

Multicultural clients' expectations are grounded in a sociocentric context. Consequently, these individuals pay inordinate attention to their clinicians' relational style. To illustrate, most American Indians (and other multicultural clients) expect clinicians to be empathic, warm, respectful, connected, and genuine (Trimble, Fleming, Beauvais, & Jumper-Thurman, 1996). Remember that many Latinos may expect you to engage in a *plática*, or the informal small talk that breaks the ice before discussing serious topics. Make sure to exercise your clinical judgment in discerning when plática is a defense, a cultural talk, or an evaluation of your cultural credibility. However, do not overanalyze a cultural practice. Sometimes a cultural cigar is just a cultural cigar. When in doubt, ask. In short, balance your clinical judgment with cultural sensitivity as you assess a client's expectations of your role.

Most collectivistic clients perceive therapy as an education and expect you to be a wise teacher (Yi, 1995). Within this framework, clients may expect you to act as a coach, mentor, guide, facilitator, or all of these roles. Moreover, some multicultural clients may see you as a wise elder. Likewise, they may anticipate that you will act as a philosopher versed in life lessons. The use of folk wisdom expressed through *dichos* (sayings; see Chapter 8 for a detailed explanation), proverbs, stories, fables, and other narratives are common ways of communicating life lessons among many people of color. Furthermore, most sociocentric clients bring their holistic views into your practice. For example, some Asian clients may expect you to be an expert of the heart (Chao, 1992), because they frequently translate emotional problems into an aching heart (Bernstein, Lee, Park, & Jyoung, 2008). Readers can see an illustration of an aching heart in a case vignette I presented in Chapter 2. I introduced Steve, a Filipino man, who was referred by his internist to a psychologist because of symptoms of heart ache without a physical basis. The research findings linking depression with cardiac problems (Penninx et al., 2001) seem consistent with the "aching heart" syndrome. Such holistic expectation recognizes the interconnection of mind with body. Indeed, alternative medicine and indigenous healing acknowledge the interaction of mind (thoughts), heart (emotions), body (somatic symptoms), and energy (spirit). Accordingly, many multicultural clients expect their clinician to recognize the role of balance and harmony in healing. Moreover, some clients may expect their clinician to act as a folk healer because of their familiarity with indigenous healing. To illustrate, some of my clients call me *curandera* (healer–shaman; see Chapter 8 for a description of *curanderismo*) or psychic, simply because they associate my psychotherapist role with the function of a folk healer. These clients may not be that far off, because there are similarities between psychotherapy and folk healing (see Chapter 8 for a discussion on this topic).

Atkinson, Thompson, and Grant (1993) identified diverse intersecting roles that multicultural clients assign to their clinicians. These authors stated that low-acculturated clients expect clinicians to act as advisor, advocate, facilitator of indigenous support systems, or all three roles. They identified clinical strategies such as modeling, selective self-disclosure, and psychoeduction as congruent with the expectations of low-acculturated clients. These authors asserted that more acculturated clients may expect their clinician to behave as a consultant, change agent, counselor, psychotherapist, or all of these roles.

Of course, clients' presenting problem, level of distress, stage of therapy, developmental status, cultural identity, and sociopolitical factors, among other contexts, influence their expectations of treatment and of their clinicians. To examine the interaction of these factors, Comas-Díaz, Geller, Melgoza, and Baker (1982) studied the pretherapy expectations of people of color. The results of our investigation suggested that although clients of color expected to obtain relief from their distress, they also expected to work in therapy to overcome their contribution to their problems. Moreover, clients of color expected clinicians to be active, give advice, teach, and guide them. They believed that psychotherapists would help them to grow emotionally in a process that would at times be painful. In other words, clients of color exhibited psychological mindedness, viewed psychotherapy as a process for working through their problems, and endorsed complex expectations of their clinicians. In summary, multicultural clients expect their clinician to wear several hats and to engage in multiple helping roles such as advisor, advocate, change agent, coach, consultant, counselor, elder, expert of the heart, family member, guide, healer, mentor, philosopher, psychotherapist, role model, teacher, witness, and other roles.

CULTURAL FATIGUE

Clinicians can develop cultural fatigue when they experience difficulties negotiating clients' expectations of the therapeutic relationship. A term coined in the sojourn literature, *cultural fatigue* refers to the exhaustion that results from the adjustments required to function in a different culture (Textor, 1966). These cultural adjustments involve the need to suspend automatic judgments, create new interpretations to seemingly familiar behavior, and develop constant alterations in activity, leaving individuals to feel fatigued (Textor, 1966). Similarly, as you adjust to work with multicultural clients, you may expend an inordinate amount of energy and feel fatigued. I use the term *cultural fatigue* in multicultural care to designate clinicians' exhaustion due to their adjustment to working with culturally different clients. Needless to say, cultural fatigue strains the multicultural therapeutic relationship. As you cope with cultural discord, you can develop frustration, defensiveness, and even hostility toward your clients. In fact, you can experience cultural fatigue in four stages: honeymoon, anxiety, rejection or regression, and adjustment (Textor, 1966). In the honeymoon stage, you may be fascinated by the differences between you and your culturally different clients. When you enter the anxiety stage you may experience frustration, fears, and perhaps impotence due to the weariness of interacting with multicultural clients. During the rejection or regression stage, you may encounter ruptures in the therapeutic alliance and consequently, you may question your cultural competence. In extreme cases, you may even want to retire from your multicultural work. Finally, in the last stage you adjust to the complexities of working with culturally different clients and feel more at home with the development of your cultural competence. Cultural fatigue can trigger missed empathic opportunities. In other words, when clients address cultural issues and clinicians ignore the topic, clinicians miss an empathic opportunity (Suchman, Markakis, Beckman, & Frankel, 1997). In contrast, you earn your multicultural clients' trust when they feel that you empathize with them.

MANAGING THE MULTICULTURAL THERAPEUTIC RELATIONSHIP: CULTURAL EMPATHY

A foundation of any therapeutic relationship is the clinician's ability to empathize with his or her clients. Enhancing empathy with multicultural clients is a fundamental task in one's development as a culturally competent clinician. Within a multicultural context, empathy is a means of connection that involves the recognition of the self in the other. Such recognition is crucial because of people's tendency to like people who remind them of themselves, which can inhibit empathy toward individuals who are different. Cognitive empathy helps you to understand your clients so as to be able to witness their experience (Kleinman, 1988), and affective empathy facilitates the development of a subjective experience of being like the other (Kaplan, 1991). How do you experience being like your culturally different client? This can be particularly challenging when you try to recognize yourself in your client. In the words of Robert Desnos, how do you *become* your culturally different client?

To be multicultural caring, you need to expand your concept of empathy. Consider the following vignette.

Dr. Weinstein was working with Ann, a Cherokee woman. A Jewish Holocaust survivor, Dr. Weinstein felt deep empathy for Ann's history of cultural oppression. During a poignant session when Ann was relating her ancestors' experience with the Trail of Tears, Dr. Weinstein said, "I, too, know what it is like to experience exile." Ann felt hurt by her therapist's statement. She terminated treatment and told the referring physician that Dr. Weinstein did not understand what it is like to be exiled from one's own land and to slowly commit suicide with alcohol. Unfortunately, Dr. Weinstein's comment seemed to equate the Jewish genocide with the

American Indian genocide. Ann felt that Dr. Weinstein's statement invalidated her experience of belonging to a community that internalized cultural oppression as self-destruction. Moreover, Dr. Weinstein's comment appeared to ignore Ann's specific reality of being an American Indian woman who struggles with contemporary racism, neocolonialism, and sexism. As a lesson learned, it is important to recognize that all types of cultural oppression are unique and not interchangeable.

You can enhance your effectiveness with multicultural clients when you commit to develop cultural empathy. Simply put, *cultural empathy* is the ability to place yourself in your client's cultural shoes while acknowledging differences and similarities between the two of you. Indeed, Ridley and Lingle (1996) advanced the concept of cultural empathy as a process of taking the perspective of the other, using a contextual framework as a guide for recognizing cultural differences and similarities between self and other. These authors defined cultural empathy as "clinicians' learned ability to accurately understand the self-experience of multicultural clients informed by clinicians' interpretations of cultural data" (p. 32). Ridley and Lingle proposed a cultural empathy model that integrates a variety of perceptual, cognitive, affective, and communication skills, and places empathetic understanding and cultural responsiveness at the center of healing. Their model suggests a perspective taking—using a cultural framework as a guide for understanding the client from the outside in—as well as the recognition of cultural differences between you and your client. To convey accurate understanding of your clients' reality, you can explore their whole experience using sensitivity and asking clarifying questions.

Cultural empathy is similar to *affective attunement*—the process whereby the clinician focuses on the internal world of the client and in turn, he or she feels understood and connected (Stern, 1985). Cultural empathy requires that you manifest vicarious affect and express genuine concern. In other words, you express vicarious affect when you use similar experiences in your own life to understand your client's reality. Likewise, you show expressive concern as you manifest real concern for your clients' challenges and assert their achievements. A key factor in cultural empathy is to help clients to mitigate the negative effects of cultural disconnection and to reconnect in an empowering manner. When you exhibit cultural empathy, you can help clients to benefit from multicultural experiences without compromising their cultural legacy and identity.

I extend the notion of cultural empathy to include the concept of cultural resonance. Defined as the ability to understand the other through clinical skill, cultural competence, and intuition, *cultural resonance* promotes a convergence between you, the clinician, and your multicultural client (Comas-Díaz, 2006b). Accordingly, you can use yourself as an instrument to culturally empathize with your client. For example, when you rely on body language, vibes, and intuition, you "resonate" with your client. Indeed, intuition is an effective means of communicating and relating during the multicultural encounter. An intuitive empathy relates to a preconscious nonverbal communication through hunches, dreams, imaging, and artistic creations that allows you to pick up your client's feelings of others to be aware of bodily sensations (Becvar, 1997). In my experience, intuition allows you to capture part of your client's unconscious as well as collective unconscious. Because there are no cognitive explanations, the transrational ways of knowing including images, sensations, and feelings, facilitate the deepening of an underlying connection. Similarly, anthropologist Joan Koss-Chioino (2006) identified a type of intuitive relatedness in which intra and interindividual differences converge into one field of feeling. She named this type of relatedness *radical empathy*. Remember to maintain an essential objectivity and avoid overidentification with your client, while sustaining the empathic connection during the transformative energy to bring about deep change (Bolen, 1985). Indeed, the results of a study on clinicians' use of intuition in psychotherapy suggested that you can enhance clinical intuition as you become open to this phenomenon, quiet your mind, develop a sense of feeling of connection with clients, and allow your sensations to surface without engaging in premature analysis (Dodge Rea, 2001). Finally, when you integrate cognitive, affective, cultural, and radical empathy into your multicultural work, you enhance your multicultural clinical presence. A multicultural clinical presence requires a combination of empathy, judgment, intuition, insight, acumen, style, awareness, communication, resonance, and cultural competence.

Awareness of cultural parameters in transference and countertransference is a critical aspect of multicultural clinical presence.

ETHNOCULTURAL TRANSFERENCE AND COUNTERTRANSFERENCE

An African American woman said to her White therapist, "How can I trust you? Although we are both women, you will never be able to feel what I feel." A Latina told her Latino therapist: "It's difficult for me to openly disagree with you. I respect you the same way I respect my father." A White male Vietnam veteran said to his female Chinese American therapist, "You have helped me very much, but I still feel I have to protect myself from you." How do you feel about these clinical interactions? Have you experienced similar clinical situations?

Although all of these clinical exchanges are presented out of their clinical context, they illustrate the complex effects of culture, race, and ethnicity on the therapeutic relationship. Because every therapeutic encounter is replete with conscious or unconscious messages, or both, about culture, clients tend to raise these messages in a subtle, nonsubtle, direct, or nondirect manner. Certainly, racial, gender, and ethnocultural factors are available targets for projection in multicultural clinical practice (E. E. Jones, 1985). Moreover, projections are frequently manifested through the cultural parameters of the therapeutic relationship.

Unfortunately, mainstream clinicians who endorse a culture- and race-neutral position ignore the role of cultural projections in psychotherapy (Pinderhughes, 1989). For example, identification and projection are defense mechanisms relevant to people who have experienced personal or historical colonization, or both. Identification plays an important role in people of African descent, according to Peltzer (1995), because child and adult development depend on changing multilateral identifications during the life span. Peltzer argued that participatory projection provides a defense against powerlessness and frustration. Moreover, he added that participatory projection increases self-esteem because it helps individuals to participate in the omnipotent powers of authority figures. Likewise, oppression engenders intense reactions of rage, shame, and/or guilt on both client and clinician. Minimizing these reactions or solely focusing on the negative aspect of oppression inhibits the exploration of cultural resilience and survival among many multicultural individuals.

Clinicians should be mindful of the projection iceberg floating in multicultural therapeutic waters. Indeed, multicultural practice tends to foster cultural fatigue and cultural disorientation because it provides more opportunities for empathic and dynamic stumbling blocks. Certainly, you can minimize empathic breaks in the healing relationship when you examine the cultural parameters of transference and countertransference. Regardless of your theoretical orientation, it is important to be aware of the cultural parameters of the therapeutic relationship because clients' references to race, ethnicity, or culture frequently signal the development of transference (Varghese, 1983; Zaphiropoulos, 1982).

My partner, Frederick M. Jacobsen, and I identified several types of ethnocultural transference and countertransference within the interethnic and the intraethnic psychotherapeutic dyads (Comas-Díaz & Jacobsen, 1991). We believe that the reactions that occur within the interethnic dyad need to be differentiated from those emerging in the intraethnic therapeutic dyad.

Within the interethnic clinical dyad, some of the transferential reactions include

- overcompliance and friendliness (when there is a societal power differential between you and your client),
- denial (when your client avoids disclosing racial, ethnocultural, gender, and other diversity variables issues),
- mistrust and suspiciousness (when your culturally different client questions whether you can understand him or her), and
- ambivalence (your client may struggle with negative feelings toward you while simultaneously developing an attachment to you).

For example, people of color in an interethnic psychotherapy dyad frequently struggle with negative feelings toward their clinicians while also developing an attachment to them. Moreover, issues of identification and internalization within the interethnic dyad may strengthen the client's ambivalence. Some of the countertransferential reactions within the interethnic clinical dyad include

- denial of cultural differences,
- the clinical anthropologist's syndrome (you may feel excessive curiosity about multicultural clients' ethnocultural backgrounds at the expense of their emotional needs),
- guilt (results from societal and political realities that dictate a lower status for clients of color),
- pity (a form of guilt or an expression of sociopolitical impotence),
- aggression, and
- ambivalence (if you are ambivalent about your own cultural background class, national origin or other diversity variable, be careful of projecting such feelings onto your client).

It is equally important that you examine the ethnocultural projections within the intraethnic clinical dyad. Therefore, within the dyad, the transferential reactions may include

- omniscient and omnipotent clinician (your client may idealize you, aided by the fantasy of the reunion with the perfect parent, promoted by the ethnic similarity),
- traitor (your client exhibits resentment and envy at your success—equated with betrayal and the "selling out" of culture and race),
- autoracist (clients do not want to work with you because you are a member of their own ethnicity, and they project societal negative feelings about your shared ethnic group onto you), and finally,
- ambivalent (your clients may feel comfortable with the shared ethnocultural background, but at the same time fear too much psychological closeness to you).

Within the intraethnic therapeutic dyad, some of the countertransferential reactions are

- overidentification (you may lose your clinical compass if you overidentify with your client),

- "us and them" mentality (shared victimization due to ethnocultural discrimination may contribute to your overidentification, and consequently you risk neglecting your client's intrapsychic issues),
- distancing (you may feel too close to home and engage in distancing as a defense mechanism),
- survivor's guilt (you may feel guilty at having escaped the socioeconomic realities and harsh circumstances of your ethnic community, leaving family and friends behind),
- cultural myopia (you can develop an inability to see clearly because of cultural factors that obscure the therapeutic relationship),
- ambivalence (working through your own cultural ambivalence), and
- anger (being too ethnoculturally close to ethnically similar clients may uncover unresolved emotional issues).

The examination of ethnocultural transference and countertransference advances the psychotherapeutic process. Just as clinicians monitor regular transference and countertransference, it is important to monitor ethnocultural elements of these phenomena. Succinctly put, ethnocultural transference and countertransference play a significant role in the multicultural therapeutic relationship because clinicians and their clients bring their imprinting of ethnic, cultural, and racial experiences into the clinical arena. These reactions offer a blueprint for the relationship between self and other.

CLINICIAN OF COLOR AND WHITE CLIENT DYAD

Although the therapeutic dyad involving a clinician of color and a White client is presently uncommon, the demographic projections suggest that people of color will constitute a significantly greater proportion of the labor force (Toossi, 2006). This movement will include the increased presence of multicultural clinicians. The clinician of color and White client dyad can evoke strong projections because there is a power reversal in this dyad, because historical and racial divisions of labor and class are more consistent with a White clinician and a client of color dyad. However, White clients may see themselves as outsiders, and by working with a clinician of color, they may consciously or unconsciously identify with the alienness of the clinician (Varghese, 1983). These clients may struggle with unresolved marginality issues and the clinician's racial visibility may facilitate the rapid unfolding of their struggle. However, the dynamics present in the clinician of color and White client tend to reflect the racial dynamics of the historical era.

My partner and I (Comas-Díaz & Jacobsen, 1995a) examined the specific ethnocultural transference and countertransference occurring within the clinician of color and the White client dyad. We identified the prevalent transferential reactions within this special dyad as

- cognitive dissonance (manifested through the client's resistance and a greater use of defense mechanisms),
- reaction formation (your clients may perceive you as being immensely superior because of the sociopolitical difficulties ethnic minorities have to overcome),
- tokenism (your client's unconscious antiminority mind-set and aversive racism may lead him or her to question your qualifications and assume that you are a token),
- cultural xenophobia (your clients may question your ability to help them because you are not White),
- fear of abandonment (your clients exhibit a fear that you will abandon them to move "back" to country of origin, or abandon them for clients of color),
- alien transformation anxiety (some White clients get anxious regarding your power over their lives, and may fear that they will "become" a member of your ethnocultural group),
- ethnocultural disinhibition (clients may confront you and act out more than with a White therapist due to the lower societal status assigned to you as a person of color), and
- racial guilt and shame (your clients may exhibit guilt towards you because of their struggle with White privilege).

The ethnocultural countertransferential reactions present in the clinician of color and White client dyad include

- the need to prove competence (if you have a conflicted cultural identity, you may struggle with superiority/inferiority issues and thus may fear being perceived as less competent than a White clinician),
- anger and resentment (while attempting to prove competence, you can become angry and resentful, potentially compromising the therapeutic relationship),
- avoidance (you can engage in emotional inhibition and self-censoring to avoid working with White clients, particularly if you have an expectation of working with clients of color),
- impotence (you may rationalize your client's excessive use of cultural factors as barriers to treatment and hence feel impotent to examine their dynamics),
- guilt (you may experience guilt at not working exclusively with clients of color),
- good enough concerns (you may feel concerned about not being good enough to work with White clients as a response to the client's defensive ethnocultural projections), and
- fear (sociohistorical power differentials between you as a person of color and your White client can disempower you and induce fear).

CONCLUSION

The multicultural therapeutic relationship is a crucial healing factor in multicultural care. You can develop cultural empathy, use power differential analysis, and monitor the cultural aspects of the relationship to help you see yourself in your culturally different client. Be aware of ethnocultural transference and countertransference (in both interethnic and intraethnic clinician–client dyads) because they can serve as catalysts for issues such as trust, anger, intimacy, ambivalence, and acceptance of disparate aspects of the self. Managing the relationship between self and other is a building block in the cultural competence journey. Below is a list of key multicultural clinical strategies presented in this chapter.

MULTICULTURAL CLINICAL STRATEGIES

- Become familiar with clients' collective history of oppression.
- Monitor cultural fatigue.
- Aim to develop cultural empathy.
- Bear in mind that all types of cultural oppression are unique, not interchangeable.
- Think about dealing with hostility, discomfort, and defenses as a result of cultural discord.
- Unpack invisible and unacknowledged areas of privilege.
- Make the invisible visible: Be aware of unintentional micro-aggressions.
- Conduct power differential analyses between the clinician and client.
- Consider an expansion of clinician style.
- Recognize that the multicultural therapeutic relationship has more opportunities for projections based on cultural issues.
- Examine ethnocultural transference and countertransference, both in the interethnic and intraethnic therapeutic dyads.

6

Psychopharmacology and Psychological Testing: Engaging in Cultural Critical Thinking

Your neighbor's vision is as true for him [or her]
as your own vision is true for you.

—Miguel de Unamuno

Connie: My mother is in the hospital.

Dr. Duncan: What happened?

Connie: The doctors said that she tried to commit suicide.

Dr. Duncan: How come? Your mother is a devout Catholic.

Connie: She got sick after she took the medication you prescribed me.

Dr. Duncan: I don't understand, she's not my patient.

Connie: [*Begins to sob.*] The pills helped me so I thought they could help her . . .

How do you feel about this clinical encounter? Do you work with clients who take psychotropic medications? Are your clients satisfied with their psychopharmacological treatment? Do you collaborate with your clients' psychopharmacologist or psychiatrist? Do you know whether your multicultural clients share medications? Do you prescribe psychotropic medications?

Cultural, sociopolitical factors, ethnic traditions, explanatory models, and lifestyle issues affect the psychopharmacological treatment of multicultural individuals. As shown in the above vignette, Connie, a Mexican American woman, shared her psychotropic medication with her mother because "the pills helped [Connie]." This vignette illustrates the cultural practice of sharing medication among many members of collectivistic societies. The cultural value of familism—with its dictum that illness is a family affair—tends to reinforce the sharing of medications with significant others among many Latinos (Jacobsen & Comas-Díaz, 1999). Unfortunately, this scenario is common, and it can have serious and even fatal consequences.

In this chapter, I advocate for clinicians' engagement in cultural critical thinking. When you engage in cultural critical thinking, you use a cultural analysis to examine assumptions, recognize unstated values, identify objectives, evaluate "evidence," conduct interventions, and interpret conclusions. I illustrate the use of cultural critical thinking in two major areas of clinical practice: psychopharmacology and psychological testing. Although these areas can be of tremendous benefit, lamentably, many clinicians working in these fields have neglected the needs of multicultural individuals. Adding a cultural critical thinking component to your work with clients who require psychopharmacology and/or psychological testing increases your cultural competence and clinical effectiveness.

PSYCHOPHARMACOLOGY AND MULTICULTURAL CLIENTS

When multicultural individuals enter the mental health system, many receive poor psychopharmacological treatment. Moreover, prescribers' lack of awareness of racial and ethnic differences in drug metabolism and responses has resulted in psychopharmacological mistreatment of many people of color (Melfi, Croghan, Hanna, & Robinson, 2000). Fortunately, there is a growing awareness that ethnic and cultural influences can alter

PSYCHOPHARMACOLOGY AND PSYCHOLOGICAL TESTING

an individual's responses to medications. Research has shown ethnic differences in the clinical presentation, treatment, clinical response, and outcome of mental illnesses (Chaudhry, Neelam, Duddu, & Husain, 2008). As a mental health clinician, it is essential that you understand how ethnicity and culture affect a client's response to psychotropic medications. Lamentably, clinicians' bias against culturally diverse patients is a factor in the inappropriate prescription of psychoactive medications (Garcia Campayo, 2003). Therefore, to increase your cultural competence, you can learn about the ethnocultural aspects of psychopharmacology. When you introduce a cultural analysis and interpretation into your clinical practice, you recognize the influence of ethnocultural factors on psychopharmacological treatment. Even if you do not have prescribing privileges, a significant number of your clients may need to take psychotropic medications. And of course, if you do prescribe medications, such an assessment is particularly relevant.

Interface of Multiculturalism and Psychopharmacology

A major problem in psychopharmacotherapy is the lack of appropriate representation of culturally diverse individuals in clinical research trials. Regrettably, most drugs have been tested only on White men, and thus such findings are not necessarily generalized to multicultural individuals and women. In other words, psychopharmacological treatment can be inappropriate and, at times, harmful when gender, race, and ethnicity are not taken into consideration. As a case in point, gender matters in the medication and required doses (Hamilton, Jensvold, Rothblum, & Cole, 1995). Unfortunately, the lack of female participation in basic research in animals (i.e., most participating animals are male) and in clinical trials in humans has resulted in a dearth of effective drug treatments for diseases that predominantly affect females, such as chronic pain, depression, and autoimmune problems (Hayden, 2010). Although the U.S. Government Accountability Office reported in 2000 that the participation of women in National Institutes of Health–funded trials had increased, there still is a serious underrepresentation of females in biomedical studies. A common explanation for researchers' preference for studying males is their concern over the potential effect on results of female estrous cycle. Nonetheless, data from tests that measure pain response do not show sex differences between the responses of male and female mice (Mogil & Chanda, 2005). However, multicultural individuals continue to be grossly underrepresented in psychopharmacological research trials, without a reasonable explanation.

Becoming a culturally competent clinician involves being aware of the combined impact of culture, ethnicity, gender, and environment on individuals' response to psychopharmacotherapy. Following this analysis, culture and ethnicity may also influence clients' response rates to psychopharmacological drugs, their reporting of side effects, compliance with the treatment regimen, and their perception of the need for such treatments compared with alternative health beliefs (Rey, 2006). The biology–ethnicity–culture interface challenges you to pay attention to the multiple factors that may influence a client's response to pharmacotherapy.

Certainly, the lack of recognition of ethnocultural differences in drug responses has resulted in the psychopharmacological mistreatment of many people of color (Melfi, Croghan, Hanna, & Robinson, 2000). For example, compared with Whites, many African Americans have been diagnosed with more severe mental health disorders and thus receive comparatively higher drug doses for the same level of symptoms. Indeed, the mental health literature has documented that African Americans with affective disorders are often treated inappropriately with antipsychotic medications (Lawson, 2000; Strickland, Ranganath, & Lin, 1991). Moreover, compared with other ethnic groups, African Americans tend to have more side effects with standard doses of lithium, have significantly faster responses to benzodiazepines, and have higher risks of adverse effects from tricyclic antidepressants (e.g., Elavil; Baker, & Bell, 1999). Of interest, the dosage prescription pattern of antipsychotic medications in most sub-Saharan African countries is lower than the United States' standard prescription guidelines for African Americans (Bakare, 2008).

This series of problems adds to the mistrust that many African Americans have for the medical establishment, particularly regarding the prescription of medications. Tom, the biracial self-identified African American fashion photographer discussed in Chapter 4, provides an illustration of this mistrust. Although Tom used melatonin to treat his sleep problems, his insomnia worsened. Dr. Winston added cognitive behavior therapy to treat Tom's insomnia. The client's symptoms improved some, but unfortunately Tom continued having sleeping problems. At that point, Dr. Winston suggested a psychopharmacological consultation. Tom adamantly refused to follow such recommendation. He told Dr. Winston, "No way—my great uncle was in the Tuskegee medical experiment." (You can find detailed information on the Tuskegee experiment in J. H. Jones, 1981.)

An aggravating factor in psychopharmacotherapy for people of color, besides the history of medical apartheid (Washington, 2007), is ethnic variation in the metabolization of drugs. Individuals' metabolism affects the amount of the drug in the circulation. According to the surgeon general of the United States (Satcher, 2001), a slow rate of metabolism leaves more drug in the circulation, and too much drug in the circulation typically leads to heightened side effects. On the other hand, a high rate of metabolism leaves less drug in blood circulation, reducing its effectiveness.

Multicultural clients' wide racial and ethnic variation in drug metabolism can result in higher amounts of medication in the blood, which causes adverse effects (Satcher, 2001). For example, 33% of African Americans (K. M. Lin, Poland, & Anderson, 1995) and 37% of Asians (M. Chen, 2006; K.-L. Lin & Cheung, 1999) are slow metabolizers of several antipsychotic medications and antidepressants, such as tricyclic and selective serotonin reuptake inhibitors. Consequently, these clients may require different doses of psychotropics compared with their White counterparts. Consequently, because of the differences between Asians and non-Asians in the metabolization of drugs, several psychopharmacology experts have documented the need to start Asian American clients with half of the standard dosage of all psychotropic medications (K.-L. Lin & Cheung, 1999; Pi & Gray, 2000). This prescription practice is known as the "start low and go slow" norm with multicultural clients. Along these lines, African American clients have been overmedicated with antipsychotic drugs. The combination of slow metabolism and overmedication of antipsychotic medications in African Americans can yield very painful extrapyramidal side effects (Lawson, 1996; Strickland, Ranganeth, & Lin, 1991).

Latinos are a widely diverse group. However, like other clients of color, Latinos have been treated inappropriately with psychopharmacology, partly because of their variable rate of drug metabolization (Jacobsen & Comas-Díaz, 1999; Lam, Castro, & Dunn, 1991; Mendoza & Smith, 2000). As an example, Latinos tend to respond better to lower doses of risperidone (Mendoza & Smith, 2000). In addition, they tend to have side effects with even half the doses of tricyclic antidepressants prescribed for European Americans (Mendoza & Smith, 2000). To add complexity to this picture, prescription practices in Latin America vary from those in the United States. For instance, psychopharmacologists in Latin America frequently prescribe lower doses of medication than do their counterparts in the United States (Mendoza & Smith, 2000). Moreover, pharmacists in Latin America can prescribe psychotropic medications (Jacobsen & Comas-Díaz, 1999). Although this practice expands the freedom of choice for Latinos, it allows them to obtain psychotropics from Latin America without a prescription from their U.S. treating clinician.

A number of ethnically specific variations affect the pharmacokinetics and dynamics of psychotropic drugs. The nongenetic, ethnic-based variables that potentially influence clients' responses to psychopharmacotherapy include culture, diet, lifestyle issues, perceptions, and attitudes. As a result, the cultural, ethnic, and environmental contexts of psychopharmacology need to be considered in the prescription of psychotropic medications to multicultural clients.

Ethnopsychopharmacology

Psychopharmacology's cultural insensitivity and lack of ethnocultural specificity gave birth to *ethnopsychopharmacology:* the study of the effects of psychoactive drugs on culturally and ethnically diverse patients. This emerging field is influencing clinical practice (Ng, Lin, Singh, & Chiu, 2008). Succinctly put, ethnopsychopharmacology studies cultural variations and biological differences that influence the effectiveness of psychopharmacotherapies. The ethnic and racial variations and differences are both genetic and psychocultural. The factors that affect these variations include individuals' differences in drug metabolism, enzymatic characteristics, lifestyle, diet, medication adherence, placebo effect, and concurrent use of mainstream and alternative healing methods (K.M. Lin, Anderson, & Poland, 1995).

Biological differences interact with cultural, environmental, and socio-economic factors, particularly among multicultural clients. Ethnopsycho-pharmacologists aim to prescribe psychotropic drugs within their clients' ethnic, gender, age, body size, and sociocultural contexts. Although ethno-psychopharmacologists acknowledge the significant racial mix among individuals, for pragmatic reasons, they tend to divide racial populations on the basis of genetic differences. In other words, time separation in evolutionary trends in Africans, Asians, and Caucasians is a possible explanation for the observed racial variation in activities of cytochrome P 450 (CYP; Bakare, 2008). The CYP enzyme system is the main pathway of drug metabolism, and this enzyme system is responsible for the metabolism of most psychopharmacological agents (Smith & Mendoza, 1996). Thus, ethnic differences in drug metabolism appear to be related to polymorphic variation of the same enzyme, attributable to evolutionary pressures on the CYP system. These genetic variations alter the activity of several drug-metabolizing enzymes. Multicultural clients' inactivation or reduction in activity in the enzymes can result in higher amounts of medication in the blood, causing side effects (Satcher, 2001). In sum, the differences in the genetic structure of drug-metabolizing enzymes can explain most of the ethnic variations in psychopharmacological responses (Ruiz, 2000). Nonetheless, the drug metabolism story seems to be complex. For example, Latinos in the United States are a mixed racial and genetic group (indigenous, African, and Spaniard). Of interest, about 5% of Spaniards possess two or more copies of the P450 2D6 enzyme, and as a result, they metabolize some commonly prescribed psychotropics, such as Prozac, Paxil, tricyclic antidepressants, and most antipsychotics, at such a rapid pace that it can be difficult to reach therapeutic blood levels (Agúndez, Ledesma, Ladero, & Benítez, 1995). Lam et al. (1991) reported that compared with other ethnicities, Mexican Americans have faster 2D6 metabolism in addition to lower numbers of slow metabolizers. These findings suggest that whenever possible, clinicians should identify multicultural clients' specific ethnicities when exploring their medication regimen.

Other biological factors affecting psychopharmacological treatment of people of color include body size and composition. These factors often vary across ethnic groups, and therefore the volume of distribution of drugs can vary, particularly with drugs that are absorbed by fatty tissue (Ruiz, 2000). Small but crucial genetic differences can also affect how a person of color's body reacts to the often-substituted generic forms of prescription drugs. Many generic brands have "fillers," such as lactose, that can change the effectiveness of the medication for African Americans and Latinos who tend to be lactose intolerant (Campinha-Bacote, 2007). (I am well aware of this issue because my own lactose intolerance prevents me from taking pain medication that contains lactose fillers.) In addition, culturally informed behaviors, such as diet, response to placebo, health beliefs, and lifestyle choices, also influence clients' drug metabolization (K.-L. Lin, Anderson, & Poland, 1995).

Sociocultural Factors

As I have discussed previously, help-seeking behavior and adherence to treatment are encased in a cultural context. To illustrate, many multicultural clients enter the mental health system through a referral from their primary physicians. This referral source may shape their expectations toward a medical orientation and receiving medication. Therefore, it is essential that you examine the meaning your clients attribute to medication. For instance, the mind–body orientation of many multicultural individuals tends to influence their expectations regarding psychopharmacotherapy. Some clients may expect to be prescribed drugs or other biological treatment because they believe their emotional status affects their physical functioning and vice versa. For example, Ethiopians and Eritreans place faith in medications, and if their physicians do not prescribe drugs these patients tend to feel dissatisfied and terminate treatment.

Similarly, when Latinos are prescribed medications, many tend to expect rapid relief from their symptoms. Unfortunately, because several psychotropic medications do not have an immediate effect, these clients' perception of a lengthy delay in improvement often leads them to discontinue treatment (Jacobsen & Comas-Díaz, 1999).

Culture shapes how people interact with medications. For example, Asian and Asian American clients often use complementary and alternative medicine (CAM), such as herbal remedies, with psychotropic medication (K.-L. Lin & Cheung, 1999; Pi & Gray, 2000; Ruiz, 2000). Although the use of herbal remedies may be harmful, some ethnic groups find it to be helpful. For instance, many Latinos have historically used herbal remedies, such as St. John's wort, to treat emotional distress (López-Muñoz, Garcia-Garcia & Alamo, 2007). However, multicultural clients' combined use of psychopharmacotherapy and CAM can be harmful because of the potential interaction between CAM and psychotropic medication. For example, chamomile (*manzanilla*) tea, a common Latino remedies for insomnia, can interact with sedatives and statins and can have a side effect of allergic anaphylactic reactions (Ortiz, Shields, Clauson, & Clay, 2007).

As a clinician, you may want to keep an open mind with regard to clients' CAM use. Consider Aimee's experience. A 40-year-old Vietnamese-French woman, Aimee worked as an economist in an international organization. She saw Dr. Carr, a psychiatrist who is a White American of Scottish ancestry, for depression. Dr. Carr prescribed Wellbutrin. When he asked Aimee about her CAM use, she replied that she was taking the over-the-counter dietary supplement S-adenosylmethionine (SAM-e) for her depression. Dr. Carr questioned Aimee's use of SAM-e. In response, she shared with Dr. Carr data supporting the effectiveness of a combined use of antidepressant with SAM-e (Papakostas, Mischoulon, Shyu, Alpert, & Fava, 2010).

The consumption of herbal remedies among some multicultural clients may be related to the hot and cold theory of illness and healing. This theory originates from Hippocrates' humoral theory of illness, in which the body's four humors, namely, blood, phlegm, yellow bile, and black bile, are classified according to their physical properties as hot, cold, moist (wet), or dry (Harwood, 1971), respectively. Interestingly, within the Asian perspective of the hot and cold theory, yin is cold and yang is hot. The humoral theory proposes that illness occurs when the humors become imbalanced, and consequently treatment targets the restoration of balance. Health is restored by taking a cold medication for a hot illness, and vice versa (Harwood, 1971). Thus, if psychopharmacologists prescribe a hot drug for a hot condition, the patient may be noncompliant. For example, some Latinos identify *cólera* (rage), thick blood, *susto* (a Latino culture-bound syndrome in which fear predominates—see Chapter 8), and nervousness as hot illnesses. Therefore, if a client believes that her medication for her "nerves" is a hot substance, she will not take the psychotropic pill. Instead, she may take cold remedies such as linden (*tila*), lemon juice, passion flower (*pasionara*) tea, or *sapodilla* (*zapote blanco*). It is not surprising that because of self-prescription practices and the use of alternative medicine, many Latinos appear to be noncompliant with psychopharmacological treatment (Comas-Díaz & Jacobsen, 1995b). Following this analysis, research has documented that African Americans and monolingual Latino patients have lower medication adherence rates than their White counterparts (Díaz, Shields, Clauson, & Clay, 2005).

Clinical Implications

You may want to explore your multicultural clients' experiences with medication when they are prescribed psychopharmacotherapy. For example, you can ask the following questions:

- How do you feel about taking medication?
- How do you feel about taking this particular psychotropic medication?
- What do you expect from the medication?
- How do you feel about the medication doses?
- Are you aware of any restrictions, such as avoiding excessive sun, foods (e.g., cheese), dietary supplements, or others while taking the medication?
- What do you expect from the prescribing clinician?
- What do you expect from me [in case you are not the prescribing clinician]?
- Do you get the medication in the United States, in another country, or both?
- Do you take the medication as prescribed?
- If you stop talking the medication, do you inform your prescribing clinician?
- Do you share your medication with others?

- Do you take medication prescribed to others but not prescribed to you?
- Do you use alternative or complementary medicines such as herbal remedies and others, with your psychotropic medication?

Your clients' responses may help you to engage in psychoeducation around their use of medication. Needless to say, clinicians should combine clinical judgment with cultural critical thinking when exploring these areas. You exercise your cultural critical thinking when you consider the following suggestions (Comas-Díaz & Jacobsen, 1999; K. M. Lin, Smith, & Ortiz, 2001; Pi & Gray, 2000):

- Examine the cultural meaning medication has for your clients.
- Be aware that cultural, ethnic, and environmental factors interact with clients' biology.
- Advocate for the use of ethnopsychopharmacology.
- Promote "the start low and go slow" norm: Remember that some multicultural clients require half of the standard dosage of all psychotropic medications.
- Aim to identify your clients' ethnicity and its relationship with CYP enzymes.
- Assess your clients' beliefs and expectations related to psychotropic treatment.
- Be aware of your clients of color's sociopolitical history with medications.
- Examine clients' use of CAM.
- Be aware of the possibility of drug interaction with herbal remedies, dietary supplements, and other CAM modalities.
- Psychoeducate your clients about the use of psychotropics and the danger in sharing medications with significant others.
- Be aware of the cross-cultural differences in dosage prescription of psychotropic medications.
- If you do not prescribe medications, develop a collaborative relationship with the clinician who is prescribing psychotropic medication to your clients.

In summary, cultural critical thinking can foster your clinical effectiveness with clients who take psychotropic medication. Specifically, you can use psychoeducation and ethnopsychopharmacological principles in your multicultural caring practice. Following this analysis, you can exercise your cultural critical thinking, in other aspects of your clinical practice, such as psychological testing.

PSYCHOLOGICAL TESTING
AND MULTICULTURAL CLIENTS

Juan, a 35-year-old man who moved to the United States from Puerto Rico 3 months prior, was rushed into the emergency department with agitation and aggressive behavior. Several medical tests yielded no physical signs of illness. "The devil is in my head," Juan screamed when questioned about his symptoms. After administering a mental status examination, Dr. Cooper, a White Jewish American psychiatry resident, declared Juan disoriented, anxious, and with inappropriate affect. Assessing his intellectual capacity, Dr. Cooper asked Juan to define *winter,* and Juan responded, "a warm and wet season." Being from a Caribbean country, Juan did not define *winter* as a cold, snowy season. To the question, "What is the meaning of the following sentence: 'Shallow brooks are noisy'?" Juan responded that brooks "carry a lot of things." The clinician noted that this was a concrete answer.

On the basis of this assessment, Dr. Cooper diagnosed Juan as having a psychosis accompanied by a borderline intelligence. Because of Juan's culture and language (Spanish native tongue and English as a second language), the chief resident asked Dr. Cortina, a Latino psychiatry resident, to interview Juan in Spanish. Dr. Cortina conducted a more culturally relevant mental examination following the explanatory model of distress. He found Juan to be well oriented to person, date, and place. In addition, Juan knew why he was in the hospital. Dr. Cortina asked Juan his understanding of the cause of his illness and its potential cure. Juan clarified that his pain was so severe—metaphorically, as if the devil was in his head—as opposed to Juan's assertion in English that the devil was inside his head. Juan admitted that the pain was so severe that he had contemplated suicide. Having had no previous psychiatric history, Juan's story seemed more congruent with a severe pain. Dr. Cortina interviewed Juan's wife, Carmen, who confirmed Juan's report. Indeed, Lu (2004) recommended clinicians to actively involve family members in the clinical care of culturally diverse clients. Subsequently, Dr. Cortina ordered a complete neurological exam and a magnetic resonance imaging scan. The results indicated that Juan had a brain tumor.

The Need for Cultural Interpretation

Juan's ethnicity, language, social class, and migrant status distorted the emergency department clinician's diagnosis. As I discussed in previous chapters, relating to culturally diverse people frequently causes miscommunication, misinterpretation, and frustration because clinicians feel more comfortable with those who are like them. Some of the diagnostic errors due to cultural differences include

- *overpathologizing,* or inappropriately perceiving patients as more disturbed;
- *minimizing,* or inappropriately judging symptomatology as normal for members of a group;
- *overdiagnosing,* or inappropriately applying a diagnosis as a function of group membership; and
- *underdiagnosing,* or inappropriately avoiding application of a diagnosis as a function of group membership (S. R. López, 1989).

Juan became a victim of both overdiagnosis (psychosis) and underdiagnosis (brain tumor).

Regrettably, diagnostic errors also occur with "objective" assessment methods (Comas-Díaz & Ramos-Grenier, 1998; Escobar, Burnam, & Karno, 1986; Helms, 1992; Lu, Lim, & Mezzich, 1995; Westermeyer, 1993). If you use standardized assessment instruments, make sure to become aware of their cultural bias (Valenstein et al., 2009), as well as their linguistic problems (E. C. Lopez, Lamar, & Scully-DeMartini 1997). For example, if you use the Diagnostic Interview Schedule (Reiger et al., 1984; Robbins, Helzer, Croughan, & Ratcliff, 1981; an instrument developed for the Epidemiologic Catchment Area study) with Puerto Ricans, you need to modify your interpretation of certain items to accommodate belief in *espiritismo* (see Chapter 8 for an explanation of this folk healing) and transpersonal experiences, to properly differentiate between cultural beliefs and psychotic symptoms (Guernaccia et al., 1992). In Chapter 3, I recommended a process-oriented multicultural assessment. As we saw in Juan's vignette, diagnostic errors can occur in cross-cultural situations even when clinicians use "objective" assessment methods, such as the Mini-Mental State Exam (Folstein, Folstein, & McHugh, 1975) and mental status examination (Comas-Díaz & Ramos-Grenier, 1998; Escobar et al., 1986; Lu et al., 1995; Westermeyer, 1993). For example, various cultural groups use different calendars, and their degree of attention or inattention to time can affect when you assess orientation to date (Westermeyer, 1993). Likewise, the usefulness of fund of knowledge can vary according to educational differences. Moreover, seasons vary around the world, and the description of, for example, winter in one geographic area will be different from that in another (as you saw in Juan's vignette). Assessing the cognitive function of abstraction through the use of proverbs may be difficult because proverbs' meaning and wording vary between cultural groups. Furthermore, short-term memory tests can be adversely affected if you use culturally irrelevant items on linguistically different clients (or those for whom English is a not a first language; S. R. López & Taussig, 1991; Lu et al., 1995).

It is instructive to note that general intelligence—and the controversial IQ tests, fund of knowledge, as well as the ability to take traditional psychological tests generally depend on education and past experience, as well as knowledge of the information presented in the questions. Regrettably, psychological IQ testing has contributed to the history of medical apartheid (Hilliard, 1996). To illustrate, many Native Americans and African Americans were tested with IQ tests, and the results were used to justify their sterilization (Painter, 2010). Indeed, psychological tests were used at Ellis Island to restrict immigrants of color and those from Southern and Western Europe from entering the United States (Kraut, 1994). For recent immigrants (like Juan), the psychological testing results may be more reflective of their translocation, adaptation, and acculturation process than of their cognitive abilities (Comas-Díaz & Ramos-Grenier, 1998). Culture shock often produces cognitive disorientation (Jalali, 1988), influencing the results of intellectual assessment and, subsequently, clouding an accurate estimation of the client's potential functioning. Unfortunately, cognitive assessment can still present diagnostic dilemmas even with those individuals who have successfully undergone cultural translocation.

The use of clinical rating scales may be helpful in diagnosis and treatment; however, many of these instruments contain bias and ambiguity. Thus, questioning their use with many culturally diverse populations is appropriate. On the other hand, self-report scales are susceptible to response bias sets (C. Chen, Lee, & Stevenson, 1995) and use terms that are often not clearly defined, causing respondents to be uncertain of what they are being asked (Beere, 1990). For example, the original Minnesota Multiphasic Personality Inventory (McKinley & Hathaway, 1944) did not include ethnic minority individuals in its standardization sample; moreover, it contained several culturally biased items. Even though the Minnesota Multiphasic Personality Inventory–2 (MMPI-2; Butcher, Dahlstrom, Graham, Tellegen, & Kaemmer, 1989) improved in this area, Hersen, Hilsenroth, and Segal (2004) warned clinicians about misinterpreting data when using the MMPI-2 with multicultural clients, particularly if the clients are recent immigrants and/or have limited English proficiency. For example, MMPI-2 Item 24, *Evil spirits possess me at times,* may have a weak psychotic disorder content validity for those multicultural clients who believe in *espiritismo* (Rogler, 1999). Moreover, Hersen et al. recommended that if you use the MMPI-2 computer-based interpretation, you should make sure to complement it with other information, such as clinical interview, history, and clinical observations.

The APA Ethics Code, Standard 9.06, Interpreting Assessment Results (APA, 2010b), addresses the issue of competence in assessment and encourages psychologists to be aware of the limitations of assessment practices, ranging from intakes, to the use of standardized tests, to the effects of cultural differences when interpreting test data. Moreover, APA Multicultural Guideline 5 states that psychologists are encouraged to know and consider the validity of a given test or assessment instrument they use. This includes the appropriate interpretation of standardized assessment for the cultural and linguistic characteristics of the person being evaluated, as well as the test's limitations for culturally diverse individuals.

Language and Psychological Testing

Certainly, clinical practice has not paid appropriate attention to the effect of clients' language on assessment and/or treatment (Acosta & Cristo, 1981; Clauss, 1998). To illustrate, monolingual clinicians do not fully understand or appreciate bilingual and multilingual clients' experiences (Santiago Rivera & Altarriba, 2002). Such attitudes underestimate the multiple layers of meaning that language and bilingualism provide to people's lives. As a case in point, bilinguals do not associate the same emotion of the Spanish concept (*cariño*) with an English translation ("liking"; Altarriba, 2003).

As I previously discussed, APA Multicultural Guideline 5 (APA, 2003) urges psychologists to respect clients' language preferences and to ensure accurate translation of documents by providing informed consent about the language in which the assessment and treatment will be conducted. In addition, this multicultural guideline encourages psychologists to respect clients' boundaries by not using interpreters who are unskilled in the area of mental health, are family members, or are community authorities. Although the use of interpreters in psychological testing needs to be a last resort (Nieves-Grafals, 1995), a significant number of school psychologists use interpreters while conducting psychological assessment (Ochoa, Powell, & Robles-Piña, 1996). However, selecting and using interpreters requires special consideration. Ideally, interpreters should be trained and function as language specialists, bilingual workers, bicultural or bilingual coclinicians, or they should meet all of these qualifications (Tien, 1994). You can consult Acosta and Cristo (1981), Marcos (1979), Mollica and Lavalle (1988), Paniagua (1994), C. A. Vasquez and Javier (1991), and Westermeyer (1990) for detailed discussions of the use of interpreters in evaluating multicultural clients.

In addition, clinicians need to consider the cultural linguistic validity of translated tests (Allalouf, 2003; van de Vijver & Hambleton, 1996). For example, Marin and Marin (1991) suggested the use of back-to-back translations (i.e., translating an item from Language A to Language B and, then, independently from Language B to Language A). Notwithstanding their potential benefits, many translated tests are not necessarily culturally and linguistically validated for multicultural individuals. Rogler (1999) stated that in the translation of clinical tests, the word of equivalence must not be interpreted literally; instead, it must be culturally construed. Rogler presented an example of the Center of Epidemiological Studies Depression Scale's (Radloff, 1977) item *I felt I could not shake off the blues, even with the help of my family and friends.* An appropriate Spanish translation would be *Me sentí tan desanimado(a) que ni mi familia ni amigos me podían animar.* According to Rogler, the colloquialism "shake off the blues" carries connotations of a mild but unpleasant depression. Moreover, he observed that a literal translation of the word *blue* would be inappropriate because this word in Spanish (*azul*) does not designate mood.

Decreasing Psychological Tests' Cultural Bias

APA Multicultural Guideline 4 encourages culturally sensitive psychological researchers to recognize the importance of conducting culture-centered and ethical psychological research among persons from ethnic, linguistic, and racial minority backgrounds. This guideline was developed in response to the cultural bias present in many psychological tests and assessment tools.

Westermeyer (2004) offered a clinical suggestion to decrease cultural bias when using an assessment instrument. First, Westermeyer discussed the CAGE (Mayfield, McLeod, & Hall, 1974; see below for spelled-out form) substance abuse questionnaire, and then he questioned its multicultural applicability. To illustrate, clinicians using CAGE to explore clients' drinking can examine the following areas (Westermeyer, 2004, pp. 95–96):

- Cut down (Have you ever felt you should cut down on your drinking?),
- Annoyed (Have people annoyed you by criticizing your drinking?),
- Guilty (Have you ever felt guilty about your drinking?), and
- Eye opener (Have you ever taken an eye opener [drink first in the morning] to steady your nerves or get rid of a hangover?).

Westermeyer (2004) proposed to decrease the CAGE's cultural bias by expanding the areas examined. For example, clinicians can explore clients' substance abuse history, medical history, review of symptoms (e.g., hangover symptoms), family history, social history, examination (evidence of physical complications), and laboratory data (e.g., abnormal liver functions) and can include collateral sources (significant others) and clinical course (noncompliance to treatment) plus other related information. I concur with Westermeyer's analysis that the CAGE questionnaire tends to reflect an individualist worldview orientation and, thus, needs to be culturally adapted when applied to multicultural clients. In addition to Westermeyer's suggested areas, I routinely explore the cultural context of clients' use of substance. This exploration can unlock potential levels of resistance to substance abuse treatment. Consider the following example.

A local university counseling center referred Leonor to me for depression treatment. My assessment revealed that Leonor was having a drinking problem. When I shared my diagnostic impression with her, she said, "I'm not an alcoholic; I only drink socially. Besides, I'm from Puerto Rico, the rum capital of the world." When I asked her to elaborate on her statement, Leonor simply replied, "We drink alcohol like gringos drink Coca Cola." Unfortunately, she dropped out of treatment.

Going beyond the use of culturally sensitive assessment tools, some multicultural experts explored the development of culture-specific psychological tests. An example of this approach is Tell Me a Story (TEMAS). TEMAS is a projective psychological test like the Thematic Apperception Test (Murray, 1943), initially developed with Latino culturally relevant stimuli (Costantino, Dana, & Malgady, 2007). TEMAS is a multicultural test and can be used with diverse ethnic minority children and youth. TEMAS comprises two sets of structured stimuli cards with pictorial problem solving scenarios—one for ethnic minorities (African Americans and Latinos) and the other for Whites.

Certainly, developing psychological tests for the multiple ethnic groups can be arduous and difficult. Conversely, if you use psychological tests, you may want to follow the APA Multicultural Guideline 5. This guideline encourages clinicians to know about issues related to test bias, test fairness, and cultural equivalency. In this vein, you need to minimize psychological testing cultural bias (Dana, 1993; Lonner & Ibrahim, 1996; Nieves-Grafals, 1995; Roysircar-Sodowsky & Kuo, 2001) as follows:

- conduct an assessment of acculturation;
- provide a culture-specific service delivery (including behavioral etiquette);
- use multiple methods of assessment;
- consider constructivist approaches (e.g., content analysis of clients' responses, journal work);
- use the client's preferred language;
- when deemed necessary, use nonverbal cognitive tests;
- select assessment measures appropriate for client's cultural orientation;
- use translated measures with linguistic and construct equivalence;
- exercise caution in using computerized reports due to their omission of cultural issues; and
- use a culture-specific strategy when informing the client about findings derived from the assessment process.

The use of appropriate psychological testing with subsequent cultural interpretation of the tests' findings is a useful tool in clinical practice. As a case in point, with the aging of populations of all colors, the need for neuropsychological assessment is pressing. Experts on this assessment area have suggested the following clinical guidelines for the use of neuropsychological tests with multicultural clients (Cuéllar, Arnold, & Maldonado, 1995; Wong, Strickland, Fletcher-Janzen, Ardila, & Reynolds, 2000):

- Make the testing situation a culturally holding environment. In other words, aim to increase the cultural sensitivity of the testing environment by attending to the physical needs, and explaining to the client the testing process. Moreover, you can use the suggestions presented in Chapter 2 to make the testing situation a culturally holding environment.
- Make sure to conduct a comprehensive clinical interview, including clients' explanatory model of distress. The goal of this interview is to identify the client's cultural influences that may affect his or her test scores.
- Do not use translations of tests unless they have cultural validation and reliability.
- Do not use interpreters because linguistic variables interfere in interpreting the results.

- Consider acculturation status when evaluating migrant individuals.
- When you write the psychological testing report, include information regarding cultural biases in the test, interpretation, and examiner.

In her discussion of neuropsychological testing, Hays (2008) recommended the combined use of a hypothesis-testing approach with a testing the limits strategy. Within the hypothesis-testing approach, you start with a number of hypotheses based on the referral questions, the client's history, and your initial clinical impressions. Afterward, you choose the specific tests. As testing progresses, you refine the general hypotheses into specific ones, eliminating diagnostic possibilities, a process that may lead to a relatively conclusive diagnosis. After that, you can use the strategy of testing the limits to interpret the neuropsychological testing results. According to Hays, following the standard test administration, this strategy involves exploring the potential reasons for clients' poor performance. In other words, when you ask clients why they think they missed an item, this strategy offers a fuller understanding and allows their perspectives to emerge.

When you use a hypothesis-testing approach, you engage in critical thinking. You can apply critical thinking in combination with the previously discussed suggestions to decrease cultural bias in psychological tests. As an illustration, J. Sandoval (1998) advised clinicians to use critical thinking in the following ways when interpreting psychological test results with culturally diverse individuals:

- Identify your preconceptions—avoid selective perceptions through the use of cultural self-assessment.
- Develop complex conceptions of clients' group—cultural competence can help you to create new, more complete, and accurate conceptions that allow you to understand your clients in context.
- Actively search for disconfirmatory evidence—avoid confirmatory bias and do not attribute clients' difficulties solely to internal states; instead, make sure that you consider environmental causes as well. Ask yourself, "Did the client have an opportunity to learn the information or to express it on the test?" (p. 46).

- Resist a rush to judgment—avoid impulsivity to judge, be reflective, and use personal culturally relevant data.

- Seek supervision, consultation, or both—if you are not familiar with the client's culture, consult with a colleague who has experience with your client's population.

- Distrust memory—memory can be subjected to confirmatory bias—instead, document impressions with objective means.

CONCLUSION

It is essential that clinicians exercise cultural critical thinking when examining clients' responses to psychopharmacotherapy and psychological testing. Cultural critical thinking entails openness to cultural information and analysis, awareness of multiple interacting contexts, use of alternative frameworks, prudence in making judgments, and on-going self-reflection. Despite the controversy on what the concepts of ethnicity and race actually mean and measure, these variables are important proxies for a person's culture, diet, beliefs, health behaviors, and attitudes (Chaudhry, Neelam, Duddu, & Husain, 2008). For example, if your clients receive psychopharmacological treatment, you can enhance your cultural competence when you become familiar with ethnopsychopharmacology.

There is hope that culturally relevant psychopharmacological research can result in a better understanding of the way that cultural and biologic processes, separately and in interaction with each other, mediate psychopharmacological treatment responses. Such knowledge will represent a significant contribution to the field of psychopharmacology and will be crucial for the optimal pharmacotherapeutic care of the majority of patients, who will increasingly be of diverse ethnic and cultural backgrounds (K. M. Lin, Smith, & Ortiz, 2001). Likewise, if you engage in cultural critical thinking when you use psychological testing with culturally diverse clients, you will behave in an ethical, culturally congruent, and multicultural caring way. Below is a list of key multicultural clinical strategies presented in this chapter.

MULTICULTURAL CLINICAL STRATEGIES

- Exercise cultural critical thinking, particularly when dealing with psychopharmacology and psychological testing.
- Be cognizant of ethnic, racial, and gender differences in the metabolism of psychopharmacological drugs.
- Promote the "start low and go slow" norm when prescribing (or working with prescribers) psychotropic medication to multicultural clients.
- Aim to identify your clients' ethnicity and its relationship with the CYP enzymes if they are taking psychotropic medications.
- Explore your clients' use of CAM.
- Be aware that some people of color tend to use herbal remedies in addition to medications.
- Examine the potential interaction of herbal remedies with psychotropic medications.
- Enhance your knowledge of psychopharmacology and in particular, ethnopsychopharmacology.
- Use psychoeducation with clients who require ethnopsychopharmacolgical treatment.
- Be aware that a client's psychological test results may not be valid.
- Exercise cultural critical thinking in interpreting multicultural clients' psychological tests' results.
- If appropriate, implement the strategies to reduce psychological tests bias presented in this chapter.

7

Multicultural Treatment: Part 1. Fostering Empowerment

Each person carries his (her) own doctor inside him (her). They come to us not knowing that truth. We are at our best when we allow the doctor who resides in each client a chance to go to work.

—Dr. Albert Schweitzer

Dr. Carlson: You sound like you have been in therapy before.

Raul: Yeah. I did network therapy.

Dr. Carlson: So, you had addiction problems . . .

Raul: Actually, I'm referring to the Native American Network therapy, not the substance abuse treatment.

Dr. Carlson: Oh, I didn't know. What kind of therapy is this?

Raul: One that empowers by reminding you of who you are.

How do you feel about this clinical encounter? If you were Raul, how would you feel about Dr. Carlson's assumption? Are you familiar with empowering psychotherapies?

Historically, multicultural individuals have resorted to diverse sources of healing. Just to name a few, these sources include empowerment approaches, such as ethnic psychotherapies, folk healing, and spiritual practices. For instance, network family therapy emerged from a Native American context to use individuals' relational network in support of the healing process (Attneave, 1990). As a result, mainstream counselors borrowed and incorporated network therapy into substance abuse treatment (Galanter, 1993; see Chapter 8, this volume, for a fuller description of network therapy).

Multicultural care promotes the incorporation of diverse healing modalities into mainstream treatment. This means that multicultural caring clinicians aim to empower their clients by complementing their treatment orientation with varied approaches. In fact, several multicultural experts recommend the use of a plurality of interventions in clinical practice (D. W. Sue & Sue, 2008).

In this chapter, I present multicultural treatment as an empowering approach. First, I present a cultural adaptation of mainstream clinical practice. Then, I discuss empowerment as an example of a culture-centered clinical treatment. A clinical case illustrates the empowering focus of multicultural treatment. I conclude with a discussion of the ethics of being a multicultural caring clinician.

CULTURAL ADAPTATION OF MAINSTREAM MENTAL HEALTH PRACTICE

Seeking mental health services can be a paradox for multicultural individuals. Although people of color have a significant need, unfortunately, the history of service delivery to these populations is fraught with obstacles and missed opportunities. To illustrate, most people of color have to overcome a history of medical research abuses and subsequent mistrust toward the health care delivery. Regrettably, this medical legacy affects those clients of color whose primary care practitioners refer them to mental health treatment. Moreover, numerous multicultural individuals perceive clinical practice as being monocultural, ethnocentric, and insensitive to their cultural and spiritual experiences (G. C. N. Hall, 2001; D. W. Sue, Bingham, Porche-

Burke, & Vasquez, 1999). As such, clinical practice tends to reflect dominant cultural values and to ignore multicultural worldviews. Consequently,
many culturally diverse individuals fear that dominant mental health practice is a stigmatizing and acculturative institution (Ramirez, 1991). In contrast, when multicultural clients encounter clinicians who respect, hear,
understand, and care for them, they tend to remain in treatment. Certainly,
cultural competence is the key to engage multicultural clients to treatment.
For instance, research found clinician's cultural competence, compassion,
and sharing their clients' worldview were more important factors than ethnic matching between client and clinician (Knipscheer & Kleber, 2004).
Consequently, clinicians' lack of cultural competence is one reason many
multicultural individuals resort to alternative sources of healing.

Although some clinicians have questioned the applicability of dominant clinical practice to multicultural clients (Bernal, Bonilla, & Bellido,
1995; D. W. Sue et al., 1999), others have suggested a cultural adaptation
to mainstream clinical practice (Altman, 1995; Bernal & Scharron del Rio,
2001; Foster, Moskowitz, & Javier, 1996; Kakar, 1985). The cultural adaptation of mainstream psychotherapy consists of both the development of
generic cross-cultural skills and the acquisition of culture-specific skills.
Because every encounter is multicultural in nature, when you enhance
your generic cross-cultural skills, you improve your cultural competence
with all clients.

Nonetheless, when you develop culture-specific skills, you enhance
your ability to work with particular cultural populations. According to
multicultural experts, the development of culture-specific skills includes
(a) involvement of culturally diverse people in the development of interventions; (b) inclusion of collectivistic cultural values (such as familism, social
cohesion, contextualism); (c) attention to spirituality, religion, and faith;
(d) recognition of the relevance of acculturation; and (e) acknowledgment
of the effects of oppression on mental health (Muñoz & Mendelson, 2005).

According to Bernal, Bonilla, and Bellido (1995), a cultural adaptation of mainstream psychotherapies needs to include the dimensions of
language, persons, metaphors, content, concepts, goals, method, and context. Specifically, the language used in treatment needs to be culturally
congruent to the client's worldview; the persons must be engaged in a

good therapeutic relationship; metaphors must include symbols and concepts shared by members of the cultural group; the content of the clinician's cultural knowledge must be sufficient (i.e., does your client feel understood by you?); the concepts of the treatment must be congruent with the client's culture; the goals of therapy must be culturally congruent; the methods and instruments of therapy must be culturally adapted and validated; and the context must include the clients' ecology, including historical and sociopolitical circumstances.

An example of the incorporation of cultural factors in treatment is ethnic family therapy. As a field, family therapy has a legacy of incorporating ethnicity and culture into its theory and practice (Ho, 1987; McGoldrick, Giordano, & Garcia-Preto, 2005). Ethnic family therapy emerged out of this tradition to address the cultural context of families and to use ethnic values in treatment. Boyd-Franklin's (2003) multisystemic approach presented in her book *Black Families in Therapy* is a classic example of this perspective. As an illustration of a multicultural care treatment, ethnic family therapy requires clinicians to develop cultural competence. Family clinicians commit to cultural competence by becoming multicultural aware, avoiding ethnocentric attitudes and behaviors, aiming to achieve an insider/outsider status, and engaging in selective disclosure (Ariel, 1999).

Psychoanalysis has a long-standing tradition of examining the relationship between culture and psyche. This tradition gave birth to psychoanalytic anthropology (Devereux, 1958). Early on, psychoanalysts exhibited an interest in the relationship between oppression and psychological functioning (Kardiner & Ovesey, 1951). Along these lines, proponents of the cultural school of psychoanalysis believed that human development is rooted in environmental factors that vary across cultural contexts and historical periods (Seeley, 2000). Adherents of the cultural school of psychoanalysis, such as Eric Fromm, Karen Horney, and Harry Stack Sullivan, argued that culture shapes behavior because individuals are contextualized and embedded in social interactions (Comas-Díaz, 2011a). Some psychoanalysts are responding to the call to culturally adapt their practice through the incorporation of clients' social, communal, and spiritual orientations into psychoanalysis (Foster, Moskowitz, & Javier, 1996). As a vivid example, Altman (1995) reported using a modified object relations framework, in which he examines his clients' progress by their ability to use relationships to grow, rather than by the insight that they gain. Similarly, Indian psychoanalyst Kakar (1985) culturally adapted his clinical practice by educating, empathizing, and actively expressing warmth toward his East Indian patients.

And yet, other multicultural clinicians recommended the cultural adaptation of evidence-based practice (EBP) based on commonalities regarding mind–body connection, the role of thoughts in health and illness, and the importance of education in healing, (Muñoz & Mendelson, 2005). Lamentably, EBP approaches tend to underemphasize the role of historical and sociopolitical contexts in the delivery of clinical care to people of color and, thus, lack a contextual-ecological viewpoint to examine social and environmental problems (Rogers, 2004). To address these concerns, an American Psychological Association (APA) Presidential Task Force reconceptualized EBP as the "integration of the best available research with clinical expertise in the context of client characteristics, culture and preferences" (APA, 2006, p. 273). Although evidence-based treatments tend to lack cultural and ecological validity (G. C. N. Hall, 2001; Rosselló & Bernal, 1999), research on culture-sensitive EBPs has shown benefits for some culturally diverse populations. For example, researchers found positive gains in the areas of depression (Kohn, Oden, Muñoz, Robinson, & Leavitt, 2002; Organista, Muñoz, & Gonzales, 1994), anxiety (Sanderson, Rue, & Wetzler, 1998), obsessive disorder (Hatch, Friedman, & Paradis, 1996); attention-deficit/hyperactivity disorder, depression, conduct disorder, substance use, trauma-related disorders, and other clinical problems (Huey & Polo, 2008; Horrell, 2008) among clients of color. (The interested reader can consult Morales & Norcross, 2010, for a report on the conference "Culturally Informed Evidence Based Practices." The conference proceedings are available at http://psychology.ucdavis.edu/aacdr/ciebp08.html.)

Notwithstanding the above-mentioned gains, people of color drop out of mental health treatment more often than their White counterparts (Miranda et al., 2005; Organista et al., 1994). Unfortunately, a decontextualized manualized clinical approach (Carter, 2006; Wampold, 2007) tends to restrict access to treatment of choice (Norcross, Koocher, &

Garofalo, 2006; Rupert & Baird, 2004). To bridge this gap, experts recommend that clinicians incorporate culture-centered strategies into their clinical approaches (Bernal & Scharron del Rio, 2001). Indeed, empowerment is a central component of culture-centered clinical interventions.

EMPOWERMENT: A CULTURE-CENTERED CLINICAL INTERVENTION

APA Multicultural Guideline 5 (APA, 2003) recommends that clinicians recognize that there are situations in which adapting culture-centered interventions to their practice will increase their clinical effectiveness. In other words, this guideline asks clinicians to focus on clients' cultural contexts and to include a broad range of interventions into your practice. You can comply with this recommendation when you complement your practice with empowering, pluralistic, and holistic approaches. Given the central relationship between health and oppression in the lives of many people of color, numerous clinicians have recognized the need for empowerment approaches in multicultural care (Muñoz, 1996; D. W. Sue & Sue, 2008).

To facilitate empowerment, you can acknowledge your clients' experiences with racism, sexism, classism, homophobia, heterosexism, ethnocentrism, ableism, ageism, and other forms of discrimination. For instance, you can open a clinical space to discuss the effects of the oppression on your clients' lives. In such a space, you can become a witness and an interpreter of your clients' maladies. Dr. Cassidy and John's vignette from Chapter 2 illustrates this point. Dr. Cassidy witnessed John's experiences with oppression regarding race and sexual orientation. During their initial session Dr. Cassidy facilitated the emergence of a working alliance when he examined John's ADDRESSING areas. John's responses to the ADDRESSING tool revealed a conflict with being a gay Black man raised working class with a minister father in a Southern Baptist community. Although John reported no previous personal or family psychiatric history, he agreed to see a psychologist for anger management. John's responses to the explanatory model of distress revealed that the behavior of his White coworkers triggered his anger. He acknowledged being the victim of a combined racist and homophobic discrimination at work. John stated that a White coworker spotted him walking out of a gay bar several days before the harassment at work began. In addition, John described several incidents where he experienced racial microaggressions ("You're an affirmative action baby"). Perhaps John's combined lower social status as an African American gay man made him more of a discrimination target. As a result, John discussed with Dr. Cassidy his plan to file a discrimination complaint at work.

After analyzing the symbolic meaning of John's intended complaint, how would you handle this plan? In other words, should you advocate for, against, or remain neutral on John's plan to file an Equal Employment Opportunity complaint? Although multicultural caring clinicians do not need to be politically active, they recognize that clinical practice is grounded in a political context and, thus, can be a political action. In other words, your clinical orientation can be an instrument of the status quo, or conversely, it can be an empowering activity. You can conduct a cultural self-assessment to explore your political ideology.

Cultural Self-Assessment: Political Ideology

What is your political ideology—conservative, liberal, centrist, radical, libertarian, apolitical, or none? Do you belong to a political party? How do you feel about clients endorsing political views different from your own? How do you feel about clients endorsing your personal political views? How do you feel about the political issues affecting minority groups? For example, how do you feel about state abortion laws, same sex marriage, anti-immigration laws, and the Americans With Disabilities Act (1990)? What criteria do you use when you examine political issues in your clinical practice?

Empowerment as a Multicultural Clinical Tool

Regardless of your political orientation, remember that mainstream clinical practice's neglect of sociopolitical contexts can be detrimental to many multicultural clients. In other words, numerous people of color's realities differ from the experience of most majority group members because of their history of collective oppression and trauma (M. J. T. Vasquez, 1998). Moreover, people of color tend to internalize their oppression. Regardless of your political orientation, you can use empowerment approaches to help your clients differentiate functional adaptive responses from dysfunctional ones.

Multicultural caring clinicians use empowering approaches to foster clients' examination of their oppression to promote liberation (Pinderhughes, 1994). Therapeutic empowerment helps clients to increase their self-efficacy, mastery, agency, and control (Dass-Brailsford, 2007). For example, research findings suggested that African American adolescents empowered by cultural pride and racial socialization endorsed fewer depressive behaviors as opposed to those who reported experiences of discrimination (Davis & Stevenson, 2006). Empowerment promotes self- healing by allowing the doctor who resides in each patient a chance to go to work. When you subscribe to an empowerment multicultural model, you recognize your clients' contextual reality, accept their experience as valuable knowledge, affirm their cultural strengths, and acknowledge their perspectives on healing. In summary, a multicultural empowerment helps clients to

- increase their access to resources,
- develop options to exercise choice,
- affirm cultural strengths,
- strengthen support systems,
- promote cultural identity development,
- foster self-healing,
- develop critical consciousness,
- overcome internalized oppression,
- improve individual and collective self-esteem, and
- engage in transformative actions.

The clinical emphasis on empowerment in the United States has political roots. Civil rights movements (e.g., Black power, Chicano/Brown power; gay, lesbian, and bisexual rights) has led to the empowerment of minorities. These movements raised consciousness and attempted to redress the social and political inequities affecting marginalized minority groups. Minority empowerment movements examined the dynamics of power and privilege between dominant group members and individuals from disenfranchised groups. As a result, multiculturalism emerged to promote a critical dialogue on oppression and power and to explore models for healing and liberation.

Critical Consciousness Dialogue

Looking beyond the shores of the United States, multiculturalists found an example of such critical dialogue in Freire's (1970) education for the oppressed. A Brazilian educator, Freire identified his model as *conscienti-zacion*, or critical consciousness—a process of personal and social liberation through critical thinking. Adherents of critical consciousness teach their clients to critically perceive their circumstances, analyze the causes of their oppression, and discover new ways of action (Freire, 1970). Clinicians using critical consciousness promote clients' agency, and ask them to engage in transformative actions. Succinctly put, conscientizacion encourages clients to examine meaning, beliefs, and existential choices to critically analyze their situation, affirm ethnocultural strengths, and promote personal and collective transformation.

Because oppression robs its victims of their capacity for critical thinking, the development of conscientizacion involves asking questions to help clients to make a connection between their concerns and the distribution of power. Asking critical questions, such as What? Why? How? For whom? Against whom? By whom? In favor of whom? In favor of what? To what end? (Freire & Macedo, 2000, p. 7) can raise consciousness and initiate critical reflection and dialogue about individuals' life circumstances. This process facilitates clients' examination of their own issues against the backdrop of sociopolitical realities.

Marcia, the African American client I introduced in Chapter 5, missed the first part of a lecture because she misplaced her admission ticket. You may remember that the White female clerk denied her entrance to the conference until she found Marcia's name on a second list. Marcia expressed anger at the incident and interpreted the clerk's behavior as racist. My question about alternative explanations seemed to direct her anger toward me ("It's easy for you to ask about alternative explanations. You're not Black.").

In addition, you may remember that as a result, we engaged in a discussion about our racial differences ("You're right, I'm not Black. How do you feel about working with a non-Black clinician? Can we talk about your experiences with racism?"). This discussion resulted in a power differential analysis between us (see the power analysis in Chapter 5).

Let us see what happened when I asked Marcia the following critical consciousness questions:

Lillian: Can we examine the incident from a different perspective?

Marcia: Fine with me.

Lillian: Why do you think the clerk refused to let you in?

Marcia: You tell me . . .

Lillian: Honestly, I really want to know what you think.

Marcia: I told you she's a racist hypocrite.

Lillian: Who benefits from her behavior?

Marcia: What kind of question is that?

Lillian: Please, can you think about it? Who benefits?

Marcia: Not me!

Lillian: What happened afterward?

Marcia: I already told you, she gave the presenter his badge.

Lillian: Can you tell me more?

Marcia: Had a late night? [*Laughs*] Your memory isn't so good today.

Lillian: Come on.

Marcia: OK. The presenter was standing next to me when he asked the clerk to let him in the room. Where're you going with this?

Lillian: Please bear with me. I'm trying to help. What was the woman's purpose in letting you wait?

Marcia: I will not answer that question. [*Moves backwards into her chair.*]

Lillian: OK. It's natural to be angry.

Marcia: You may be trying to help, but . . .

Lillian: But . . . ?

Marcia: Why don't you help me with my snowballing anger?

Lillian: Snowballing?

Marcia: Yeah. My snowballing anger gets everything in its way.

Lillian: How does it get to you?

Marcia: [*Takes several deep breaths, straightens her skirt, and moves forward in the chair.*] I'm tired of fighting racism.

I remembered the power analysis (see Chapter 5) I had conducted previously, in which I compared Marcia's areas of privilege and oppression with mine. As a result, the topic of dark skin emerged as both a connection and a disconnection between us. Although I am not White, my skin color is lighter than Marcia's.

Lillian: I wonder if there is a connection between your snowballing anger and what happened?

Marcia: I don't know, maybe . . .

Lillian: What was the presenter's skin color?

Marcia: Were you there?

Lillian: I don't understand your question. [*Not addressing Marcia's ironic tone in her question*] No, I wasn't there.

Marcia: So why are you asking about his color?

Lillian: Well, a hunch.

Marcia: He was Indian, you know, from India, and his skin was quite dark.

Lillian: What do you make out of that?

Marcia moved slowly toward the box of tissues in front of her. She took one tissue. She then grabbed a second one while still holding the box in her left hand. Finally, Marcia took a third tissue. She released the box and bunched the three tissues together. Only then did Marcia's tears began to flow.

RACISM-RELATED DISTRESS

As I indicated previously, the single most common problem underlying psychotherapy with African American women is racism-related distress (Landrine & Klonoff, 1996). Marcia's encounter with the White female clerk was colored by her societal role as a Black woman, the social distance between Blacks and Whites in Washington, DC, and her exposure to personal and collective racial discrimination. Her angry reaction at the clerk's behavior uncovered a racial–gender injury, a response consistent with evidence showing that racism is a pathogen with biological consequences for its victims (Krieger, 1999). To illustrate, research has documented that African Americans show greater increases in blood pressure when exposed to a stressful task than do Whites (N. B. Anderson et al., 1988; Treiber, McCaffrey, Musante, Rhodes, Davis, Strong, & Levy, 1993). This racial difference can be understood in the context of African Americans' cumulative exposure to racial discrimination (D. W. Sue, Capodilupo, & Holder, 2008). Certainly, racial discrimination has been related to health problems among ethnic minorities (Araújo & Borrell, 2006; Williams, Neighbors, & Jackson, 2008; Williams, Yu, Jackson, & Anderson, 1997). Moreover, African Americans' history of slavery and exposure to microaggressions can result in oversensitivity toward perceived acts of disrespect, as they may be subliminally associated with historical trauma.

Lillian: Can you tell me what is like for you to be a Black woman?

Marcia: It ain't easy . . . too much stress.

Lillian: How can I help?

Marcia: You can't get it. You have light skin.

Lillian: Yes, my skin is lighter than yours. I don't experience what you do as a Black woman.

Marcia: No, you don't. [*Says this in a loud voice as she averted her eyes.*]

Lillian: How can I help? [*Asks this in a soft voice.*]

Marcia: [*Speaks after a long pause.*] Can you help me to separate my legitimate anger from overreactions?

The power differential analysis that I conducted in a previous session (see Chapter 5) offered a safe place for the discussion of racial differences. Marcia identified colorism (preference for light skin over dark skin) as a main difference between us. I attempted to remain "present" and did not shy from exploring our differences as women of color. Furthermore, by answering critical consciousness questions, Marcia confronted the possibility that she may have overreacted to the White clerk's behavior. Marcia associated her cumulative exposure to racial microaggressions with an exacerbation of her irritable bowel syndrome. It seemed that her exposure to racial stress and her "snowballing" anger culminated in physical and psychological symptoms.

Constant exposure to racism increases behavioral exhaustion, psychological distress, and physiological disturbances (Clark, Anderson, Clark, & Williams, 1999). For example, Marcia revealed a history of overreactions to neutral interpersonal situations. She reported a series of conflicts in relationships with her adult offspring, relatives, friends, and neighbors. Marcia's reactions seemed consistent with ethnocultural allodynia, a psychological reaction to cumulative pain. In medicine, *allodynia* refers to exaggerated pain sensitivity in response to neutral or relatively innocuous stimuli, resulting from previous exposure to painful stimuli. With my partner Frederick Jacobsen, we borrowed the term *allodynia* and coined the concept of ethnocultural allodynia as an increased sensitivity to ethnocultural dynamics associated with exposure to emotionally painful social, racial and ethnoracial stimuli (Comas-Díaz & Jacobsen, 2001).

Ethnocultural allodynia entails a disturbance in individuals' ability to judge perceived ethnocultural and racial insults and, subsequently, discern defiant and maladaptive responses from adaptive ones. Ethnocultural allodynia describes a pain caused by previous racial and ethnic and cultural injuries as an extreme reaction to neutral or ambiguous stimuli. Therefore, people of color can develop ethnocultural allodynia as a reaction to an increased sensitivity to ethnocultural and racial dynamics associated with past exposure to microaggressions. Marcia's ethnocultural allodynia was a maladaptive response involving an injury to her sense of self that compromised her coping.

Completing Marcia's cultural genogram offered a fuller picture of the context of her historical and contemporary trauma. To aid in this process, Marcia brought a photo album during the completion of her cultural genogram. The essential differences between a regular genogram and a cultural genogram are that the latter goes back at least five generations, emphasizes ethnoracial identity, acknowledges the sociopolitical and historical contexts, and recognizes sociocentric cultural values.

Figure 7.1 shows Marcia's cultural genogram. I included the information suggested by Hardy and Laszloffy (1995) and used the form suggested by McGoldrick and colleagues (McGoldrick, Gerson, & Petry, 2008; McGoldrick, Gerson, & Shellenberger, 1999). I modified some genogram symbols to reflect racial and ethnic identification and collectivistic cultural values. Moreover, I added more universal symbols to simplify the genogram diagram.

In addition, I completed Marcia's culturagram. As I discussed in Chapter 3, a culturagram maps your client's (and family's) journey or cultural translocation (Congress, 1994, 2002). This tool helps you to examine in more detail issues such as reason or reasons for relocation; type and nature of journey (immigration, migration, refugee, international sojourn); age at immigration (younger immigrants tend to adapt faster than older individuals); legal status; languages spoken at home and in the community; length of time in the community; health beliefs; impact of crisis events, holidays, and special events; participation in cultural spiritual and religious organizations; values about education and work; and values regarding family structure, power, hierarchy, rules, subsystems, and boundaries, among others. Marcia's culturagram appears in Figure 7.2.

Because Marcia's history of race relations was complex, we also developed a sociopolitical timeline to highlight her racial issues:

- 1827: First recording of the existence of Red slaves.
- 1863: Abolition of slavery in Aruba. Slavery in Aruba was different from other islands in the Caribbean and lasted from 1800 to 1863. Arubans' cultural identity does not highlight a history of slavery (see Regional Office for Culture in Latin America and the Caribbean, n.d.).

Marcia's Cultural Genogram

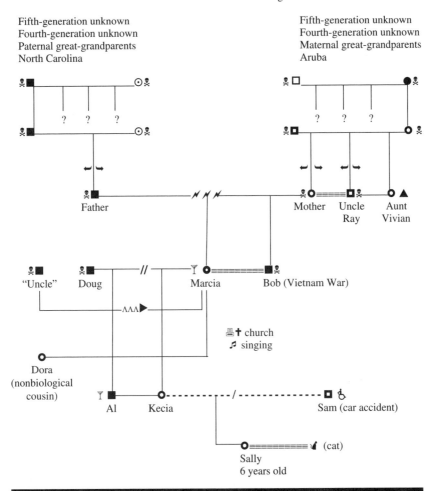

Figure 7.1

Marcia's cultural genogram. Please note that "Red slaves" are people who were kid-napped from Goajira (Venezuela) and forced into slavery (see Regional Office for Culture in Latin America and the Caribbean, n.d.). The genogram information here follows the genogram formulation by McGoldrick and colleagues (1999, 2008; genogram symbols can be viewed at http://courses.wcupa.edu/ttreadwe/courses/02courses/standardsymbols.htm). The essential differences between a genogram and a cultural genogram are that the latter goes back at least five generations, emphasizes ethnoracial identity, acknowledges the sociopolitical and historical contexts, and recognizes socio-centric cultural values. Here, some genogram symbols were modified to reflect racial-ethnic identification and collectivistic cultural values, and "universal" symbols were added to simplify the diagram. *(continued)*

LEGEND

Cultural symbols
⬤ Marcia
◯ Mixed-race woman or girl
◼ African American man or boy
◻ Mixed-race man or boy
◻ Venezuelan Red slave
⊙ Native American woman or girl
⚲ Deceased
➥|➥ Person has lived in 2 cultures
♿ Physical disability
▲ Family secret
🏛† Christian Church
⁄⁄ Conflict
♪ Music
⅄ Alcohol abuse
🐈 🐕 Pet (cat, dog)
Color (Marcia used the following colors)
◯ Orange - self-designation
◯ Gold - daughter Kecia
◻ Blue - son Al
◯ Pink - granddaughter Sally
⊙ Reddish brown - paternal Cherokee great-grandmother
◻ Red - maternal great-grandfather Red slave Venezuelan
Emotional relationship symbols
_____ Good
___⁄⁄⁄___ Basically good, some powerful arguments
⁄⁄⁄⁄⁄ Conflicted
======= Close or Enmeshed

Family and significant other relationship
Married

Cohabiting

Common law marriage

Divorced

Separated

Sexual abuse

Figure 7.1 (*Continued*)

- 1868: Trail of Tears. Marcia's Cherokee great grandmother survived in North Carolina passing as Black.
- 1950: Marcia's parents met in Aruba.
- 1954: Marcia's birth.
- 1955: Marcia and her parents immigrated to the United States.
- 1968: Bob, Marcia's brother, died in combat during the Vietnam War.
- 1985: Aruba became a separate entity within the Netherlands.

Notably, Marcia's parents' relationship with African American and with White American society community was mixed. Although her father endorsed Afrocentric perspectives and was mistrustful of Whites, Marcia's mother did not share her husband's racial mistrust. Moreover, she did not perceive slavery in Aruba as a historical influence in her life.

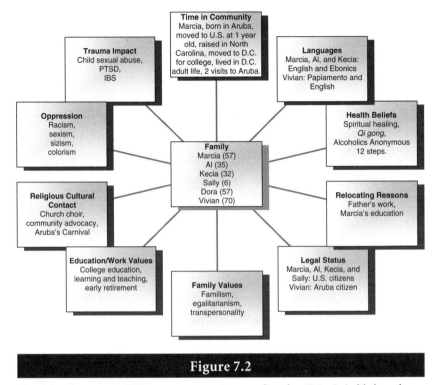

Figure 7.2

Marcia's culturagram. PTSD = posttraumatic stress disorder; IBS = irritable bowel syndrome.

In addition, Marcia self-identified as African American. She expressed pride in her Cherokee blood and acknowledged her maternal Aruba ancestry.

MULTICULTURAL TRAUMA THERAPY

Although trauma is not endemic among multicultural individuals, I suggest that you carefully explore this area during the process-oriented assessment. Certainly, experience with trauma is familiar to many people of color, whether directly, indirectly, or vicariously. At times, clients may have repressed their traumatic experience, as I now discuss regarding Marcia.

To help Marcia separate her appropriate anger from overreaction, I invited her to examine her previous injuries using the Schedule of Racist

Events (Landrine & Klonoff, 1996). I then asked her to rank the events to achieve a baseline before engaging in a cognitive–behavioral strategy. Afterwards, I adapted a systematic desensitization technique to Marcia's reality. This adaptation consisted of teaching Marcia relaxation techniques with guided imagery (Foote, 1996), using her strengths (identified in her multicultural assessment). Marcia named singing in the church choir as one of her blessings; indeed, she identified her safe place (E. R. Shapiro, 1994) as being on a North Carolina beach at dawn while singing a gospel song. Marcia responded well to the culturally centered intervention. Moreover, she learned self-regulation techniques to manage her anxiety. However, her decrease in anxiety seemed to unlock a repressed memory. Marcia reported a lucid dream in which she was sexually assaulted after attending a family reunion. The dream helped her to remember being sexually assaulted by a church minister when she was 9 years old. Incidentally, because the minister was married to her father's cousin, he visited the family frequently, and the assault occurred at Marcia's parents' house. The perpetrator, whom Marcia had to call "Uncle," forced her to perform fellatio on him. The sexual abuse lasted for about 2 years and ended when the minister moved his family to another city. Marcia never disclosed the abuse and eventually "forgot" it. She experienced a constellation of conditions associated with past child sexual abuse, including anxiety, obesity, diabetes, substance abuse, domestic abuse, interpersonal difficulties, and dissociation (Banyard, Williams, & Siegel, 2001; Chu, 1998). It is interesting to note that Marcia described her dissociation as "being in the spirit." In other words, she further identified her dissociative experiences as "the spirit helps me to disconnect from the pain and instead, lifts me up." Indeed, dissociation may be the most prevalent psychotherapeutic procedure used in the world (Kakar, 1982; Prince, 1980). It is also interesting to note that some ethnic groups view dissociation as an adaptive response to oppression (A. Castillo, 1995), a perspective that suggests cultural resilience in interacting within a hostile environment (Comas-Díaz, 2006b). In this vein, I accepted Marcia's explanatory model of dissociation and did not challenge it. Consequently, I encouraged her to offer testimony at her church.

Initially, Marcia was reluctant to give testimony at church. However, she spoke to the minister's wife, who encouraged her to give testimony on her sexual abuse as a child. Her church brothers and sisters met her testimony with compassion and support. Held by the church family, Marcia was able to forgive her deceased abuser. During a therapy session, she communicated that she had received a message through a vision. Marcia reported that her "betrayed soul needed healing." In response, I recommended a trauma therapy approach consistent with eye movement desensitization and reprocessing (EMDR; F. Shapiro, 1995). As a trauma- and EMDR-trained clinician, I culturally adapt EMDR to my clients. Indeed, clinical reports describe a similar adaptation to clients of color (Rittenhouse, 2000). For Marcia's treatment, I followed a method developed by Marcelo Urban, a physician and healer (personal communication, May 30, 2000). Urban adapted a Sufi soul healing technique (see Kakar, 1982, pp. 31–42) into an EMDR-like psychospiritual approach using spiritual affirmations as positive cognitions. This approach seemed consistent with Marcia's spiritual orientation.

During this phase of treatment, Marcia exhibited an ethnocultural transference consistent with idealizing me with the fantasy of a reunion with a perfect parent (omniscient clinician). The clinician's role in mind–body spirit approaches (similar to a healer) may have precipitated the ethnocultural reaction: "You remind me of my aunt Vivian—she's a psychic who lives in Aruba." It is interesting to note that during the course of treatment, Marcia's ethnocultural transference ranged from an interethnocultural transference of ambivalence to an intraethnocultural transference of omniscient clinician. I frequently witness ethnocultural transferences range from reactions typical of interethnic dyad to those typical of an intraethnic dyad in my therapeutic work with clients of color.

Marcia responded well to the multicultural trauma therapy. Fortunately, she was not using alcohol at the time of treatment. However, during the completion of the cultural genogram Marcia mentioned that she had been "married to alcohol" for many years. She returned to her cultural genogram and added alcohol as a deceased spouse. My previous clinical experience in a mental health and substance abuse clinic alerted me to the comorbidity of mental illness and substance abuse. Therefore, I recommended Alcoholics

Anonymous (AA) meetings to Marcia to help her contain excess anxiety arising during the EMDR treatment. I hoped that the AA approach could help
her manage a potential relapse and provide her with a holding environment.
Parenthetically, for those individuals who do not profess faith or religion, I
suggest that they ignore the AA spiritual component and, instead, concen-
trate on the rest of the AA 12 steps.

Marcia accepted my self-help recommendation and joined a mixed-
race AA group. She found the AA group experience helpful. Marcia found
AA's emphasis on the higher power to be congruent with her spirituality. In
addition, Marcia met Margot, an African American woman with a similar
history of child sexual abuse, in the AA group. Margot became Marcia's program sponsor and mentor. She introduced Marcia to *Qigong,* an Eastern
form of personal cultivation, as well as a healing approach. A self-care practice, Qigong works with the *qi,* or vital energy, to flow in the body, working
though obstacles and leading to greater health and well-being (Rubik, 2007).
Marcia embraced Qigong and subsequently credited this practice with her
ability to center herself.

Feeling grounded, Marcia remembered a promised she made to herself. She decided to visit Aruba during its carnival or Bacchanal celebration.
Aruba's Carnival is an expression of creativity, music, and merriment.
Moreover, Aruba's Carnival is considered a special preparation to cleanse
people's sins. Born in Aruba and raised in the United States, Marcia considered her cultural identity to be African American with Arubian ancestry. Marcia's parents (African American father and mother from Aruba)
moved to the United States when she was 6 months old. Marcia, who had
not been to the island since she was 15 (for a funeral), visited her Aunt
Vivian during the carnival. Considered to be a folk healer, this 70-year-old
aunt shared with Marcia many family stories. Among the genealogical
information, she revealed a family secret: Vivian's paternal uncle sexually
molested her when she was 9 years old. Both Vivian and Marcia cried
together and consoled each other. Afterward, Vivian counseled Marcia that
she needed to heal others.

Upon her return from Aruba, Marcia reported that she felt energized
as a result of her reconnection with her birthplace, her maternal extended

family, and the island culture. "You receive a special blessing when you return to the land you were born," Marcia announced. "I recharged my batteries the moment my feet touched Aruba's soil." Marcia's experience seemed consistent with the Antaeus effect. According to Greek mythology, the wrestler Antaeus was the son of the earth goddess Gaia. Consequently, he drew his strength from his mother every time he was thrown down on the earth. Several of my immigrant clients experience the Antaeus effect upon their return to their original country. Moreover, second-generation individuals may "find themselves" when they visit their parents' country of origin. Marcia validated this clinical observation when she asserted, "I became empowered to be myself."

During her last phase of treatment, Marcia followed Vivian's suggestion. She focused on her survivor's identity by becoming an advocate. Within her advocate role, she decided to educate the children at her church about sexual abuse. Previously, Marcia had identified her singing and spirituality as strengths in her multicultural assessment. Consequently, Marcia presented a proposal on a sexual abuse prevention program to her church. She based her training on didactic information, movement (Qigong), music (singing), and art (drawing and painting). The church clergy offered Marcia their full support. As Marcia empowered herself, she empowered others.

At the end of her treatment, Marcia's mood was within normal limits. She reported sleeping and eating well. Her child sexual abuse prevention program was successful, and she had expanded it to a second church. During our last therapy session, Marcia announced that she wanted to commemorate our work with a gift. She regaled me a song. Marcia sang the gospel from her safe place exercise.

CONCLUSION

Multicultural care entails a pluralist, holistic, and empowering method of treatment. When you expand your range of psychological interventions, you enhance your cultural competence. The cultural adaptation of dominant psychotherapies and the infusion of empowerment and culture-specific healing approaches into dominant clinical practices is a model of meeting the mental health needs of multicultural individuals. Below is a list of key multicultural clinical strategies presented in this chapter.

MULTICULTURAL CLINICAL STRATEGIES

- Use a cultural analysis to critically examine Western-based psychological paradigms for their relevance to culturally diverse individuals, families, groups, and communities.
- Tolerate ambiguity, particularly of a cultural nature.
- Examine the potential cultural factors contributing to a clinical impasse.
- Acknowledge acculturation, biculturation, language, spirituality, racism, oppression, and discrimination as important variables in treatment for many culturally diverse clients.
- Remember that multicultural clients prefer clinicians to be culturally competent, not necessarily ethnically matched.
- Expand your range of clinical interventions.
- Balance individualism, collectivism, holism, and their interaction in your treatment approach.
- Foster your clients' empowerment.

Multicultural Treatment: Part 2. Incorporating Culture-Specific Healing

The initial step in healing is caring for others.

—Claudia, a *curandera*

Sonia: Can you read my aura?

Dr. Jenkins: I'm not sure what you mean.

Sonia: You know, can you read the energy around my body?

How do you feel about this clinical encounter? Have you had similar requests from clients? If so, how do you handle these requests? Do you have clients who use culture-specific therapies? How do you feel about folk healing and complementary and alternative medicine (CAM)? How do you feel about clients who use folk healing? Do your clients disclose their use of folk healing to you?

Methods of healing emerge from their cultural context. Furthermore, they evolve to meet individuals' needs within their life experiences (Moodley & West, 2006). Culture-specific healing methods validate the importance of racial, ethnic, historical, and political contexts of oppression and thus are anchored in an empowerment foundation (Comas-Díaz, 2007). Although individualistic psychotherapies tend to emphasize freedom of choice, culture-specific healing methods foster clients' grounding in history, context, and place (Kakar, 1982). Succinctly put, these methods provide resources for rescuing ancestry and cultural archetypes and grounding ethnic identity into a collective self while affirming collective survival. Moreover, culture-specific healing approaches emphasize interconnectedness and holism. Contrary to many individualistic members, who may prefer a verbal healing that works through and promotes change by moving from the unconscious to the conscious, most collectivistic members prefer a holistic healing approach that acknowledges nonverbal communication and promotes change by moving from the conscious to the unconscious (Tamura & Lau, 1992). For these reasons, many multicultural persons favor culture-specific healing perspectives, such as ethnic psychotherapies, indigenous traditions, and folk healing. Of course, not all multicultural individuals endorse syncretistic therapies, nor do they all subscribe to folk healing.

In this chapter, I discuss culture-specific healing approaches, including folk healing, CAM, and ethnic psychotherapies. My goal is to help readers understand the power of these healing practices, incorporate the skills of these practitioners when appropriate, and above all, respect clients' reliance on these approaches as valid and efficacious. First, I introduce syncretism as a broad approach to integrating traditional culture-specific healing with dominant psychotherapies. Next, I provide an overview of traditional folk healing, including types of folk healers, how they develop and function in specific cultural contexts, and the culture-bound afflictions that they seek to heal. I then discuss CAM and ethnic psychotherapies as two syncretistic ways to incorporate culture-specific healing into mainstream psychotherapy.

SYNCRETISM: A MEETING OF EAST, WEST, NORTH, AND SOUTH

Culture-specific healing approaches respond to the relational and contextual needs of multicultural individuals as they promote connection with significant relationships. Partly because of the belief that relationships do not necessarily end with death, numerous people of color continue their relationship with the deceased as they honor ancestors. Accordingly, culture-specific approaches, such as folk healing and ethnic psychotherapies, promote ancestral and sacred affiliations in the treatment process.

Many multicultural individuals use a *syncretistic* approach—that is, a combination of mainstream treatments and culture-specific healing. You may remember from my discussion in Chapter 6 that clients may combine psychopharmacology with folk remedies. Similar to integrative medicine (Snyderman & Weil, 2002), syncretism combines the use of mainstream clinical practice with CAM. Indeed, multicultural individuals who require a combined mind, body, and spirit treatment approach favor culture-specific healing. Of interest, many contemplative psychotherapies (Walsh, 2011), non-Western healing practices, and examples of CAM have roots in traditional folk healing.

Folk healing and mainstream clinical practice are meeting at a cultural crossroads. People of all colors and ethnicities use a combination of Western medicine, ethnic psychotherapies, and folk and indigenous healing practices (Kaptchuk & Eisenberg, 1998). Instead of generating conflict, these perspectives can complement each other. Numerous multicultural individuals favor a syncretism of these two paradigms (Factor-Litvak, Cushman, Kronenburg, Wade, & Kalmuss, 2001). A syncretistic approach for the multicultural individual involves the integration of folk healing with culturally adapted mainstream clinical practice.

The popularity of CAM is fostering a paradigmatic shift in health care. For example, the National Center for Complementary and Alternative Medicine (NCAM; n.d.) identified the following mind–body interventions as examples of CAM: progressive relaxation, hypnotherapy, guided imagery, biofeedback, yoga, tai chi, Qigong, lifestyle interventions, and psychosocial social groups, among others. Many of these alternative healing practices are part of the general public's collective consciousness. Moreover, the definition of CAM varies across cultures. What is considered an alternative and complementary practice in one country may be considered a mainstream healing practice in another country (Fernando, 2003). Along these lines, multicultural clients may not disclose their use of culture-specific healing to their clinician for fear of being negatively judged. Of interest, people who use CAM tend to be highly educated adults who suffer from anxiety and depression, older adults, and people who frequently use mainstream medicine (Astin, 1998; Eisenberg et al., 1998).

Researchers examining a large multiethnic sample of midlife women who participated in the Study of Women's Health Across the Nation found that half of the participants had used some form of CAM during the previous year (Blair et al., 2002). In 2005, the Institute of Medicine reported that a third of Americans reported using CAM in conjunction with mainstream medicine. This number will most likely continue to increase, as these practices encourage self-care, self-healing, and recognition of clients' spiritual contexts. A 2007 survey found that 38% of adults and 12% of children in the United States used CAM: specifically, acupuncture, herbal remedies, breath work, meditation, yoga, and other alternative therapies (Stein, 2008). Likewise, a third of the psychotherapy clients surveyed reported using CAM modalities such as relaxation, imagery, meditation, hypnosis, biofeedback, herbal therapies, herbs, yoga, acupuncture, massage, and spiritual healing in combination with dominant psychotherapy (Elkins, Marcus, Rajab, & Durgam, 2005).

Mainstream clinicians are learning from alternative healers (Walsh & Shapiro, 2006). Currently, numerous clinicians are incorporating non-Western practices, such as meditation, guided imagery, visualization, yoga, rituals, breath work, among others, into their therapeutic practices. For example, the success of Simonton and colleagues (1978) in treating cancer patients with the addition of guided imagery and visualization is a classic illustration of the impact of non-Western healing practices. Moreover, mindfulness has been successfully integrated into stress reduction programs (Kabat-Zinn, 2003) and cognitive behavior therapy (Bennett-Goleman, 2001). Other mainstream clinicians are using non-Western healing modalities, such as meditation (Epstein, 1995); mindfulness (Segal, Williams, & Teasdale, 2002); guided imagery (Gawain, 2002; Rossman, 2000); yoga (Criswell, 2007); mindfulness and acceptance (Hayes, Strosahl,

& Wilson, 2003); acupuncture (J. J. Allen, et al., 2006); and wise mind, or inner guide exercise (Linehan, 1993), among others.

Culture-specific healing approaches have survived the test of time and continue to evolve to meet the needs of individuals and groups. As a result, ethnic practices and folk healing offer a syncretism of Western, Eastern, Southern, and Northern healing practices. Jung was the first Western psychiatrist known to have affirmed that Eastern, indigenous, and spiritual disciplines make important contributions to healing. Similarly, Watts (1961) argued that Eastern traditions such as Buddhism, Taoism, Vedanta, and yoga resemble Western psychotherapy in their goals of attaining consciousness and liberation.

Many scholars have recognized the value of a syncretism between East and West, North and South. In the early 1970s, Ornstein (1972) discussed the psychology of consciousness as a synthesis of Western and Eastern orientations. He described the bifunctional human brain, in which analytical and rational Western thought follows the left brain hemisphere and the holistic and intuitive Eastern thought follows the right brain hemisphere. Ornstein concluded that because Western and Eastern orientations—like the right and left sides of the brain—are complementary, healers need to synthesize these two modes of consciousness.

Some multicultural clinicians have advocated for the syncretism of North and South wisdom in healing. For instance, Duran and Duran (1995) proposed a syncretistic healing with the use of Native American worldviews to analyze psychological processes and outcomes in their incorporation of indigenous healing into Western psychology. It is interesting to note that these authors merged an indigenous healing approach with a Jungian psychological perspective. Relatedly, several multicultural scholars have argued for an integration of Eastern, indigenous (Bankart, Koshikawa, Nedate, & Haruki, 1992; Comas-Díaz, 1992), and African (Holdstock , 2000; Watson, 1984) healing traditions into Western mental health treatment.

Jacobs (2003) continued the discussion on syncretism when he argued for the need to balance the thinking mind with the ancestral mind. He defined the *ancestral mind* as an older, more unconscious, ancestral intelligence. The ancestral mind is a deeper, wiser guide to well-being, and according to Jacobs, embodies the source of a more integrated concept of self. Jacobs went on to say that people's ancestors developed their cognitions and emotions far differently than do people of today because they were not burdened by modern circumstances. By contrast, our contemporary internal monologue depends on a verbal form of communication and reasoning that results from the use of language as a form of communication. On the other hand, our early ancestors' behaviors were based on a deeper connection to their emotions, feelings, and environment—in other words, they were guided by their ancestral mind. Jacobs concluded that there is a need to balance the thinking mind with the ancestral mind to enhance people's connection to self, others, and environment. Accordingly, a similar approach can be applied to healing. The syncretism of folk healing (right brain hemisphere) with dominant clinical practice (left brain hemisphere) combines intuitive healing with rational (analytical) treatment. Such a syncretistic model can foster the development of an expanded sense of daily awareness, promote powerful positive emotions, and foster healthy mind–body connection. An illustration of this concept is philosopher Wilber's (2000, 2006) integral model of spirituality and psychology, one that joins the enlightenment of the Eastern traditions (which cultivate higher states of consciousness) with the illumination of the West (which offers psychology's research findings).

Before explaining how clinicians can incorporate culture-specific healing into their clinical practices, I first discuss folk healing as a traditional form of culture-specific healing.

FOLK HEALING

Folk healing is a holistic attempt to restore balance among the individual, family, community, and environment. Many multicultural individuals use folk or indigenous practices during times of crisis, when dominant clinical treatment fails, when the clinical services are culturally irrelevant, or in all of these circumstances (Ruiz & Langrod, 1976). For example, a sample of people of color reported that they coped with the September 11,

2001, attacks by engaging in religious and spiritual activities and consulting folk healers (Constantine et al., 2005). As I indicated in Chapter 6, clinicians' lack of cultural competence is one reason many multicultural
individuals resort to alternative sources of healing. Unfortunately, some
mainstream clinicians believe that only poor or unacculturated individuals use folk healing. In reality, many people of color, regardless of social
class and education, have used some type of folk medicine in the form of
home remedies. Certainly, people of color seek folk remedies for the treatment of minor afflictions (those not requiring a physician), when access
to medical care is limited, and to preserve agency and mastery. These individuals may use the folk remedies at their home, at a relative's residence,
or at a folk healer's home (hence the term *home remedies*).

Similarities to, and Differences From, Western Therapeutic Practice

Folk healing shares common elements with Western therapeutic
approaches. According to Frank (1973), these similarities include the existence of (a) a trained healer whose healing powers are accepted by the sufferer and the sufferer's network, (b) a sufferer who seeks relief from the
healer, and (c) systematic contacts between the healer and sufferer in which
the healer attempts to reduce distress by changing the sufferer's behavior.
Both systems recognize the preeminent role of the healer–sufferer and the
clinician–client relationship in treatment (Hammer, 1990). Moreover,
researchers have found universal elements, called common factors, operating in psychological and spiritually-based therapies across cultures. The
common factors behind psychotherapy and folk healing include the
acknowledgment of the role of unconscious motivation, the need for
catharsis, and the therapeutic power of working through (Torrey, 1986).
In this vein, most types of folk healing share similarities with psychotherapy, because healers use the concepts of ego, id, and superego in their
treatment (Lubchansky, Egri, & Strokes, 1970). Certainly, folk healers
provide crisis intervention, in addition to individual, family, group, and
community counseling.

Notwithstanding their commonalities, there are differences between folk healing and dominant clinical practice. The main differences consist of folk healers' commitment to spiritual development (for both healers and clients), their service to humanity, and care for global welfare. As a result, folk healers use healing strategies consistent with their spiritual beliefs. To illustrate, healers aim to reach deep feeling states such as benevolent love, empathy, and compassion to provide life-enriching experiences to their clients. This process is similar to the Buddhist concept of compassionate, loving heart (Kornfield, 2008). In other words, healers aim to develop compassion and lovingkindness for their clients. As Claudia, the *curandera* (folk healer) quoted at the beginning of this chapter, said, the initial step in healing is caring for others. Moreover, healers enter a variety of states of consciousness, including trance states, attained through ritual performance such as spirit possession, prayer, sensory deprivation, or a combination of these methods. As previously mentioned, these states of consciousness help healers to gain intuitive understanding and knowledge of a client's suffering to intentionally direct their energy to heal and enhance well-being (Sollod, 1993).

Although Western and folk healing traditions include a shared worldview, the healing qualities of the therapist, the client's expectations, and an emerging sense of mastery (Torrey, 1986), folk healers culturally contextualize these therapeutic elements. Whereas Western approaches emphasize individualism and dismiss the interdependence among people, community, and cosmos (Smolan, Moffitt, & Naythons, 1990), folk healing highlights individuals' connection to a larger context. As folk healers acknowledge that suffering causes separation from other people, they foster their clients' reconnection with their culture. In addition, most of the folk healers come from the ethnic community they serve. Therefore, they operate within a context that facilitates their cultural empathy and responsiveness to clients' life experiences. Folk healers are culturally attuned and prepared to address the needs of sociocentric individuals. They diagnose by looking at their clients' reflection in the relational mirror. This means that folk healers include client's significant others, community, ancestors, spirits, and cosmic affiliations in treatment. Certainly, a central objective in folk healing is to help sufferers integrate their psychological distress and at the same time, to strengthen their collective self (Moodley, 1998). Moreover, folk healing operates at a symbolic representational level (Kakar, 1982). In other words, folk healers attempt to connect individuals with their cultural roots to reach deep into their collective unconsciousness.

Similarities to, and Differences From, Western Scientific Research

Indigenous and folk healing knowledge is based on a holistic paradigm that recognizes spiritual, physical, emotional, and mental well-being (Yeh, Hunter, Madan-Bahel, Chiang, & Arora, 2004). According to some authors (Battiste & Youngblood Henderson, 2000, as cited in Quinn, 2007; Bigfoot, 2008; Grenier, 1998; Koss-Chioino, 1992), indigenous knowledge follows a scientific approach because it is empirical, experimental, cumulative, dynamic, and systematic. Nonetheless, there are several differences between indigenous and Western knowledge regarding the study, purpose, methodologies, outcome measures, and issues regarding control and ownership of research (Grenier, 1998; Quinn, 2007). For example, the purpose of indigenous knowledge is to achieve wisdom by understanding *why*, as opposed to Western science, which attempts to understand *how*, or the immediate causality. Indigenous knowledge is culture specific, high context, and related to survival needs. The methods used in indigenous knowledge include talking with elders, prayer, meditation, and traditional ceremonies. Conversely, Western methods include analyzing data through measurement or breaking things down to their smallest parts. Moreover, the outcome measures in indigenous knowledge entail finding a balance with the natural world, in contrast to Western science, which offers a report of findings through data analysis. The indigenous investigator follows a subjective mode with an informal style, putting himself or herself into their study, as opposed to the Western scientist, who separates himself or herself from the research. Moreover, indigenous knowledge designates the community as the owner of the research, whereas Western science assigns control to the scientist expert. Furthermore, indigenous knowledge recognizes spirituality as an interconnected variable that infuses everything, whereas Western science separates itself from religion and spirituality.

Finally, the cumulative indigenous knowledge is transmitted orally, whereas the Western knowledge is disseminated through the scientific and professional literature. Table 8.1 summarizes these differences.

Examples of Folk Healing

Many multicultural clients are familiar with folk healing through cultural osmosis. In the following sections, I briefly discuss shamanism, *curanderismo, espiritismo, Santería,* and *Ho'oponopono* as examples of folk healing practices prevalent among several people of color.

Shamanism

Shamanism is the oldest spiritual healing practice. It entails the belief that spirits surround people and that they can commune with these forces. The

Table 8.1
Indigenous Knowledge Versus Western Knowledge

Area of emphasis	Western knowledge	Indigenous knowledge
Premise	Understanding	Wisdom
Question	How	Why
Purpose	Nonsurvivalist	Survivalist
Foundation	Evidence based	Spiritual, ancestral
Approach	Analytic	Holistic
Mode	Objective	Subjective
Style	Formal	Informal
Context	Low (Independent)	High (Dependent)
Culture	Nonspecific	Specific
Methods	Data collection	Traditional
Result	Data analysis	Balance, harmony
Power, Ownership	Expert	Community
Dissemination	Scientific literature	Oral

Note. Please also see Battiste and Youngblood Henderson (2000), as cited in Quinn (2007); Bigfoot (2008); Colorado (1988); Grenier (1998); Koss-Chioino (1992); and Mehl-Madrona (2003).

shaman is the intermediary who facilitates such communication (Villoldo, 2000). Shamans see life as sacred, recognize a creative energy, believe in the circular nature of time, do not try to dominate nature, and accept the presence of mystery (Cowan, 1996). As healers, shamans heal ailments by mending the sufferer's soul. According to Tedlock (2005), the shamanic worldview contains several fundamental perspectives, outlined below.

1. All entities have a holistic life force, vital energy, consciousness, soul, or spirit that permeates everything.
2. A web of life connects all things in an interdependent cause and effect relationship.
3. The world is constructed as a series of levels connected by a central axis in the form of a world tree or mountain. Shamans can travel to diverse worlds by moving through these cosmic levels.
4. Shamans understand events and can change them through normal or alternative states of consciousness, fasting, undertaking a vision quest, engaging in lucid dreaming, ingesting hallucinogens, or some combination of these activities.
5. Shamans recognize forces, entities, or beings whose behaviors in alternative worlds or realities affect individuals in the ordinary world.

Shamans use a diversity of healing strategies. They can prescribe a specific diet, a period of rest, or a particular ritual. A change in diet can help clients to readjust their biochemical functions. Moreover, they can pray, chant, and play the drum for healing purposes. Shamans use purification in the healing process. Within this purification the sufferer/client is called to destroy his or her "sick" existence to increase awareness and to experience life more fully (Kalweit, 1989). Such a catharsis helps clients to balance their emotional status. At times, shamans may reach the deepest level of unconsciousness to engage the client in individual healing as in healing of the collective self.

A vivid example of shamanistic healing is the interrogation of the distress (spirit, problem energy, or essence). In this technique, the healer and the client enter into a trancelike state in which the interrogation occurs and the "spirit" (sufferer's wise mind or unconsciousness) suggests ways to solve the problem. Healers may ask the spirit (distress or problem) that is afflicting the sufferer the following types of questions (L. Mehl-Madrona, personal communication, August 10, 2006):

- Who are you?
- Where did you come from?
- Why are you here?
- Where are you going?
- What would you look like if the distress [sorrow, problem, illness] were not here?
- What is that you really meant to ask for?

Answering these kinds of questions can offer potential solutions to the problem and enhances the client's self-healing capacities.

Curanderismo

Curanderismo is a Latin American folk healing system and a folk psychiatry (Kiev, 1968). The Spanish word curar means to heal. Curanderos (male healers) or curanderas (female healers) are shamans who devote themselves to curing physical, emotional, and spiritual illnesses (Harding, 1999). They use a holistic perspective to balance the body with the living elements of the earth, including plants, animals, air, water, fire, and divine entities.

Curanderismo integrates the indigenous shamanism from the Americas with Catholic elements such as images of saints, Jesus and the Virgin Mary, holy water, crucifixes, candles, and other religious icons. Like other forms of folk healing, curanderismo has a spiritual foundation. Some of the Latino indigenous spiritual principles are identified in Cervantes (2010, p. 529) and are listed below.

- The earth is a living system with an interconnection with humans.
- A holistic approach to life helps to nurture a relational self.
- Systemic causality allows the acceptance of the interconnection of events.
- Life is a great mystery that embraces sacred stories, ancestral teachings, visionary, and prophetic experiences.

- Knowledge is holistic and recognizes that every aspect in nature contains wisdom that can be revealed.
- Songs, dance, prayer, meditation, and ceremony are methods to unearth indigenous wisdom.
- Humans can use dreams, intuition, trance, and other transrational means to communicate with nonhuman entities.
- Spirits, cosmic energies, and a creative life force are core elements of Latino spirituality.

Curanderos consider their healing ability as a *don*, or gift from God. As such, curanderos use prayer, massage (the curandera who specializes in massage is called *sobadora*), herbal remedies, spiritual cleansing, rituals, and others.

According to Maduro (1983), the curanderismo model comprises eight major philosophical premises:

1. The sufferer has strong emotional states (e.g., rage, fear, envy, mourning of painful loss).
2. The sufferer is out of balance or harmony with his or her environment.
3. The sufferer is the innocent victim of malevolent or misguided forces.
4. The sufferer's soul may become separated from the body (*susto,* or loss of soul).
5. Cure requires the participation of the entire family, network, or both.
6. The natural world is not always distinguishable from the supernatural.
7. Illness or affliction often serves the social function through increased attention and rallying of the family around a sufferer or of reestablishing a sense of belonging (resocialization).
8. Latinos respond better to an open interaction with their curandero or curandera.

Espiritismo

Espiritismo is a religion and a Latino folk psychotherapy (Comas-Díaz, 1981). Espiritismo involves the belief that spirits of the dead intervene in the affairs of the living. Because the family structure among many people of color includes the relationship with the deceased (Council of National

Psychological Associations, 2003; E. R. Shapiro, 1994), *espiritistas* act as mediums to facilitate the communication between the living and the dead. Espiritismo flourished in Latin American and in the Caribbean, nurtured by Kardec's (1957) concept of spiritualism (Harwood, 1971). However, espiritismo differs from spiritualism in that it is primarily used as a folk healing and as a spiritual development practice. Espiritistas respond to individuals' personal circumstances as well as to their sociocultural contexts (Harwood, 1977). For example, espiritismo emerged in the Caribbean as an affirmation of ethnic roots and as a coping mechanism against social discontent. In this vein, espiritismo helps individuals to cope with powerlessness and oppression; in other words, "I become powerful with the help of the spirits."

Espiritistas assist clients to make meaning and to positively reframe events in their lives. Consider the following example. Maria brought her cousin Rosa to meet her clinician, Dr. Duffy, an Irish American psychologist. With Maria's consent, Dr. Duffy invited Rosa to attend the session. Maria reported that she saw her own funeral in a dream the previous night. Upon hearing this dream, Rosa congratulated Maria. Confused, Dr. Duffy asked why Rosa congratulated Maria. An espiritista, Rosa explained that dreaming about a funeral means that there will be a wedding. Consequently, Rosa was certain that Maria would be getting married soon.

Espiritistas diagnose clients/sufferers through communication with the spirits or *buscando la causa* (looking for the spiritual cause). They view problems as part of clients' spiritual development. Similar to shamans and curanderos or curanderas, espiristas treat clients with rituals, possession, prayers, and *remedios* (herbal remedies). Moreover, espiritistas involve the clients/sufferers' family in the healing process. Table 8.2 offers a comparison between dominant psychotherapy and espiritismo healing (data are from Comas-Díaz, 1981; Harwood, 1977; Kardec, 1957; Koss-Chioino, 1992).

Ho'oponopono

Ho'oponopono, which means "to make things right," is a Hawaiian indigenous healing. This practice of reconciliation and forgiveness attempts to restore and maintain positive relations among family members and

Table 8.2
Mainstream Psychotherapy and Espiritismo

Psychotherapy	Espiritismo
	Diagnosis
Diagnostic intake	Searching for the spiritual cause
Client verbalizes problems	*Espiritista* channels (divinizes) problems.
Client receives diagnostic label	Sufferer is viewed as evolving spiritually
	Treatment
Psychotherapy, psychopharmacology	Rituals, prayers, possession, *remedios*
Clinician may or may not communicate culturally and linguistically	*Espiritsta* communicates both culturally and linguistically
Family may or not be involved	Nuclear/extended family is involved
Clients are responsible for their behavior	Sufferers are not responsible for their behavior
Focus on adaptation and reduction of problems	Emphasis on spiritual development
Absence of spiritual component	Presence of spiritual component

between the sufferer and supernatural energies (D. W. Sue & Sue, 2008). Many people throughout the South Pacific believe that individuals' errors, including sexual misconduct or anger, can cause illness. Therefore, Ho'o-ponopono healers ask sufferers/seekers to confess, repentant, and forgive.

According to Tseng and McDermott (1975), Ho'oponopono healing ritual begins with a prayer—an invocation to tell the truth. Afterwards, the assembled family members, just like in a family therapy mode, discuss and confront each other with the conflict or transgression. A resolution process emerges out of a collective participation. After the members resolve the problem, they engage in releasing, or letting go of, the distress. As an illustration, the participants release their distress when they go to the sea and "give" the problem to the ocean. The ritual ends with a ceremonial feast—an offering of food to the gods and to the participants (D. W. Sue & Sue, 2008).

Santería

Santería, also known as *la regla lucumí,* is an African-based religion transplanted to the Americas by slaves from Nigeria and Benin (Yoruba people; Gonzalez-Wippler, 1974). The Santería religion has one god, Olorun, and the Orichas are his emissaries (Nuñez, 1992). Because the African slaves were forbidden to worship their deities, they disguised their Orichas as Catholic saints to practice their religion. As a result, the term *Santería* originated from the masking of the Yoruba Orichas as Catholic *santos* (saints; Gonzalez-Wippler, 1989). This camouflage designated Olorun as Jesus Christ, Elegua as the Holy Child of Atocha, Changó as Saint Barbara, Yemayá as Virgin of Regla, Ochún as our Lady of Charity, Ogún as Saint Peter and Saint Miguel, Oyá as Virgin of Candelaria, Obatalá as Our Lady of Mercy, Ochosi as Saint Norbert, Ourula as Saint Francis, and Babalú-Ayé as Saint Lazarus (see *Santería Religion,* 2010). The Orichas, or Santos, rule over every aspect of life and communicate with humans for guidance purposes. Gonzalez-Wippler (1974) described the orichas and their aspects as follows: Obatalá is associated with peace and purity; Elegua, with messages; Orunla, with divination; Changó, with passion and enemies; Ochosi, with hunting; Oggún, with war and employment; Babalú-Ayé, with illness; Yemayá, with womanhood; Ochún, with love and gold; and Oyá, with death.

Santería has millions of followers throughout the United States, the Caribbean, and Central and South America (Nuñez, 1992). Besides being a religion, Santería is a healing, magic, and divination practice.

Syncretism in Folk Healing

Most of the above-discussed folk healing and indigenous practices are currently being integrated into a syncretism. As you saw in the previous section, Santería, the way of the saints, provides an early example of syncretism. Currently, a dynamic syncretism of Santería and espiritismo is replacing the model of the Latino folk healing (Baez & Hernandez, 2001). As a result, *santerismo* is a syncretism of espiritismo and Santería (Olmos & Paravisini-Gebert, 1997).

In an interesting syncretism, Native American healers and constellation clinicians are uniting efforts with these two forms of healing. This approach, called "all my relations constellation," combines the wisdom of Native American traditions with the constellation therapy concept of family soul, transgenerational trauma, and the release of positive emotions (see http://allmyrelationsconstellations.com). Bert Hellinger, a German former missionary Catholic priest in South Africa, developed constellation therapy as a syncretism of Zulu cultural and spiritual beliefs with family therapy (Hellinger, Weber, & Beaumont, 1998). Constellation clinicians use the family energy field, or family soul, as the principle for diagnosis and treatment. Constellation family therapy is very popular among Latin Americans and other sociocentric individuals.

Cane's (2000) research provides an elegant example of a multicultural syncretistic treatment. She used a holistic approach with self-healing practices such as tai chi, Pal Dan Gum, acupressure, visualization, and breath work. Cane combined these alternative healing practices with Freire's (1970) critical consciousness (see Chapter 7). She treated victims of violence, indigenous peoples, refugees, prisoners, and battered women and children from El Salvador, Nicaragua, Honduras, and Guatemala with this syncretistic approach. Cane's study findings indicated a lessening of symptoms related to traumatic stress and posttraumatic stress disorder.

How Folk Healers Develop

Many folk healers adhere to indigenous knowledge, undergoing a training not necessarily accredited by mainstream institutions but recognized by their community. The community certification of these healers helps multicultural individuals to differentiate fake healers from folk healers. Folk healers commit to a code of ethics that includes a commitment to spiritual development, development of wisdom, exercise of compassion, and the engagement of service to humanity (Espin, 1996; Koss-Chioino, 1992). Most folk healers view unethical behavior as arising from destructive and negative thoughts that inflict harm (Walsh, 2011). Folk healers' ways of knowledge include intuition, spirituality, experience, observation, nature, balance, harmony, ancestors, history, and humor (Bigfoot, 2008), among others. They connect with these sources of knowledge by embracing honor, listening, being respectful, revering, collaborating, teaching, and learning.

Certainly, folk healers commit to a lifelong spiritual development. Most indigenous practitioners believe that everyone has the potential to be a healer. Therefore, they foster self-healing as part of helping the client's own development as a healer. Certainly, folk healers aim to awaken the healer within. For example, Eastern traditions such as Ayurvedic medicine attempt to awaken one's inner healer as a means of aligning oneself with the universal healing intelligence (Lad, 1993). The connection of personal healing with a cosmic or universal intelligence is also prevalent among many ethnic psychologies. Consequently, folk healing fosters development of the inner healer as an innate source of power and connection to the cosmos.

Although some folk healers inherit their curative ability from their ancestors, others become healers after receiving a message from a dream, a vision, or after experiencing a life-transforming event. At times, this transformative event is known as the *wounded healer syndrome.* Suffering, or the condition of being wounded, has been identified as a necessary quality for healing in shamanistic societies, Greek mythology, as well as in the Christian religion (symbolism of the crucifixion). Within shamanism, wounded healers embark upon a spiritual journey taken during a crisis usually involving a symbolic encounter with death. During this journey, shamans develop ways to order the chaos and confusion of their lives, achieving new meaning within their shamanic mission (Halifax, 1982). This process is symbolized by the shamans' confrontation of demonic forces that torture and dismember them, yielding a spiritual transformation and a renewal of the self. The shaman's mastery of chaos springs from direct experience, enabling him or her to be compassionate and to transform adversity into healing. Such a wounded healer transformation provides the shaman with the necessary power to help others. Likewise, Remen (1989) discussed the wounded healer syndrome as an essential element in the curative process. According to her, this syndrome represents two people in a healing rela-

210

tionship, where both are peers, wounded, and with healing capacity. In other words, the healer's woundedness allows him or her to connect to the client's woundedness in a nonjudgmental way.

How Folk Healing Works

Several mental health professionals have studied the curative elements of folk healing (Harding, 1999; Harwood, 1977; Kakar, 1982; Kiev, 1968). Sollod (1993) summarized the core aspects of diverse traditions healing methods as follows:

1. The healer engages in an altered state of consciousness, different from waking consciousness, that facilitates a variety of therapeutic processes.
2. The healer's perception of the sufferer/healee as a person free of limitations, instead of deficient, enhances healing.
3. The healer uses intuitive understanding.
4. There are no clear boundaries between the processes of the healer and those of the sufferer/healee.
5. Both healer and healee use visualization.
6. The healer uses trance induction to alter the sufferer/healee's state of consciousness.
7. The healer uses a spiritual or transpersonal paradigm to explain illness and recovery.
8. The spiritual paradigm emphasizes the potential for change.
9. The restoration of health implies the reestablishment of a conscious relationship with the divine or universal laws.
10. Prayer, faith, and meditation are considered therapeutic activities.

Although the popularity and effectiveness of most folk and indigenous healing have been attributed to the placebo effect (power of suggestion, faith, belief), K. M. Lin (2010) asserted that folk healing provides therapeutic benefits because it is embedded in clients' sociocultural contexts, fosters hope and expectations of recovery, and thus maximizes the placebo effect. Moreover, K. M. Lin stated that placebo responses are frequently accompanied by physiological changes (e.g., changes in blood pressure, neurohormonal levels, brain imaging characteristics) that are indistinguishable from those seen with pharmacological agents.

What Folk Healing Targets: Culture-Bound Syndromes and Ailments, or Cultural Disconnection

Folk healers acknowledge the existence of forces, energies, and spirits that can be personal, ancestral, animal, ecological, natural, divine, and/or cosmic. These energies, spirits, and entities can interact and influence people. Such a perspective is consistent with the sociocentric concept of *transpersonality*—the spiritual value that acknowledges the role of supernatural factors in people's lives (see Chapter 4). Within the folk healing belief system, illness is the result of imbalance, disharmony, disconnection, or all three. Consequently, folk healers treat ailments related to a client's imbalance in his or her life. An example of imbalance is the development of culture-bound syndromes.

The American Psychiatric Association's *Diagnostic and Statistical Manual of Mental Disorders* (4th ed., 1994; 4th ed., text rev. [*DSM–IV–TR*], 2000) cultural formulation acknowledges the cultural expression of distress in an appendix listing several culture-bound syndromes. A culture-bound syndrome is a recurrent, strange, or at times aberrant, illness, affliction or behavior that may be or not associated with a *DSM IV–TR* diagnosis (American Psychiatric Association, 2000). You may find useful getting familiarized with culture-bound syndromes, particularly if you work with immigrant, internationals, or ethnic minority clients. When you assess culture-bound syndromes, you need to consider your clients' (a) main forms of manifesting the disorder (e.g., spirits, nerves, fatalism, possession, unexplained misfortune, bad luck), (b) explanatory models, and (c) preference for folk and indigenous healers for treatment of these conditions (American Psychiatric Association, 2000). In addition, you may want to assess your clients' degree of connection or disconnection with their culture of origin.

Following are examples of culture-bound syndromes presented in the *DSM–IV–TR*.

- *Amok.* The word *amok* in Malay means being mad with uncontrollable rage. This dissociative disorder involves an outburst of aggressive violence and homicidal behavior toward people as well as objects. This ailment has been observed in Malaysia, Laos (*cathard*), Polynesia, the Philippines, Papua New Guinea, Puerto Rico (*mal de pelea*), and among the Navajo (*iich'aa*). This disorder is more predominant among men than women.

- *Ataque de nervios* ("attack of nerves"). This is an idiom of distress prevalent among Latinos from the Caribbean but is also known among many Latin American and Latin Mediterranean groups. Symptoms include uncontrollable attacks of crying, shouting, trembling, verbal and physical attacks, dissociation, and seizurelike or fainting episodes. Ataques are triggered by a stressful event related to a significant other (e.g., death, divorce, accident, interpersonal conflict) or situations in which the sufferer feels victimized. Individuals with ataques frequently feel being out of control.

- *Bilis* ("bile") and *cólera* ("rage"). These syndromes result from an excessive emotional distress, such as strong anger or rage. A major consequence of a powerful emotion such as anger is the disturbance of the body's humoral balance (see Chapter 6 for a discussion of the hot and cold theory of illness) and between the material and spiritual aspects of the body. Symptoms include acute nervous tension, headache, stomach problems, screaming, trembling, and chronic fatigue. In some extreme cases, the person can experience loss of consciousness. *Bilis* and *cólera* are common among Latinos (in the United States) as well as Latin Americans.

- *Dhat.* This term is used in India to denote severe anxiety and hypochondriacal concerns associated with the discharge of semen and feelings of weakness and exhaustion.

- *Falling out* or *blacking out.* These syndromes tend to occur in southern United States and in Caribbean groups. Symptoms include a sudden collapse preceded by feelings of dizziness. People who experience this usually hear and understand what is happening around them but are unable to move.

- *Ghost sickness.* This syndrome refers to a preoccupation with death and the deceased. Usually observed around American Indians, symptoms of ghost sickness include weakness, feelings of danger, loss of appetite, fear, bad dreams, confusion, feelings of doom, and a sense of suffocation.

- *Hwa-byung.* This term means "anger syndrome" in Korean. Also known as *wool-hwa-byung,* this affliction is attributed to the suppression of anger and includes symptoms of insomnia, fatigue, panic, fear of impending death, anorexia, generalized aches and pains, and other somatic symptoms.

- *Koro.* This refers to a sudden and intense anxiety accompanied by a fear that the penis (or vulva in females) will recede into the body and probably cause death. Koro has been reported in Malaysia, China, Thailand, and other regions of East Asia.

- *Mal de ojo* ("evil eye"). Sufferers are usually women and children. Symptoms include fitful sleep, crying without an apparent cause, diarrhea, vomiting, and fever. This disorder is prevalent in Latino and Mediterranean groups.

- *Nervios.* This syndrome entails a wide range of symptoms of emotional distress, somatic problems, and difficulties in functioning. It is a common idiom of distress among Latinos (in the United States) as well as Latin Americans. Nervios differ from ataques de nervios in intensity and severity. Whereas nervios range from mild to moderate nervousness, ataques de nervios are more severe and may overlap with panic disorder (Liebowitz et al., 1994) and dissociation (Lewis-Fernández et al., 2002).

- *Rootwork.* Roots, hexes, or spells can be "put" on the victim and result in a variety of emotional and somatic problems, including anxiety, gastrointestinal complaints, weakness, dizziness, and others. If a folk healer (root doctor) does not take off (eliminate) the root, the victim will fear death (voodoo death). You can read about the effect of rootwork in Tom's clinical vignette in Chapter 4. Prevalent in the southern United States, rootwork is known as *mal puesto* or *brujería* among Latinos.

- *Susto* ("fright"). Also known as *espanto* ("fright") and *pérdida del alma* ("soul loss"), susto is attributed to a frightening event that literally causes the soul to leave the body and results in sorrow and sickness.

Susto is a prevalent culture-bound syndrome among people in Latin America as well as among Latinos in the United States.

- *Taijin kyosfusho* ("anthrophobia"). A phobia that afflicts the Japanese, this culture-bound syndrome entails an individual's guilt about offending others because of the fear that his or her body's appearance, odor, and movements, among other body characteristics, embarrass other people.

- *Zar* ("possessing spirit"). This syndrome entails the possession by alien spirits that can cause disease. Symptoms may include dissociation, shouting, weeping, laughing, self-damage, and other expressive episodes. Originating in Ethiopia, zar is prevalent in many other countries in Africa, as well as in the Middle East, such as Algeria, Egypt, Kenya, Morocco, Nigeria, Somalia, Sudan, Tanzania, the Arabian Peninsula, and Iran. Healing includes the ritualistic placation of the possessing sprits.

Culture-bound syndromes are not exotic conditions that afflict only people abroad. Some immigrants in the United States, and even their offspring, may experience culture-bound afflictions as an expression of acculturative stress. Culture-bound syndromes can be interpreted as a metaphor for a cultural disconnection. Moreover, there are other culture-bound syndromes not listed in the *DSM–IV–TR*. Clinical and popular lore describes these culture-bound afflictions. To illustrate, below I present an incomplete list of Latino ailments (adapted from Martin, 2002, and from many Latina mothers and grandmothers).

- *Corriente de aire.* Being exposed to cold air can result in coughing, chest cold, or pneumonia. This affliction brings secondary gains such as not "exposing" yourself to unnecessary or unwanted interactions by staying home.

- *Cuerpo cortado.* This refers to a general sense of malaise, or feeling unwell. It relates to a pain in one's body usually associated with the common cold. Sometimes this problem entails a lack of energy and an inability to do anything. Cuerpo cortado can be a sign of depression.

- *Musarañas.* This refers to obsessive thoughts that can affect a person's mood.

- *Fiaca.* This is a feeling of weariness, boredom, dissatisfaction, and anomie (Argentina).
- *Saladerra.* This is when a person develops acute anxiety (without somatic symptoms) as a consequence of being the victim of a series of continuing misfortunes and bad luck (Dobkin de Rios, 1981; Peru). A version of this condition is known as *salazón* (literary, being "salted by life") in Puerto Rico.
- *Los diablos azules* ("the blue devils"). This affliction refers to an incidence that grips a person and makes him or her lose possession of his or her faculties (Chile and Peru).
- *Patatún* or *patatús.* This is a fainting spell caused by emotional, as well as physical, causes (Caribbean).
- *Telele.* This affliction causes sufferers to change their mood.

The above-mentioned culture-bound illnesses illustrate the power of the cultural context in shaping the development and expression of mind–body–spirit afflictions. In treating culture-bound syndromes, folk healers use strategies to help clients foster a significant connection to themselves, others, community, and culture. They aim to enhance self-healing and agency. Healers help clients to make meaning out of adversity, reframe their problems into spiritual challenges, and embark on a psychospiritual journey.

The Benefits of Addressing Folk Healing in Mainstream Psychotherapy

As I mentioned before, many people of color use folk approaches in conjunction with mainstream clinical practice. In other words, they favor integrative, holistic, and syncretistic healing approaches. APA Multicultural Guideline 5 recommends psychologists expand their range of interventions by acknowledging ethnic and indigenous psychologies. To enhance your cultural competence, you can learn about non-Western helping practices and healing traditions that may be appropriately included in your clinical practice. When deemed appropriate, APA Multicultural Guideline 5 (APA, 2003) encourages psychologists to recognize and enlist the assistance of recognized indigenous healers such as shamans, medicine men or women, curanderos, astrologers, espiritistas, clairvoyants, psychics, santeros, and others with their clients.

Following a similar line of reasoning, the U.S. Surgeon General (Satcher, 2000) concluded that Western psychological interventions could benefit from incorporating core assumptions and practices of ethnoindigenous healing. The inclusion of culture-specific approaches does not imply that you have to abandon your theoretical orientation or become an alternative healer. Instead, it reflects your ability to adapt your treatment to multicultural clients. You can enhance this ability when you elicit your clients' explanatory models, recognize their healing perspectives, and empower them to connect with the "doctor who resides in each client."

Depending on your theoretical orientation and therapeutic style, you can incorporate aspects of folk healing into your practice when you recognize the mind–body–environment connection, acknowledge spirituality as a dimension in healing, use empowering approaches, and endorse syncretistic healing perspectives. You can address the culture-bound syndromes and ailments described above using mainstream psychotherapy approaches, as well as culture-specific approaches that are rooted in folk healing, such as CAM and ethnic psychotherapies. In the rest of this chapter, I discuss how mainstream psychotherapy, CAM, and ethnic psychotherapies can be used with multicultural individuals.

USING MAINSTREAM PSYCHOTHERAPY TO ADDRESS CULTURE-BOUND SYNDROMES AND AILMENTS IN CLINICAL PRACTICE

Mainstream psychotherapy approaches and referrals to other CAM healers can be used alongside more traditional folk healing. For example, I saw Gordon, a Chinese neuroscientist, who was completing a research fellowship in the United States. Gordon sought therapy because he suffered from extreme anxiety. During the completion of the multicultural assessment, Gordon revealed that his anxiety stemmed from a breakup with his fiancée. Consequently, I incorporated elements of grief therapy into our clinical work. However, Gordon's anxiety worsened until he revealed that he suffered from koro, the above-mentioned culture-bound syndrome in which he feared that his penis could retract into his body. Incidentally, individuals suffering from koro tend to see mainstream clinicians for treatment (Mattelaer & Jilek, 2007). Gordon stated that he developed koro after he found out that his fiancée was seeing another man. In therapy we worked on Gordon's castration fears and on his needs to "redeem himself as a man." In addition, I used guided imagery. Moreover, I referred him to an acupuncturist. Gordon consulted a folk healer, who recommended that he practice tai chi. The combination of talk psychotherapy, experiential therapy (guided imagery), and folk healing helped to reduce Gordon's anxiety. After 6 months of treatment, Gordon's symptoms subsided. In a similar vein, R. J. Castillo (1997) described the successful treatment of a man with *dhat* (anxiety associated with the discharge of semen) with psychotherapy, yoga meditation, and visualization.

Sonia, the client from the beginning of this chapter, provided an example of the role of culture-bound afflictions in Latinos' lives. You may remember that in a vignette in Chapter 1, I introduced Sonia as a victim of domestic abuse, who wanted to "castrate" her husband, Dale. During the middle phase of therapy, Sonia expressed concern about communicating with her mother. Sonia told Dr. Jenkins that if she disclosed her plan to divorce Dale, her mother would have a susto (fright) and could die. Certainly, many Latinos believe that strong emotions such as fear, rage, susto, envy, mourning, and others can induce physical and mental health problems (Maduro, 1983). In turn, Dr. Jenkins suggested assertiveness training to Sonia. Unfortunately, Sonia adamantly rejected Dr. Jenkins's suggestion, claiming that she could develop an ataque just thinking about it. The value of familism appeared to reinforce Sonia's intense relationship with her mother. Indeed, Sonia's concern was consistent with second-generation young adults' tendency to maintain more frequent contact with their parents after leaving home, when compared with their White American peers (Tummala-Narra, 2004). Finally, Dr. Jenkins suggested a Latino cultural assertiveness training (Comas-Díaz & Duncan, 1985). Sonia agreed to try it but stated that she would consult a curandera to prevent the development of an ataque.

COMPLEMENTARY AND ALTERNATIVE MEDICINE

The popularity of CAM approaches among the general public could potentially land clients at your clinical door. To illustrate, I have numerous clients who, during their initial consult, asked for mind–body approaches. If you consider incorporating CAM into your practice, make sure to examine the compatibility of these methods with your clinical approach and style. For example, if you are a cognitive–behavioral therapist, you could incorporate mindfulness (Segal et al., 2002), schema work (Bennet-Golman, 2001), or both, into your clinical work. However, if you are a Jungian psychotherapist, you may feel at home with guided imagery (Foote, 1996) and with creative visualization (Gawain, 2002).

Moreover, if you endorse experiential therapies, you could be familiar with mind–body healing. In particular, if you work with trauma victims, you can use therapies such as eye movement desensitization and reprocessing (EMDR; F. Shapiro, 1995), somatic experiencing (Levine, 1997), or both, among others. Incidentally, EMDR borrowed its healing light stream technique from yoga (F. Shapiro, 1995). Conversely, if you do not subscribe to experiential approaches, you may want to consider techniques that are relatively easy to integrate into your practice. As an illustration, Gendlin (1982, 2001) developed focusing, a technique for personal growth, psychotherapy, and counseling. Similar to Buddhist psychotherapy (Epstein, 1995), focusing-oriented psychotherapists aim to help individuals achieve a deeper understanding of their lives within a larger context (Gendlin, 2001). In brief, the focusing technique comprises six steps, where you can help your clients to

1. *clear a space* to be with themselves;
2. *feel or sense* the problem in their body;
3. *handle* and describe a quality or image of the felt sense itself;
4. *resonate*, or check how the felt sense and the image resonate with each other;
5. *ask* if they can change the image so it does not hurt as much; and
6. *encourage them to receive* whatever understanding and life lesson that come with the experience.

In choosing which CAMs to incorporate into your practice, allow yourself to explore holistic methods consistent with your psychotherapeutic approach.

ETHNIC PSYCHOTHERAPIES

Another way to incorporate culture-specific healing into psychotherapy is through ethnic psychotherapies. Ethnic psychotherapies are similar to folk healing in that they are a type of culture-specific healing. However, although folk healing is embedded in a spiritual context, ethnic psychotherapies are embedded in cultural wisdom. In other words, whereas folk healing approaches promote spiritual development, ethnic psychotherapies help individuals to cope in a culturally relevant manner. Following this analysis, ethnic psychotherapies can be placed at the center of a healing continuum, with traditional folk healing at the left and dominant psychotherapies at the right.

Ethnic psychotherapies arise from ethnic and indigenous holistic practices that aim to connect individuals to a larger context. Because healers interpret distress as a result of individuals' disconnection from their cultures of origin, ethnic psychotherapies provide resources to rescue clients' ancestry as they ground their cultural identity into a collective self (Comas-Díaz, Lykes, & Alarcón, 1998). In the same way that folk healers promote clients' involvement with significant relationships for treatment purposes, ethnic psychotherapies respond to clients' needs of familism in addition to the Native American value of all my relations in healing. Ethnic psychotherapies are anchored in an empowerment foundation and validate the importance of racial, ethnic, historical, and political contexts of oppression.

You can increase your clinical repertoire by becoming familiar with ethnic psychotherapies. I present selected examples of ethnic psychotherapies next.

Testimonio (Testimony)

Storytelling can be a reason for living. For instance, many survivors of death camps found that the drive to tell their story provided the impetus to survive (Kay, 1998). Chilean psychologists developed *testimonio,* a narrative healing approach, to help individuals and communities sustain the catastrophic context of the political terrorism during the Augusto Pinochet dictatorship. Testimonio is a first-person account of one's experiences, with attention to experiences of loss, trauma, and oppression (Cienfuegos & Monelli, 1983). As a verbal healing journey to the past, testimonio facilitates a catharsis and helps individuals to integrate fragmented experiences.

Mainstream trauma therapists have been successfully incorporating testimony into their clinical practice (Aron, 1992). Testimony validates personal experience as a basis for truth and knowledge in an empowering manner. To illustrate, Marcia's sexual assault testimony (see Chapter 7) to her church community empowered her through validation and support. As a holistic approach, testimony addresses the needs of clients who have suffered individual, collective, and multigenerational oppression. Moreover, testimony helps individuals to restore a sense of purpose and usefulness through helping others (Fischman & Ross, 1990). Certainly, Marcia found meaning and a way to help others when she empowered herself to develop a child sexual abuse prevention program. An ethnic psychotherapy, testimonio addresses the sociopolitical context of oppression through a verbal healing journey. In short, testimony can transform adversity into consciousness and action.

Dichos (Proverbs)

Another ethnic narrative healing approach is *dichos*. Dichos are a form of popular psychology that captures folk wisdom (Aviera, 1996; Zuñiga, 1991, 1992). This healing approach involves Spanish proverbs or idiomatic expressions used to communicate about every single aspect in life. Also known as *refranes,* dichos have cultural credibility and validity. For example, you can use dichos as a type of flash therapy consistent with sociocentric clients' worldview. Indeed, several multicultural clinicians have used dichos in adapting dominant psychotherapy to foster culturally relevant cognitive restructuring and address cultural obstacles in managing relational conflicts (Comas-Díaz, 2006a). For example, you can use the dicho *El mal escribano le echa la culpa a la pluma* ("The poor writer places the blame on the pen"), meaning that people tend to blame their problems on external causes rather than examine their own contribution to address clients' use of externalization.

In addition, I have found the use of dichos to be effective in cognitive–behavioral interventions. For example, the dicho *Gato escaldado del agua fría huye* ("A scalded cat runs away from cold water") means that the scalded cat avoids both hot and cold water without differentiating between them. In other words, this dicho conveys that traumatized individuals generalized their responses to neutral or nontoxic stimuli. To promote positive change, you can use the dicho *Nunca es tarde para bien hacer; haz hoy lo que no hiciste ayer* (loosely translated as "It is never too late to do a good thing; do today what you didn't do yesterday"). Moreover, the dicho *No hay curva mala pasándola despacio* ("There is no bad curve, as long as you pass it slowly") can be used to foster confidence though the use of self-regulation.

When appropriate, I use dichos to communicate in a high-context style with sociocentric clients. For example, in working with religious African American clients, I quote Biblical proverbs as a culturally congruent treatment approach. To illustrate, the biblical proverb "Ask and it shall be given to you; seek and you will find; knock and it shall be opened onto you" (Matthew 7:7–8) can be used to combat resistance against asking for psychological help. Another example, proverbs like "A gentle answer turns away wrath, but a harsh word stirs up anger" (Proverbs 15:1) can provide a forum for a discussion of racial microaggressions, and conversely, as an interpersonal anger management.

Cuentos (Storytelling)

Many collectivistic groups use storytelling to answer questions, educate, communicate, and transmit knowledge. Along these lines, storytelling is a means to preserve collective memory by maintaining history, culture, and mythology (E. R. Shapiro, 1998). Indeed, many multicultural psychotherapists use narrative approaches congruent with sociocentric people's oral and storytelling legacies (Semmler & Williams, 2000). *Cuentos* (literary meaning "stories") help individuals to create personal narratives that lead to healing and empowerment (K. Anderson & Jack, 1991). This cultural-centered therapy emerged out of a Latino sociocentric context to emphasize a relational self and to promote family unit. Moreover, clinicians use Latino folk tales and adapted cuentos to promote culturally relevant adaptive interpersonal behaviors. In other words, they use cuentos to foment youngsters' identification with a culturally relevant hero or heroine, as well as with antiheroes, such as fools or tricksters, to teach valuable lessons (Costantino, Malgady, & Rogler, 1986). A main goal of cuento therapy is to promote a bicultural adaptation and synthesis among ethnic youngsters who live in two cultures. To enhance this goal, clinicians use psychoeducation: "What is the hero [or heroine's] lesson [or lessons]?" To achieve this goal, clinicians engage the assistance of their clients' mothers as storytellers. Afterward, mothers and their children participate in group psychotherapy. Research has demonstrated the efficacy of cuento therapy with Puerto Rican children in reducing anxiety and aggression and improving social judgment (Costantino et al.).

Network Therapy

Remember Raul, the man in the vignette at the beginning of Chapter 7? Raul responded to Dr. Carlton's inquiry about previous treatment by stating that he had been in network therapy. Native American psychologist Carolyn Attneave developed network therapy as a means of recreating the entire social context of a clan's network in order to activate and mobilize a person's family, kin, and relationships to assist in the healing process (Attneave, 1990; Speck & Attneave, 1973). This strategically oriented, culture-specific therapy relies on the client's network members in an extended family treatment and group intervention (Speck & Attneave, 1973). The network members' influence and pressure are integral parts of the treatment in helping clients to change. As a result, network therapy is a holistic community-based form of healing. Mainstream substance abuse counselors have incorporated network therapy into their treatment. A classic exponent of this approach, Galanter (1993) recommended the use of clients' network system as a supportive and cohesive team to assist them in achieving abstinence. In additionally, network therapy for substance abuse promotes self-healing through clients' attendance at AA and other self-help groups.

Morita Therapy

Morita therapy is a culture-centered Zen healing approach. Shoma Morita, a Japanese psychiatrist, developed this treatment and called it *experiential therapy*. The experiential aspects include clinicians' prescription of rest, life renormalization, rehabilitation, and related experiential activities to his or her clients. During the first Morita treatment stage (ranging from 1 to 2 weeks), clients get deprived of sensory and social activity and are confined to bed to rest. Clients in their second treatment stage write a daily diary and engage in housework to avoid obsessing about their symptoms (Morita, 1998). In turn, clinicians comment on clients' journal to help them to accept reality and develop an appreciation of life. To change their life attitude, clients learn to accept things as they are, become action oriented, and accept Zen teachings (e.g., "Perceive every day as a good day"; Reynolds, 1980). Partly due to Morita therapy's emphasis on Zen philosophy, many Chinese clinicians use Morita therapy.

Naikan Therapy

Another culture-centered treatment is *naikan* therapy. Ishin Yoshimoto, a Japanese Buddhist monk, developed this approach in which self-inspection (i.e., self-assessment) is the central principle of treatment (Reynolds, 1980). Within this context, clients examine their life with a focus on significant relationships, particularly parental figures (Tseng, 2001). The self-evaluation helps clients to change their view of life through the development of insight, appreciation, joy, and the expression of gratitude toward others. Naikan clinicians use cultural sociocentric values to restore relations through the reappraisals of primary relationships and a discouragement of narcissistic views. The Japanese Shinto concept of *sunao* or a harmonious state of mind associated with honesty, humility, and simplicity is at the root of naikan therapy (Tseng, 2001). Both Morita and naikan therapies incorporate elements of meditation in their approach.

Psychotherapy of Liberation

Psychotherapy of liberation is a culture-centered healing approach born in Latin America. Based on Latino theology of liberation, this healing approach emerged as a response to sociopolitical oppression. Psychology of liberation is grounded in spiritual–social action that resonates with Black liberation theology, Africanist traditions, and African American psychology. Ignacio Martin-Baro (in Blanco, 1998), the architect of psychology of liberation, was both a priest and a psychologist. He identified three main goals in the liberating process of overcoming internalized oppression: (a) the recovery of historical memory, (b) de-ideologizing everyday experience and sociopolitical reality, and (c) using the cultural strengths of the people (Blanco, 1998). Indeed, psychology of liberation's spiritual basis affirms clients' strengths through ethnocultural and indigenous traditions and practices (Comas-Díaz, Lykes, & Alarcon, 1998). Liberation clinicians attempt to work with people in context through strategies that enhance awareness of oppression and of the ideologies and structural inequality that have kept them subjugated and oppressed. In addition, these clinicians help individuals recognize the relationship between intrapersonal or interpersonal dynamics and the sociopolitical context (Blanco, 1998). They use Freire's (1970) concept of critical consciousness to promote social action. You may remember that I asked Marcia critical consciousness questions in Chapter 7. Liberation practitioners collaborate with the oppressed in developing critical analysis and engaging in transformative actions. As in the example of network therapy, mainstream clinicians are incorporating psychotherapy of liberation approaches into their treatment.

CONCLUSION

Numerous multicultural individuals use culture-specific healing, such as ethnic psychotherapies, because these approaches offer them a restored sense of centrality in time and context. A significant number are exposed to folk healing through cultural and family osmosis. During times of crisis, many multicultural individuals resort to folk healing. In addition, these individuals may combine their use of ethnic, indigenous, and alternative practices with mainstream treatment. Succinctly put, ethnic psychotherapies, indigenous traditions, and folk healing offer empowerment, meaning, and cultural support to suffers, clients, and supplicants.

Several mainstream clinicians are incorporating aspects of folk healing into their practices. Although you do not need to become a folk healer, learning from culture-specific healing is a way to increase your cultural awareness, as well as a means to expand your clinical repertoire. Below is a list of key multicultural clinical strategies presented in this chapter.

MULTICULTURAL CLINICAL STRATEGIES

- Identify culture-specific and culture universal aspects of helping and healing.
- Attempt to familiarize yourself with culture-specific healing, such as ethnic psychotherapies and folk healing.
- Aim to educate yourself about the general use of CAM and the cultural-specific CAM practices.
- When appropriate, consider referring clients to an alternative healer for conjoint treatment.
- If appropriate, integrate holistic models of health into your practice.
- Recognize spirituality as a dimension in healing for many multicultural individuals.
- Familiarize yourself with culture-bound syndromes and afflictions.
- Explore ways to incorporate client's healing perspectives into your clinical practice.

9

Multicultural Consciousness: Extending Cultural Competence Beyond the Clinical Encounter

Cultural competence is the process of becoming, not a state of being.

—Josepha Campinha-Bacote (2003)

John: I saw you at the rally on Sunday.

Dr. Cassidy: Oh, really? I didn't see you.

John: What do you think about the speaker?

How do you feel about this clinical interaction? What would you do if you were in Dr. Cassidy's position? Have you been in similar situations with your clients?

As presented in John and Dr. Cassidy's vignette, your clients may encounter you outside the clinical hour. The cultural competence journey is incomplete if you do not extend your self-assessment outside the clinic. In other words, your cultural competence does not need to stay behind when you leave the consulting room.

In this chapter, I examine cultural competence as a process of becoming. I use the concept of multicultural consciousness to designate a practice for living with cultural competence. Within this context, *multicultural consciousness* refers to the process of internalizing and incorporating cultural competence into your everyday activities. Multicultural consciousness involves a lifestyle because your journey into cultural competence is reflected in every aspect of your behavior.

CULTURAL COMPETENCE AS A PROCESS IN ORGANIZATIONS

Cultural competence goes beyond being aware of the impact of culture on your clinical practice. Certainly, how you exercise cultural competence in your life is a personal choice. However, cultural competence is an inclusive process because who you are as a clinician is not isolated from the rest of your persona. Moreover, if you work within a system, your clinical services will be embedded in the organizational culture. For example, when you support the development of your organization's cultural competence, you definitely enhance your clinical effectiveness. To illustrate, the American Psychological Association (APA) Multicultural Guideline 6 encourages psychologists to use organizational change processes to support culturally informed organizational policy, development, and practices. Consequently, you can foster the development of cultural competence into those organizations you interact with. In other words, you can promote cultural competence at the organizational, community, and even societal levels.

The demographic projections in the United States mean that both organizations and clinicians will need to be culturally competent: By 2050, half of the workforce is predicted to be multicultural individuals (Toossi, 2006). Of course, the process of influencing and changing an organization is arduous and, at times, frustrating. In addition, there is no right way to influence organizations' cultural competence. Interventions that prove to be effective in one organization may not necessarily be successful in another setting.

Like individuals, organizations have a culture. An organizational culture comprises a pattern of beliefs, values, and expectations shared by its members (Hellriegel, Slocum, & Woodman, 1998). The power holders in the organization are the individuals who shape its culture by influencing its assumptions, norms, principles, and ideologies (Ragins, 1995). These individuals entrust management with the coordination of the organizational policies and the supervision of their implementation. As most of the power holders in the United States are White European Americans, they tend to reflect the mainstream culture and thus use ethnocentric perspectives to define the assessment of performance (Ragins, 1995).

Applegate (2009, p. 25) postulated that an organization is considered culturally competent when

- constituency groups involved in the organization understand how cultural competence is connected to the organization's mission;
- individuals perceive the organization to reflect the attitudes, values, behaviors, and policies described in the mission;
- commitment to inclusion is evidenced in behaviors, structures, publications, policies, plans, programs, and practices;
- power holders, board members, executive leaders, administrators, staff members, and volunteers demonstrate their commitment to cultural competence;
- the organization incorporates the needs and perspectives of a diverse workforce into decision making and delivery of services and programs;
- the organization recruits and retains diverse staff, board members, and volunteers to reflect the composition of the community they serve;
- the organization invests in developing group-processes skills at the levels of board members and staff leaders; and
- there is a culture of learning (beyond involving diverse individuals) that encourages perspectives from diverse cultural groups.

An organizational culture that lacks cultural competence can be detrimental to its multicultural workers. Helms (1990b) discussed the concept of racial climate in organizations as influenced by a variety of structural and nonstructural factors, including perception of power, group racial norms, and racial identity coalitions. The *perception of power* refers to the extent to which the individual or group in the organization is perceived as having influence. These perceptions are informed by ascribed status as well as psychological power, or the extent to which the individual perceives that he or she can influence the workplace. According to Helms, *racial group norms* refer to a particular unit's behavior regarding race on a daily basis and are maintained by those seeking homeostasis, while those disrupting the norms face resistance. As a result, racial identity coalitions involve subgroups that share similar dominant racial identity attitudes. Such coalitions can potentially influence the racial identity development of a particular organizational unit. Likewise, organizations have a multicultural environment that includes gender, age, sexual orientation climate, or some combination thereof. An organizational culture, climate, and environment can profoundly affect our clients. To illustrate, let us return to John, the client from the vignette at the beginning of this chapter.

John is an African American gay man who worked as a senior engineer in a medium-sized company. I compared John and Dr. Cassidy's ADDRESS-ING areas in Chapter 2. John contemplated the decision to file an Equal Employment Opportunity complaint against his company because he felt harassed in the workplace. The harassment began when a colleague "outed" him at work after he saw John leaving a gay bar. John discussed this issue with Dr. Cassidy and decided against filing the complaint. He continued working in therapy on his difficulties with his father, a Southern Baptist minister who rejected John's sexual orientation. While working on these issues, John's professional behavior changed. As a coping mechanism against the harassment at work, John stopped going the extra mile. Consequently, his work supervisor did not assign him substantive projects. John did not assert himself, and in his own words, he became "the stereotypic Affirmative Action employee." This behavior is consistent with the experience of many visible people of color being the only professional of color in a work group and thus the association with the perception of stereotype threat. Indeed, members of ethnic minorities are susceptible to *stereotype threat*—where individuals avoid or do poorly on tasks in which their responses could be judged as confirming racial stereotypes, in sharp contrast to their performance on the same tasks when their ethnicity will not be identified (Steele & Aronson, 1995).

An examination of the racial climate in John's workplace revealed a tense atmosphere. Kamisha, an African American female engineer, was recently fired for poor performance. Besides John, Kamisha was the only African American professional in the organization. As in other contexts in life, stereotype and discrimination are the basis of racial and gender inequality in the workplace (F. Dobbins, Kalev, & Kelly, 2007). Regrettably, John lost his only racial ally in the organization. Around the time of Kamisha's dismissal from the organization, John perceived that several male coworkers targeted him with racial microaggressions. He consulted a lawyer, who advised him against legal action because of the subtle nature of the microaggressions.

These dynamics seem to resemble Bion's (1961) concept of *basic assumption group*. Within this conceptual framework, members of a group (or organization) act collectively to alleviate anxiety and to achieve an unstated goal. In John's situation, his coworkers harbored an unspoken concern against affirmative action. According to the basic assumption group concept, members collude (including John, who acted the racial stereotypy of a token by not going the extra mile) to perpetuate the members' unstated accusation of reverse discrimination. Dr. Cassidy explored John's occupational professional work history. An occupational inventory aims to facilitate clients' knowledge, development, and enhancement of occupational experiences during previous and current work. Dr. Cassidy helped John to examine the following areas:

- meaning of work for the person, family, peer group, and community;
- family history of educational level and occupational attainment;
- previous and current work (paid and pro bono);
- occupational success and failure;
- occupational socialization;
- discrimination in the work setting (including microaggressions);
- racial and ethnocultural reactions to discrimination (e.g., anger, rage, passive aggression);
- previous and current occupational coping skills (functional and dysfunctional);
- occupational fears, fantasies, family scripts, and wishes;
- projection of family, personal, and career goals;
- assessment of racial climate in the workplace;
- assessment of organizational cultural competence;
- perception of the work setting as a safe place to engage in difficult dialogue; and
- professional or occupational achievements.

As John responded to the occupational inventory, he realized that his workplace was not a safe environment for him. Consequently, he decided to look for a work environment where he felt safe and had an appropriate person–environment fit. Unfortunately, John's experience in the workplace may be common among professionals of color. In their well-known study, F. Dobbins et al. (2007) examined the efficacy of promoting diversity strategies in organizations. These researchers analyzed how 829 companies implemented the diversity challenges and how they collected data for 31 years. They asked participants a simple question, "If a company adopts a particular diversity program, what effect does it have on the share of minority and women in management?" The study participants identified the following diversity strategies: diversity training (to eliminate stereotypes), evaluations (to provide feedback to staff making hiring and promotion decisions), task force, network, minority managers, and mentor programs. Based on their findings, F. Dobbins et al. concluded that diversity evaluations and network programs had no positive effect on the average workplace. The results indicated that diversity trainings that focused on cultural awareness were more efficient than mandatory ones that focused on legal issues, such as the threat of a lawsuit. Task forces headed by a manager who had a clear responsibility for diversity were deemed successful. However, the most effective diversity initiatives were mentoring and fostering culturally competent managers. These researchers concluded that mentoring was an efficient strategy because organizations offered this program to minorities, women, and majority members, and thus it did not generate a backlash. Unfortunately, individuals from minority groups (like John) can be targeted and become victims of organizational power dynamics.

CULTURAL SELF-ASSESSMENT: TARGET AND NONTARGET GROUP MEMBERSHIP

Applegate (2009) discussed Bates's concept of *target group*. People of color and other minority group members are in the target group; as such, they are viewed as different and inferior by dominant group members. Conversely, nontarget group membership promotes a dominant viewpoint and benefits from unearned privilege, such as higher employment, easier access to credit, and higher incomes. In brief, nontarget membership is similar to White privilege (see Chapter 5, this volume, for a discussion of White privilege). Applegate (2009, p. 29) developed self-assessment questions to help clinicians discern their position in target and nontarget locations:

- When have you been a member of a target group?
- When have you been a member of a nontarget group?
- What strengths resulted from your experiences as a member of either group?
- Can you describe a time when you were treated better than others as a result of membership in a nontarget group?
- Can you describe a time when you found yourself treating a person in a target group as less than yourself?

STANDARDS FOR CULTURAL COMPETENCE IN HEALTH AND MENTAL HEALTH ORGANIZATIONS

Government-sponsored health organizations have been striving to develop cultural competence. For example, the U.S. Department of Health and Human Services Office of Minority Health (2001) proposed the National Standards for Culturally and Linguistically Appropriate Services (CLAS) in health care. The goal of these standards is to contribute to the elimination of the racial, ethnic, and cultural health disparities and to promote the health of all Americans. Some of the CLAS standards in health care organizations are as follows:

- Health care organizations should ensure that patients and clients receive care that is provided in a manner compatible with their cultural beliefs and preferred language.
- Health care organizations should implement strategies to recruit, retain, and promote diverse staff and leadership that are representative of the community they serve.
- Health care organizations should ensure that all staff receive education and training in culturally and linguistically appropriate service delivery.

- Health care organizations must provide language assistance service (including bilingual staff and interpreters) at no cost to patients and clients with limited English proficiency during all hours of operation.
- Health care organizations must provide to patients and clients verbal and written information of their right to receive language assistance in their preferred language.
- Health care organizations must assure that competent interpreters and bilingual staff assist clients with limited English proficiency. Family and friends are not allowed to interpret except upon clients' requests.
- Health care organizations should develop, implement, and promote a strategic plan that describes clear goals, policies, operational plans, and management accountability mechanisms to provide culturally and linguistically appropriate services.
- Health care organizations should conduct initial and ongoing organizational self-assessments of CLAS-related activities.
- Health care organizations should develop participatory, collaborative partnerships with communities and use a variety of mechanisms to facilitate community and patient and consumer involvement in developing and implementing CLAS-related activities.
- Health care organizations are encouraged to share with the public information about their progress and innovations in implementing the CLAS standards.

You can see all the CLAS standards at U.S. Department of Health and Human Services (Office of Minority Health, 2001).

Several state governments use the CLAS standards to encourage the availability of culturally competent services in their organizations and personnel. Minnesota, a state whose culturally diverse population is increasing rapidly, provides an illustration. The Minnesota Department of Human Services (DHS) has endorsed guidelines for culturally competent organizations that affirm that the organization and its personnel are always accountable for culturally appropriate services. In addition to having culturally competent personnel and culturally appropriate services, the Minnesota DHS (2004) asks organizations to become culturally competent because

- health disparities exist between mainstream and culturally diverse populations;
- clients' access barriers limit their receiving effective services;
- law and accreditation standards increasingly demand cultural competence;
- liability exposure increases and costs rise when services are not effective; and
- competition in funding and market business favor culturally competent organizations.

The Minnesota DHS adheres to the federal guidelines for CLAS (Minnesota DHS, 2004; Appendix G) as follows:

- Promote and support the attitudes, behaviors, knowledge, and skills necessary for staff to work respectfully and effectively with patients and each other in a culturally diverse work environment.
- Have a comprehensive management strategy to address culturally and linguistically appropriate services, including strategic goals, plans, policies, procedures, and designated staff responsible for implementation.
- Utilize formal mechanisms for community and consumer involvement in the design and execution of service delivery, including planning, policy making, operations, evaluation, training and, as appropriate, treatment planning.
- Develop and implement a strategy to recruit, retain, and promote qualified, diverse, and culturally competent administrative, clinical, and support staff that are trained and qualified to address the needs of the racial and ethnic communities being served.
- Require and arrange for ongoing education and training for administrative, clinical, and support staff in culturally and linguistically competent service delivery.
- Provide all clients with limited English proficiency access to bilingual staff or interpretation services.
- Provide oral and written notices, including translated signage at key points of contact, to clients in their primary language informing them of their right to receive interpreter services free of charge.

- Translate and make available signage and commonly used written patient educational material and other materials for members of the predominant language groups in service areas.
- Ensure that interpreters and bilingual staff can demonstrate bilingual proficiency and receive training that includes the skills and ethics of interpreting, and knowledge in both languages of the terms and concepts relevant to clinical or nonclinical encounters. Family or friends are not considered adequate substitutes because they usually lack these abilities.
- Ensure that the clients' primary spoken language and self-identified race and ethnicity are included in the health care organization's management information system as well as any patient records used by provider staff.
- Use a variety of methods to collect and utilize accurate demographic, cultural, epidemiological and clinical outcome data for racial and ethnic groups in the service area, and become informed about the ethnic/cultural needs, resources, and assets of the surrounding community.
- Undertake ongoing organizational self-assessments of cultural and linguistic competence, and integrate measures of access, satisfaction, quality, and outcomes for CLAS into other organizational internal audits and performance improvement programs.
- Develop structures and procedures to address cross-cultural ethical and legal conflicts in health care delivery and complaints or grievances by patients and staff about unfair, culturally insensitive or discriminatory treatment, or difficulty in accessing services, or denial of services.
- Prepare an annual progress report documenting the organizations' progress with implementing CLAS standards, including information on programs, staffing, and resources.

Notably, because of its significant Native American population, Minnesota adopted the Federal Indian Child Welfare Act (1978) as the Minnesota Indian Family Preservation Act (1999). This act emphasizes the state's interests in supporting the preservation of the cultural heritage of Indian children and recognizes tribes (nations) as powerful resources. The law states that "there is no resource more vital to the continued existence and integrity of the Indian Tribe than their children" and that there has been a failure by non-Indian organizations "to recognize the essential tribal relations of Indian people and the culture and social standards prevailing in Indian communities and families" (Minnesota DHS, 2004, Appendix H).

ORGANIZATIONAL CULTURAL SELF-ASSESSMENT

You can use organizational self-assessment tools to analyze your agency's cultural competence. The Cultural Competence Self-Assessment Protocol for Health Care Organizations and Systems (Andrulis, Delbanco, Avakian, & Shaw-Taylor, n.d.) examines four areas of cultural competence: (a) a health organization's relationship with the community it serves, (b) the administration and management's relationship with their staff, (c) inter-staff relationships, and (d) client or client and provider or clinician encounter (Management Sciences for Health, n.d.).

The Minnesota DHS recommends the use of an organizational self-assessment that examines

- service delivery and quality management;
- human resources practices;
- governance, community relations, and marketing;
- administration and policy; and
- organizational culture.

See Minnesota DHS (2004; Appendix H) for the full self-assessment instrument.

HOW YOU CAN ENHANCE YOUR ORGANIZATION'S CULTURAL COMPETENCE

You can foster cultural competence in the organization where you provide clinical services by asking organizational stakeholders (e.g., board of directors, administrators) to do the following (Howard-Hamilton, Phelps, & Torres, 1998):

- evaluate the institution's mission statement and policies to determine whether they include diversity issues;
- assess policies with regard to diversity;

- evaluate how people of color may perceive specific policies;
- acknowledge within-group diversity;
- be aware that diversity requires examination from both the individual and the institutional levels; and
- recognize that multicultural sensitivity may mean advocating for culturally diverse people.

When you advocate for multicultural people in an organizational setting, be mindful to do so in a culturally appropriate manner. This entails endorsing solidarity and collaboration. In other words, when you become an ally, seek feedback from multicultural individuals. Moreover, you can contribute to and enhance your organization's cultural competence by asking your agency's power holders to (Wu & Martinez, 2006)

- include community representation and input at all stages of implementation;
- integrate all systems of the health care organization;
- ensure that changes made are manageable, measurable, and sustainable;
- make the business case for implementation of cultural competency polices;
- require the commitment from leadership; and
- help to establish staff training on an ongoing basis.

STAGES OF CULTURAL COMPETENCE IN ORGANIZATIONS

Just like individuals, organizations undergo a cultural competence developmental process. T. Cross, Bazron, Dennis, and Isaacs (1989) advanced a model for the developmental stages of organizational cultural competence. Its phases form the following continuum:

- *Cultural Destructiveness.* This is the most extreme point in the continuum and is characterized by attitudes, policies, and practices that are destructive to cultures and to individuals within cultures. An illustration is the prohibition against speaking the mother tongue.

- *Cultural Incapacity.* Individuals and organizations in this stage have extreme bias. They believe in the racial supremacy of the dominant group and assume a paternalistic mode toward the "lesser" groups. They experience ignorance and unrealistic fear of culturally diverse people.

- *Cultural Blindness.* Individuals and organizations in this stage believe that all people are the same, and culture and race make no difference. They assume that the values of the dominant culture are universally applicable and beneficial. These individuals and groups presume that members of minority groups do not meet the dominant group cultural expectations because of some cultural deficiency rather than the fact that the system works for those individuals more assimilated.

- *Cultural Precompetence:* Individuals and organizations in this stage are aware of limitations in multicultural communication and desire to provide an equitable and fair treatment with cultural sensitivity. They may become frustrated when they do not know exactly how to proceed. For example, these individuals believe that a single act fulfills any perceived obligation to all ethnic groups. An illustration is "I participated in a pro-immigration rally."

- *Cultural Competence:* Individuals and organizations in this stage value and respect cultural differences, engage in continuing self-assessment regarding culture, pay attention to the dynamics of difference, continue expanding their knowledge and resources, and endorse a variety of adaptations to belief systems, policies and practices.

CRITICAL CULTURAL COMPETENCE

The concept of *critical cultural competence* is gaining popularity among several multicultural scholars. Kumagai and Lypson (2009) argued for the expansion of the traditional notions of cultural competence to foster a critical consciousness of self, other, and the world. According to these authors, the expansion of cultural competence involves a commitment to address issues of societal relevance in health care. You may remember the concept of critical consciousness from Chapter 7 as a process of personal and social liberation through critical thinking. In brief, critical consciousness involves teaching individuals to critically perceive their circumstances, analyze the causes of their oppression, and discover new ways of action (Freire, 1970).

To summarize, critical cultural competence endorses the following factors:

- *critical mindedness,* which helps to protect against experiences of oppression and fosters a critique of existing sociopolitical conditions;
- *constructive conflict,* which encourages the development of critical cultural competent communication;
- *active engagement,* which includes individuals' agentic behavior in the clinic, organizations, community, and at home to proactively and positively impact their environment;
- *flexibility,* which promotes adaptation to cognitive, emotional, social, and physical situational demands and can advance critical cultural competence across multiple contexts; and
- *communalism,* which includes the importance of social bonds and social duties, reflects a fundamental sense of the importance of collective well-being (including interdependence), and offers the impetus for connection and promotion within and across diverse cultural groups.

Applegate (2009) argued for a simple analytic tool to examine an organization's critical cultural competence. Based on Freire's (1970) critical consciousness model, the question "In whose interest is the prevailing organizational system operating?" helps to assess an organization's critical cultural competence. According to Applegate, organizations become critically culturally conscious when they

- reexamine their core values, mission, and vision;
- develop an organizational culture that examines itself through a lens of power, privilege, and oppression;
- speak openly, informatively, and compassionately about the intersection of systemic privilege, power, and oppression at play within the organization;

- speak openly, informatively, and compassionately about the diverse and overlapping cultural locations within that systemic framework; and
- endeavor to build a community of inclusion.

COMMUNITY CULTURAL COMPETENCE

Social progress emerges when communities appreciate diversity (Fuentes, 1999). You can enhance this progress when you promote cultural competence in your community. Moreover, communal cultural competence fosters society's civic benefits. The development of communal cultural competence can emerge through the following phases (Bordewich, 2005; Musil, 2003):

- *Exclusionary.* Communities are monocultural and have a civic disengagement. Only a few people benefit for a while.
- *Oblivious.* Communities are mostly monocultural and have a civic detachment. Only one party benefits.
- *Naive.* Communities have civic amnesia and, thus, are ahistorical and acultural. Only random people benefit.
- *Charitable.* Communities are multicultural and have civic altruism, but the norm is the giver's perspective. It benefits the giver's feelings and the immediate needs of the receiver.
- *Reciprocal.* Communities are multicultural, address the legacies of inequalities, value partnering, and cultural competence, and focus on civic engagement. It benefits society as a whole but only in the present.
- *Generative.* Communities are multicultural; value interconnectedness, multiple perspectives, and cultural competence; and focus on civic prosperity. It benefits everyone in the present as well as in the future.

You can contribute to your community's journey toward a generative stage. Although at this time a community generative stage may be aspirational, collaboration among clinicians, researchers, clients, and community shareholders is an initial step for the promotion of community cultural competence. Certainly, critical cultural competence is embedded in a community generative phase.

I am familiar with the importance of critical community cultural competence. When I worked as a clinician during the mid-1970s, the concept of cultural competence was still in its infancy. With my colleagues Jorge Dominguez, Delia Lebron, Julia Ramos-Grenier (nee McKay), and Miguel Suárez, we established the Puerto Rican Psychological Association of Connecticut. Our mission was to function as educators, trainers, advocates, and a support system. Accordingly, we trained clinicians and other professionals on cultural issues and health care delivery. However, the promotion of community cultural competence was essential to our organization. Julia Ramos-Grenier was trained by Paulo Freire and taught us to infuse our work with critical consciousness. Within this context, we advocated for the rights of Latino(a) and African American individuals and communities. We used the Spanish-speaking media as well as the mainstream media to educate the public about culture and mental health. This strategy proved to be a powerful element because the media is a popular forum for many Latinos in the United States. In addition, we mentored Puerto Rican youth through cultural awareness programs. Based on this work, years later several colleagues and I (Comas-Díaz, Arroyo, & Lovelace, 1982) conducted a study showing that Puerto Rican children who learned about their culture and history through a school cultural awareness program significantly improved their academic performance. Endorsing the empowering feminist principle of "the personal is political," we acted as cultural ambassadors or as cultural warriors, depending on the specific contextualized need.

A painful, and yet necessary, process in our cultural competence journey was the examination of internalized oppression at the personal and organizational levels. As members of the Puerto Rican Psychological Association of Connecticut, we held each other accountable during this process. As an ongoing process, I continue the self-assessment of my internalized oppression.

In addition, we assisted each other in the examination of our agencies' structural racism. It is interesting to note that we followed a process similar to the one St. Onge and her colleagues (2009, p. 201) advocated:

- Are cultural differences celebrated or tolerated?
- Does the organization take an active stand against inequality?

- Does the organization have a social justice mandate?
- What are the organizational power dynamics?
- Is there a single monocultural and ethnocentric lens through which reality gets interpreted for the group?
- Whose voices are on the decision making table? Whose are not?
- Who benefits from the way things are currently done? Who doesn't?
- Who benefits from the construction of reality presented by the organization? Who doesn't?

CULTURAL BROKERAGE

When you extend your cultural competence into the community, you may engage in *Cultural brokerage* (or *brokering*), which refers to the act of bridging, linking, or mediating between persons of differing cultural backgrounds to reduce conflict or produce change. Cultural brokerage is a function that many multicultural professional organizations embrace when they act as a bridge between cultural diverse groups and the dominant society. For example, four ethnic minority psychological associations—the Asian American Psychological Association, the Association of Black Psychologists, the National Latina/Latino Psychological Association, and the Society of Indian Psychologists—collectively and separately promote cultural competence at the clinical, community, and societal levels. These organizations adhere to a social justice perspective that promotes the construction and transformation of a more egalitarian future. Collectively, they form the Council of National Psychological Associations for the Advancement of Ethnic Minority Issues, an organization consisting of leaders of national ethnic psychological associations to advocate for the needs and well-being of people and communities of color (APA, n.d.).

As a cultural broker, you can assist in the development of societal cultural competence. Yontz (2009) articulated three multicultural key concepts that promote the development of a societal cultural competence. Her model relates to the generative phase of a society's cultural competence and promotes civic prosperity. The three societal cultural competence concepts are as follows:

- *Cultural strengths* ("United we stand, divided we fall")—When you focus on the strengths of a person or culture, then you see the person or culture anew and you keep things positive.
- *Cultural integration* ("We're all in this together") means that all people have an equal desire to be listened to, heard, and respected.
- *Culturally congruent* ("Just do it") means that as you engage in the process of cultural competence, you become culturally in tune with your environment and relate to others with understanding, respect, compassion, humility, and care.

CONCLUSION: DEVELOPING CULTURAL INTELLIGENCE

Cultural competence is a learning process that fosters cultural intelligence. A concept that originated in organizational psychology, *cultural intelligence* posits that understanding the impact of culture on individuals' behavior is essential for effectiveness in business (Early & Ang, 2003). You can extend the concept of cultural intelligence to all aspects of your life. Indeed, Early and Ang (2003) stated: "High CI [cultural intelligence] requires both inductive and analogical reasoning. These two forms of reasoning are essential for how a person can approach and understand a completely new context without being constrained by past experiences and preconceived ideas" (p. 72). Although these authors identified self-awareness as a core facet of cultural intelligence, they argued that a certain level of cognitive flexibility is critical because novel cultural situations require a constant adaptation of self-concept to understand a new environment. Early and Ang concluded that high cultural intelligence requires the capability to reformulate one's self-concept and concept of others in new complex configurations. In other words, knowing and appreciating diverse cultures (including your own), exhibiting cognitive flexibility, and reformulating your self-concept and concept of others can enhance the quality of your clinical practice and your relationships.

Moreover, individuals with a high cultural intelligence tend to be flexible and to successfully adapt to their environment. These individuals also tend to develop their creativity. To illustrate, Leung, Maddux, Galinsky, and Chiu (2008) showed that the relationship between multicultural experiences and creativity is stronger when people adapt (i.e., are culturally intelligent), are open to new experiences, and when the creative context favors the need for flexibility. You can foster your cultural intelligence when you experience learning as constructionism (Merrill, 1991). In other words, cultural learning is:

- *Constructed.* Your cultural competence process helps you to build an internal representation of a multicultural world.
- *Active.* You take an active role in developing cultural competence.
- *Collaborative.* Cultural competence comes from interacting with others, becoming culturally aware, developing multicultural skills, and sharing multiple cultural perspectives.
- *Situated.* Learning occurs in meaningful multicultural contexts and situations.
- *Integrated.* Cultural self-assessment is not an isolated activity. It needs to be integrated with all aspects of your life.

As you foster the development of cultural competence in your agency, community, and society at large, you advance your clinical cultural competence. As an illustration, let us return to John and Dr. Cassidy's vignette from the beginning of this chapter. But before we do this, remember John's first session with Dr. Cassidy, presented in Chapter 2. You may recall that upon seeing a family picture on Dr. Cassidy's desk, John said, "I can tell by your family photo that your son is gay." Consider the following encounter:

John: I saw you at the rally on Sunday.

Dr. Cassidy: Oh, really? I didn't see you.

John: What do you think about the speaker?

Dr. Cassidy: [*Clears his voice*]. His message about having pride in sexual orientation was powerful.

John: I was very glad to see you at the gathering.

Dr. Cassidy: I was glad to be there. And so was my son.

John's witnessing Dr. Cassidy's attendance at a political rally seemed to strengthen their therapeutic alliance. Dr. Cassidy's multicultural consciousness outside the clinical hour illustrates his commitment to community cultural competence. Below is a list of key multicultural and clinical strategies presented in this chapter.

MULTICULTURAL CLINICAL AND COMMUNITY STRATEGIES

- Aspire to develop multicultural consciousness.
- Strive to expand your cultural competence beyond the clinical hour.
- Become familiar with your organization's cultural competence developmental stages.
- Promote the use of Cultural Competence Self-Assessment tools in your organization.
- Foster organization's examination of their structural internalized racism.
- Aim to enhance your cultural intelligence.

Memoirs of Culturally
Diverse Individuals

Anders, G. (2006). *Be pretty, get married, and always drink TAB: A memoir*. New York, NY: HarperCollins.

Blacksnake, G., & Adler, J.W. (2002). *Chainbreaker's war: A Seneca chief remembers the American revolution*. Hensonville, New York, NY: Black Dome Press.

Brown, L. S. (2010). The Jewish nonsheep as lesbian feminist therapist. *Women & Therapy, 33*(3–4), 183–188.

Carson, B., & Murphy, C. (1990). *Gifted hands: The Ben Carson story*. Grand Rapids, MI: Zondervan.

Colon-Lopez, F. (2005). *Finding my face: Memoirs of a Puerto Rican American*. Victoria, Canada: Trafford.

Comas-Díaz, L. (2010). On being a Latina healer: Voice, consciousness, and identity. *Psychotherapy, 47*, 162–168.

Comer, J. P. (1988). *Maggie's American dream: The life and times of a Black family*. New York, NY: Plume.

Crow Dog, M., & Erdoes, R. (1991). *Lakota woman*. New York, NY: Harper Perennial.

Dandicat, E. (1994). *Breath, eyes, memory*. New York, NY: Vintage Press.

Fadiman, A. (1997). *The spirit catches you and you fall down: A Hmong child, her American doctors and the collision of two cultures*. New York, NY: Farrar, Straus and Giroux.

Gartrell, N. K. (2000). Swimming upstream: Voyage of a lesbian psychiatrist. In J. J. Shay & J. Wheelis (Eds.), *Odysseys in psychotherapy* (126–146). New York, NY: Ardent Media, Inc.

Greene, B., & Brodbar, D. (Eds.). (2010). A Minyan of women: Family dynamics, Jewish identity and psychotherapy practice [Special issue]. *Women & Therapy, 33*(3–4).

Griffith, E. E. H. (1998). *Race and excellence: My dialogue with Chester Pierce.* Iowa City: University of Iowa Press.

Griffith, E. E. H. (2004). *I'm your father, boy: A memoir of Barbados.* Tucson, AZ: Hats Off Press.

Halderman, D. C. (2010). Reflections of a gay male psychotherapist. *Psychotherapy, 47,* 177–185.

Hoffman, E. (1989). *Lost in translation: A life in a new language.* New York, NY: Penguin Books.

Iwamasa, G. Y. (1996). On being an ethnic minority cognitive behavioral therapist. *Cognitive and Behavioral Practice, 3,* 235–254.

Jampel, J. B. (2010). When hearing clients work with a deaf therapist. *Psychotherapy, 47,* 144–150.

Kakar, S. (2011). *A book of memory: Confessions and reflections:* New York, NY: Penguin Books.

Kelly, J. F., & Greene, B. (2010). Diversity within African American, female therapists: Variability in clients' expectations and assumptions about the therapist. *Psychotherapy, 47,* 186–197.

Kingston, M. H. (1989) *The woman warrior: Memoirs of a girlhood among the ghosts.* New York, NY: Vintage.

Latina Feminist Group. (2001). *Telling to live: Latina feminist testimonios.* Durham, NC: Duke University Press.

Lim, S. G.-l. (1997) *Among the white moon faces: An Asian American memoir of homelands.* New York, NY: The Feminist Press at the City University of New York.

McBride, J. (1996). *The color of water: A man's tribute to his White mother.* New York, NY: Riverhead Books.

Means, R., & Wolf, M.W. (1995). *Where White men fear to tread: The autobiography of Russell Means.* New York, NY: St. Martins Press.

Mirsalimi, H. (2010). Perspectives of an Iranian psychologist practicing in America. *Psychotherapy, 47,* 151–161.

Mura, D. (1991). *Turning Japanese: Memoirs of a Sansei.* New York, NY: Grove Press.

Nafisi, A. (2003). *Reading Lolita in Teheran: A memoir in books.* New York, NY: Random House.

Nezu, A. M. (2010). Cultural influences on the process of conducting psychotherapy: Personal reflections of an ethnic minority psychologist. *Psychotherapy, 47,* 19–176.

Obama, B. (2007). *Dreams of my father: A story of race and inheritance.* New York, NY: Crown.

O'Hearn, C. C. (Ed.). (1998). *Half and half: Writers on growing up biracial and bicultural.* New York, NY: Random House.

Powell, C. (1995). *My American journey.* New York, NY: Random House.

Rastogi, M., & Wieling, E. (Eds.). (2004). *Voices of color: First-person accounts of ethnic minority therapists.* Thousand Oaks, CA: Sage.

Rodriguez, L. J. (1993). *Always running: La vida loca: Gang days in LA.* New York, NY: Touchstone.

Rodriguez, R. (1982). *Hunger for memory: The education of Richard Rodriguez.* New York, NY: Random House.

Said, E. W. (2000). *Out of place: A memoir.* New York, NY: Vintage.

Santiago, E. (1994). *When I was Puerto Rican.* New York, NY: Vintage.

Senna, D. (1999). *Caucasia.* New York, NY: Riverhead Books.

Thomas, P. (1997). *Down these mean streets.* New York, NY: Vintage.

Whitaker, M. (2011). *My long trip home: A family memoir.* New York: Simon & Schuster.

Resources

CULTURAGRAMS

"The social work podcast: Visual assessment tools: The culturagram." Interview with Dr. Elaine Congress discussing how and why she developed the culturagram, the 10 assessment areas of the culturagram, and how social workers can use the culturagram to improve their services. The interview includes research and resources about the culturagram. Retrieved from http://socialworkpodcast. blogspot.com/2008/12/visual-assessment-tools-culturagram.html

CULTURAL COMPETENCE (GENERAL)

American Psychological Association. (2003). Guidelines on multicultural education, training, research, practice, and organizational change for psychologists. *American Psychologist, 58,* 377–402.

American Psychological Association. (2004). Guidelines for psychological practice with older adults. *American Psychologist, 59,* 236–260.

American Psychological Association. (2007). Guidelines for psychological practice with girls and women. *American Psychologist, 62,* 949–979.

American Psychological Association Task Force on Gender Identity and Gender Variance. (2008). *Report of the APA task force on gender identity and gender variance.* Washington, DC: American Psychological Association.

Comas-Diaz, L., & Caldwell-Colbert, T. (2006). *Applying the APA multicultural guidelines to psychological practice.* Online continuing education course sponsored by Division 42 (Psychologists in Independent Practice) of the American Psychological Association. Retrieved from http://www.42online.org/continuing-education/multicultural "Cultural Competence Assessment Tools," a list of several assessment tools compiled by Dr. Josepha Campinha-Bacote, Transcultural C.A.R.E. Associates. Descriptions, links, and reference sources provided. Retrieved from http://www.transculturalcare.net/assessment-tools.htm

Asian American Center on Disparities Research. (2008). *Culturally informed evidence based practices: Translating research and policy for the real world.* National conference proceedings, University of California, Davis. Retrieved from http://psychology.ucdavis.edu/aacdr/ciebp08.html

CULTURAL COMPETENCE AND ETHICS

American Psychological Association. (2010). *Ethical principles of psychologists and code of conduct.* Retrieved from http://www.apa.org/ethics/code/index.aspx

CULTURAL COMPETENCE AND LANGUAGE

American Educational Research Association (AERA), American Psychological Association, & National Council on Measurement in Education. (1999). Testing individuals of diverse linguistic backgrounds. In AERA, American Psychological Association, & National Council on Measurement in Education, *Standards for educational and psychological testing* (pp. 91–100). Washington, DC: AERA.

U.S. Department of Health and Human Services, Office of Minority Health. (2007). National standards on culturally and linguistically Appropriate Services Retrieved from http://minorityhealth.hhs.gov/templates/browse.aspx?lvl=2&lvlID=15. The standards are primarily directed at health care organizations, although individual providers are encouraged to use the standards to make their practices more culturally and linguistically accessible. The 14 standards are organized by themes: Culturally Competent Care (Standards 1–3), Language Access Services (Standards 4–7), and Organizational Supports for Cultural Competence (Standards 8–14). Within this framework, there are three types of standards of varying stringency: mandates, guidelines, and recommendations:

- *Mandates* are current federal requirements for all recipients of federal funds (Standards 4, 5, 6, and 7).
- *Guidelines* are activities recommended by the OMH for adoption as mandates by federal, state, and national accrediting agencies (Standards 1, 2, 3, 8, 9, 10, 11, 12, and 13).
- *Recommendations* are suggested by OMH for voluntary adoption by health care organizations (Standard 14).

CULTURAL COMPETENCE
WITH SEXUAL MINORITIES

American Psychological Association. (2000). Guidelines for psychotherapy with lesbian, gay, and bisexual clients. *American Psychologist, 55,* 1440–1451. Retrieved from http://www.apa.org/pi/lgbt/resources/guidelines.aspx

American Psychological Association. (2011). *Practice Guidelines for LGB Clients: Guidelines for psychological practice with lesbian, gay, and bisexual clients.* Retrieved from http://www.apa.org/pi/lgbt/resources/guidelines.aspx

LGBT Advisory Committee of the San Francisco Human Rights Commission. (2011). *Bisexual invisibility: Impacts and recommendations.* San Francisco, CA: Author. Retrieved from http://www.sf-hrc.org/Modules/ShowDocument .aspx?documentid=989. The findings reveal much about a community that is rarely central to the discussion of LGBT rights.

Van Den Bergh, N., & Crsip, C. (2004). Defining culturally competence practice with sexual minorities: Implications for social work education and practice. *Journal of Social Work Education, 40.* 221–238.

CULTURAL COMPETENCE VIDEOS

American Psychological Association. (Producer). (2005). *Counseling Latina/Latino clients* (with Patricia Arredondo) [DVD]. Retrieved from http://www.apa. org/videos

American Psychological Association. (Producer). (2005). *Working with African American clients* (with Thomas A. Parham) [DVD]. Retrieved from http:// www.apa.org/videos

American Psychological Association. (Producer). (2005). *Working with Asian American clients* (with Jean Lau Chin) [DVD]. Retrieved from http://www. apa.org/videos

American Psychological Association. (Producer). (2005). *Working with Native Americans* (with Winona F. Simms) [DVD]. Retrieved from http://www. apa.org/videos

American Psychological Association. (Producer). (2006). *Mixed-race identities* (with Maria P. P. Root) [DVD]. Retrieved from http://www.apa.org/videos

American Psychological Association. (Producer). (2007). *Culture-centered counseling* (with Paul B. Pedersen) [DVD]. Retrieved from http://www.apa. org/videos

American Psychological Association. (Producer). (2007). *Ethnocultural psychotherapy* (with Lillian Comas-Díaz) [DVD]. Retrieved from http://www. apa.org/videos

American Psychological Association. (Producer). (2010). *Multicultural therapy over time* (with Melba J. T. Vasquez) [DVD]. Retrieved from http://www. apa.org/videos

Koskoff, H. (Producer). *The culture of emotions* [DVD]. Retrieved from Fanlight Productions at http://www.fanlight.com/catalog/films/361_coe.php

Wah, L. M. (Producer/Director). (1994). *The color of fear*. United States: Stir Fry Studios.

CULTURAL GENOGRAMS

U.S. Department of Health and Human Services. (2006.) *Transforming the face of health professions through cultural and linguistic competence education: The role of the HRSA centers of excellence.* Appendix A of this report explains how to create a cultural genogram. Retrieved from http://www.who-cc.dk/library/book-report/US%20HRSA.pdf

CULTURAL SELF-ASSESSMENT

Gargi, R. (2004). Cultural self-awareness assessment: Practice examples from psychology training. *Professional Psychology: Research and Practice, 35,* 658–666. doi: 10.1037/0735-7028.35.6.658

CULTURE-SPECIFIC AND MULTICULTURAL PERSPECTIVESS

Council of National Psychological Associations for the Advancement of Ethnic Minority Interests. (2009). *Psychology education and training from culture specific and multicultural perspectives: Critical Issues and recommendations.* Washington, DC: American Psychological Association. Retrieved from http://www.apa.org/pi/oema

DICHOS (PROVERBS)

Refranes y Dichos Populares. Popular sayings and proverbs in Spanish. Retrieved from http://www.proverbia.net/refranes.asp

Spanish Pronto! Dichos, Refranes. English translations of popular Spanish sayings and proverbs. Retrieved from http://www.spanishpronto.com/spanishpronto/spanishsayings.html

EVIDENCE-BASED PSYCHOTHERAPY WITH ETHNIC MINORITIES

American Psychological Association Presidential Task Force on Evidence-Based Practice (2006). Evidence-based practice in psychology. *American Psychologist,* 6, 271–285.

Morales, E., & Norcross, J. C. (2010). Culture-sensitive evidence-based practices [Special issue]. *Journal of Clinical Psychology, 66,* 821–829.

Zane, N., & Morales, E. (2008). *Proceedings: Culturally informed evidence-based practices: Translating research and policy for the real world.* Retrieved from http://psychology.ucdavis.edu/aacdr/ciebp08.html

INDIGENOUS KNOWLEDGE

Battiste, M. A., & Youngblood Henderson, J. (2000). *Protecting indigenous knowledge and heritage: A global challenge.* Saskatoon, Canada: Purich.

RACE AND RACISM

"Ten things everyone should know about race." Background reading for *RACE: The power of an illusion,* a three-part documentary about race in society, science, and history. Produced by California Newsreal. Retrieved from http://www.pbs.org/race/000_About/002_04-background-01-x.htm

"Where race lives—Go deeper." Background reading for *RACE: The power of an illusion.*

TIMELINES

http://www.free-timeline.com allows you to build, save, share, and print arbitrary timelines free. You can also embed shared timelines into your own websites or blogs.

Glossary

ANTAEUS EFFECT is similar to the Greek mythological wrestler Antaeus, who was the son of the earth goddess Gaia and drew his strength from his mother every time he was thrown down on the earth: Many immigrants renew their strength when they are in contact with their original country and culture.

AVERSIVE RACISM is a phenomenon involving dissociation between implicit and explicit stereotyping.

COLORISM is the preference for light skin color that results in discrimination against individuals with dark skin.

CONTEXTUALISM is a theory of behavior that promotes the propensity to describe self and other using more contextual references as opposed to dispositional references.

CRITICAL CONSCIOUSNESS, or CONSCIENTIZACION, is a process of personal and social liberation through critical thinking that can foster the empowerment of one's clients (Freire, 1970).

CRITICAL CULTURAL COMPETENCE refers to the use of critical consciousness in the development of cultural competence. It entails asking the critical question, "In whose interest is the prevailing system operating?"

CULTURAGRAM maps a client's (and family's) journey or cultural translocation (Congress, 1994).

CULTURAL ANALYSIS   is an ethnographic tool that helps a clinician to uncover the cultural knowledge his or her clients use to organize their behaviors and interpret their experiences.

CULTURAL BROKERAGE   refers to the act of bridging, linking, or mediating between persons of differing cultural backgrounds to reduce conflict, produce change, or both.

CULTURAL CODE-SWITCHING   refers to a facility to switch behavior back and forth from one cultural context to another.

CULTURAL COMPETENCE   entails the awareness, attitude, knowledge, and skills that allow one to understand, appreciate, and work with culturally diverse individuals.

CULTURAL CREDIBILITY   refers to a client's perception of the clinician as trustworthy and effective.

CULTURAL CRITICAL THINKING   refers to the use of a cultural analysis to examine assumptions, recognize unstated values, identify objectives, evaluate "evidence," conduct interventions, and interpret findings.

CULTURAL EMPATHY   is a process of perspective taking by using a cultural framework as a guide for understanding the client from the outside in (Ridley & Lingle, 1996).

CULTURAL FATIGUE   is the exhaustion that results from cultural adjustments that involve the need to suspend automatic judgments, create new interpretations to seemingly familiar behavior, and develop constant alterations in activity.

CULTURAL GENOGRAM   is a genealogy tool that provides an aggregate of personal, psychological, developmental, social, multigenerational, family ancestral, biological, ethnic, racial, and communal information (Hardy & Lazloffy, 1995).

CULTURAL ICEBERG   refers to the comparison between culture and an iceberg that holds that, like an iceberg, most of culture's content lies below the surface.

CULTURAL IDENTITY   refers to the shared ethnicity, race, religion, geography, and language of individuals who are connected through a sense of kinship.

CULTURAL INTELLIGENCE   consists of one's ability to understand the impact of culture on individuals' and groups' behavior. This concept originated in organizational psychology and posits that understanding the impact of culture on individuals' behavior is essential for effectiveness in business.

CULTURAL MALPRACTICE   results when clinicians ignore, discount, and/or neglect cultural aspects in treating multicultural individuals (C. I. Hall, 1997).

CULTURAL RESILIENCE   is a host of strengths, values, and practices that promote coping mechanisms and adaptive reactions to traumatic oppression (Elsass, 1992).

CULTURAL RESONANCE   is the ability to understand the other through clinical skill, cultural competence, and intuition; cultural resonance promotes a convergence between the clinician and his or her multicultural client.

CULTURAL SELF-ASSESSMENT   is a tool that fosters an ongoing process of critically examining one's culture, history, ancestry, and context.

CULTURAL TRAUMA   refers to victimization that individuals and groups experience due to their culture, including but not limited to their ethnicity, race, gender, sexual orientation, class, religion, political ideology, and interaction with other diversity characteristics.

CULTURAL UNCONSCIOUSNESS   involves the cultural vernacular that imparts a familiar context to life and includes unspoken rules, such as norms that regulate family relations, intimacy, identity, relationships, boundaries, and emotional space, and that give meaning to people's lives (Hoffman, 1989).

CULTURALLY HOLDING ENVIRONMENT   entails the development by a clinician of a flexible style, a culturally centered method, and a welcoming ambience (e.g., office décor). Multicultural clients expect the clinician to be culturally credible and to earn their trust.

CULTURE-BOUND SYNDROME   refers to a recurrent, or at times aberrant, illness, affliction, or behavior that may or may not be associated with a psychological diagnosis.

CULTURE-RELATED STRESS   causes distress and illness.

CULTURE-SPECIFIC HEALING PERSPECTIVES are contextual approaches that evolve within the dynamic circumstances of individuals' life experiences. Examples of culture specific healing include ethnic psychotherapies and folk healing.

DOUBLE CONSCIOUSNESS   refers to W. E. B. Du Bois's (1903/1996) concept that describes African Americans' feelings of contradiction between their sociocultural values and the experience of being Black in the United States.

ETHICAL CONTEXTUALISM   assumes that moral principles, such as respect for human dignity, justice, and freedom (among others), are universally valued cross-culturally but that the expression of an ethical problem and the correct actions to resolve it can be unique to the cultural context (Fisher, 2000).

ETHNOCENTRISM   entails the belief that one's worldview is inherently superior and desirable to those of others' (Leininger, 1978).

ETHNOCULTURAL ALLODYNIA   is an abnormally increased sensitivity to ethnocultural dynamics associated with exposure to emotionally painful social, racial, and ethnoracial stimuli.

ETHNOCULTURAL TRANSFERENCE and ETHNOCULTURAL COUNTERTRANSFERENCE   refer to the cultural parameters of transference and countertransference present in both inter- and intraclinician–client dyads.

ETHNOPSYCHOPHARMACOLOGY   is the study of the effects of psychoactive drugs on culturally and ethnically diverse patients.

FAMILISM   is a cultural value that highlights the importance of family members, both blood-related and non–blood-related, among collectivistic individuals.

HIGH-CONTEXT COMMUNICATION and LOW-CONTEXT COMMUNICATION   refer to the relative use of contextual references during conversation. In high-context communication, the messages adhere to a rich web of cultural nuances and meaning; in low-context communication, the message tends to rely on the literal meaning of words (E. T. Hall, 1976).

HISTORICAL TRAUMA   refers to the cumulative effects of oppressive events that members of a cultural group endure; it is transmitted from one generation to the next.

HOT AND COLD THEORY OF ILLNESS AND HEALTH   originates from the Hippocrates' humoral theory of illness, in which the body's four humors, namely, blood, phlegm, yellow bile, and black bile, are classified based on their physical properties as hot, cold, moist (wet), or dry.

MULTICULTURAL ASSESSMENT   is a process-oriented clinical tool to examine contextual areas under the interacting domains of ethnocultural heritage, journey, identity, and relations.

MULTICULTURAL CONSCIOUSNESS   refers to the process of internalizing and incorporating cultural competence into one's everyday activities.

NONVERBAL ACCENTS   are subtle cultural differences in the appearance of facial expressions of emotions.

NONVERBAL and VERBAL COMMUNICATION   may vary from culture to culture.

OCCUPATIONAL INVENTORY   aims to facilitate clients' knowledge, development, and enhancement of occupational experiences during previous and current work.

ORGANIZATIONAL CULTURE   comprises a pattern of beliefs, values, and expectations shared by the members of the organization.

POSTCOLONIZATION STRESS DISORDER (PCSD)   results from a historical and generational accumulation of oppression, the struggle with racism, cultural imperialism, and the imposition of mainstream culture as dominant and superior (Comas-Díaz, 2000; Duran & Duran, 1995).

POWER DIFFERENTIAL ANALYSIS   is a method in which the clinician compares (a) his or her own experiences with oppression and privilege with (b) those of the client.

RACIAL CLIMATE   refers to an organizational environment that is influenced by a variety of structural and nonstructural factors, including perception of power, group racial norms, and racial identity coalitions.

RACIAL–ETHNIC SOCIALIZATION   involves the process parents use to transmit to their children messages about the role race plays in their lives, including racial dynamics, expectations of discrimination and racism, intergroup relations, and racial pride.

SOCIOPOLITICAL TIMELINE   is a tool to diagram the influence of historical and sociopolitical events on people's life.

START LOW AND GO SLOW   norm refers to the prescription practice to treat those multicultural clients who require half of the standard dosage of all psychotropic medications.

TARGET GROUP   refers to people of color and other racial/ethnic and/or cultural minorities' experience of being viewed as different and inferior by dominant group members.

TRANSPERSONALITY   is the belief that individual identity expands beyond (*trans*) the personal to embrace a collective sense of self.

ULYSSES SYNDROME   is a type of depression with somatic reactions that some immigrants experience while living away from loved ones (Achotegui, 2003).

WHITE PRIVILEGE   refers to the advantages that White individuals accumulate, supported by unacknowledged systems that give them social power. McIntosh (1988) referred to this concept as "an invisible knapsack" that provides social power to White Americans and to males.

WORLDVIEW   refers to personal attitudes, beliefs, and behaviors that may unconsciously or consciously influence one's interactions with individuals from diverse cultural backgrounds.

References

Abelson, R., Dasgupta, N., Park, J., & Banji, M. R. (1998). Perception of the collective other. *Personality and Social Psychology Review, 2,* 243–250. doi:10.1207/s15327957pspr0204_2

Achotegui, J. (2004). Emigrar en situación extrema: El síndrome del inmigrante con estrés crónico y múltiple (Síndrome de Ulises) [Immigration under an extreme situation: The immigrant syndrome with chronic and multiple stress (Ulysses' syndrome)]. *Norte de Salud Mental, 21,* 39Z–52. Retrieved from http://es.wikipedia.org/wiki/S%C3%ADndrome_de_Ulises

Acosta, F. X., & Cristo, M. H. (1981). Development of a bilingual interpreter program: An alternative model for Spanish speaking services. *Professional Psychology, 12,* 474–482. doi:10.1037/0735-7028.12.4.474

Adams, J. M. (2000). Individual and group psychotherapy with African American women: Understanding the identity and context of the therapist and patient. In L. C. Jackson & B. Greene (Eds.), *Psychotherapy with African American women: Innovations in psychodynamic perspectives and practice* (pp. 33–61). New York, NY: Guilford Press.

Adler, N. J. (1998). Domestic multiculturalism: Cross-cultural management in the public sector. In G. Weaver (Ed.), *Culture, communication, and conflict: Readings in intercultural relations* (2nd ed., pp. 481–500). Needham Heights, MA: Simon & Schuster.

Adler, P. S. (1975). The transitional experience: An alternative view of culture shock. *Journal of Humanistic Psychology, 15,* 13–23. doi:10.1177/002216787501500403

Agúndez, J. A., Ledesma, M. C., Ladero, J. M., & Benítez, J. (1995). Prevalence of CYP2D6 gene duplication and its repercussions on the oxidative phenotype in a White population. *Clinical Psychopharmacology Therapy, 57,* 265–269. doi:10.1016/0009-9236(95)90151-5

Akhtar, S. (1995). A third individuation: Immigration, identity, and the psychoanalytic process. *Journal of the American Psychoanalytic Association, 43,* 1051–1084. doi:10.1177/000306519504300406

Akhtar, S. (1999). *Immigration and identity: Turmoil, treatment, and transformation.* Northvale, NJ: Aronson.

Allalouf, A. (2003). Revising translated differential item functioning items as a tool of improving cross-lingual assessment. *Applied Measurement in Education, 16,* 55–73.

Allen, J. J., Schnyer, R. N., Chambers, A. S., Hitt, S. K., Moreno, F. A., & Manber, R. (2006). Acupuncture for depression: A randomized controlled trial. *Journal of Clinical Psychiatry, 67,* 1665–1673.doi:10.4088/JCP.v67n1101

Allen, P. G.(1992) *The sacred hoop.* Boston, MA: Beacon Press,

Allport, G. W. (1954). *The nature of prejudice.* Cambridge, MA: Addison-Wesley.

Altarriba, J. (2003). Does *cariño* equal "liking"? A theoretical approach to conceptual nonequivalence between languages. *International Journal of Bilingualism, 7,* 305–322. doi:10.1177/13670069030070030501

Altman, N. (1995). *The analyst in the inner city: Race, class and culture through a psychoanalytic lens.* New York, NY: Analytic Press.

American Psychiatric Association. (1994). *Diagnostic and statistical manual of mental disorders* (4th ed.). Washington, DC: Author.

American Psychiatric Association. (2000). *Diagnostic and statistical manual of mental disorders* (4th ed., text rev.). Washington, DC: Author.

American Psychological Association. (2000). Guidelines for psychotherapy with lesbian, gay, and bisexual clients. *American Psychologist, 55,* 1440–1451. doi:10.1037/0003-066X.55.12.1440

American Psychological Association. (2003). Guidelines on multicultural education, training, research, practice, and organizational change for psychologists. *American Psychologist, 58,* 377–402. doi:10.1037/0003-066X.58.5.377

American Psychological Association. (2010a). *APA publication manual* (6th ed.). Washington, DC: Author.

American Psychological Association. (2010b). *Ethical principles of psychologists and code of conduct.* Retrieved from http://www.apa.org/ethics/code/index.aspx

American Psychological Association. (2011). *Practice guidelines for LGB Clients: Guidelines for psychological practice with lesbian, gay, and bisexual clients.* Retrieved from http://www.apa.org/pi/lgbt/resources/guidelines.aspx

American Psychological Association. (n.d). *Council of National Psychology Association for the Advancement of Ethnic Minority Interests.* Retrieved from http://www.apa.org/about/governance/bdcmte/ethnic-minority-interests.aspx

American Psychological Association Presidential Task Force on Evidence-Based Practice. (2006). Evidence-based practice in psychology. *American Psychologist, 6,* 271–285.

Americans With Disabilities Act (1990). Retrieved June 24, 2011, from http://www.usdoj.gov/crt/ada/adahom1.htm

Anderson, K., & Jack, D.C. (1991). Learning to listen: Interviews techniques and analyses. In S. B. Gluck & D. Patai (Eds.). *Women's worlds: The feminist practice of oral history* (pp. 11–26). New York, NY: Routledge.

Anderson, N. B., Lane, J. D., Muranaka, M., Williamns, R. B., Jr., & Houseworth, S. J. (1988). Racial differences in blood pressure and forearm vascular responses to the cold face stimulus. *Psychosomatic Medicine, 50,* 57–63.

Andrulis, D., Delbanco, T., Avakian, L., & Shaw-Taylor, Y. (n.d.). *Conducting a cultural competence self-assessment.* Retrieved from http://erc.msh.org/provider/andrulis.pdf

Anzaldua, G. (1987). *Borderlands/La frontera: The new Mestiza.* San Francisco, CA: Aunt Lute Books.

Applegate, B. (2009). My journey is a slow, steady awakening. In P. St. Onge, B. Applegate, V. Asakura, M. K. Moss, A. Vergara-Lobo, & B. Rousson. (2009). *Embracing cultural competency: A roadmap for nonprofit capacity builders.* (17–30), St. Paul, MN: Fieldstone Alliance.

Araújo, B. Y., & Borrell, L. N. (2006). Understanding the link between discrimination, mental health outcomes and life chances among Latinos. *Hispanic Journal of Behavioral Sciences, 28,* 245–266. doi:10.1177/0739986305285825

Ariel, S. (1999). *Culturally competent family therapy. A general model.* Westport, CT: Praeger.

Arizona State Senate. (2010). *Fact sheet for S.B. 1070.* Retrieved from http://www.azleg.gov/legtext/49leg/2r/summary/s.1070pshs.doc.htm

Armstrong, T. L., & Swartzman, L. (2001). Cross-cultural differences in illness models and expectations for the healthcare provider-client/patient interaction. In S. S. Kazarin & D. R. Evans (Eds.), *Handbook in cultural health psychology* (pp. 63–84). Ontario, Canada: Academic Press.

Aron, A. (1992). Testimonio, a bridge between psychotherapy and sociotherapy. *Women & Therapy, 13,* 173–189. doi:10.1300/J015V13N03_01

Arredondo, P., & Toporek, R. (2004). Multicultural counseling competencies and ethical practice. *Journal of Mental Health Counseling, 26,* 44–55.

Arredondo, P., Toporek, R., Brown, S. P., Jones, J., Locke, D. C., Sanchez, J., & Stadler, H. (1996). Operationalization of the multicultural counseling competencies. *Journal of Multicultural Counseling and Development, 24,* 42–78.

Astin, J. A. (1998). Why patients use alternative medicine: Results of a national study. *JAMA, 279,* 1548–1553. doi:10.1001/jama.279.19.1548

Atkinson, D. R., Thompson, C. E., & Grant, S. K. (1993). A three-dimensional model for counseling racial/ethnic minorities. *The Counseling Psychologist, 21,* 257–277. doi:10.1177/0011000093212010

Attneave, C. (1990). Core networks intervention: An emerging paradigm. *Journal of Strategic & Systemic Therapies, 9,* 3–10.

Aviera, A. (1996). *Dichos* therapy group: A therapeutic use of Spanish language proverbs with hospitalized Spanish-speaking psychiatric patients. *Cultural Diversity and Mental Health, 2,* 73–87. doi:10.1037/1099-9809.2.2.73

Axtell, E. (Ed.). (1985). *Do's and taboos around the world: A guide to international behavior.* New York, NY: Wiley.

Baez, A., & Hernandez, D. (2001). Complementary spiritual beliefs in the Latino community: The interface with psychotherapy. *American Journal of Orthopsychiatry, 71,* 408–415. doi:10.1037/0002-9432.71.4.408

Bakare, M. O. (2008). Effective therapeutic dosage of antipsychotic medications in patients with psychotic symptoms: Is there a racial difference? [Abstract]. *BMC Research Notes. 12,* 25.

Baker, F. M., & Bell, C. C. (1999). Issues in the psychiatric treatment of African Americans. *Psychiatric Services, 50,* 362–368.

Bankart, C. P., Koshikawa, F., Nedate, K., & Haruki, Y. (1992). When West meets East: Contributions of Eastern traditions to the future of psychotherapy. *Psychotherapy, 29,* 141–149. doi:10.1037/0033-3204.29.1.141

Banyard, V. L., Williams, L. M., & Siegel, J. A. (2001). The long-term mental health consequences of child sexual abuse: An exploratory study of the impact of multiple traumas in a sample of women. *Journal of Traumatic Stress, 14,* 697–715. doi:10.1023/A:1013085904337

Becvar, D. S. (1997). *Soul healing: A spiritual orientation in counseling and therapy.* New York, NY: Basic Books.

Beere, C. A. (1990). *Gender roles: A handbook of tests and measures.* New York, NY: Greenwood Press.

Bennett, M. J. (2004). From ethnocentrism to ethnorelativism. In J. S. Wurzel (Ed.), *Toward multiculturalism: A reader in multicultural education* (pp. 62–77). Newton, MA: Intercultural Resource Corporation.

Bennett-Goleman, T. (2001). *Emotional alchemy: How the mind can heal the heart.* New York, NY: Harmony Books.

Berlin, E. A., & Fowkes, W. C., Jr. (1983). A teaching framework for cross-cultural health care: Application in family practice. *The Western Journal of Medicine, 139,* 934–938.

Bernal, G., Bonilla, J., & Bellido, C. (1995). Ecological validity and cultural sensitivity for outcome research: Issues for cultural adaptation and development of psychosocial treatments with Hispanics. *Journal of Abnormal Child Psychology, 23,* 67–82. doi:10.1007/BF01447045

Bernal, G., & Scharron del Rio, M. R. (2001). Are empirically supported treatments valid for ethnic minorities? Toward an alternative approach for treatment research. *Cultural Diversity and Ethnic Minority Psychology, 7,* 328–342. doi:10.1037/1099-9809.7.4.328

Bernstein, K. S., Lee, J., Park, S., & Jyoung, J. (2008). Symptom manifestations and expressions among Korean immigrant women suffering with depression. *Journal of Advanced Nursing, 61,* 393–402. doi:10.1111/j.1365-2648.2007.04533.x

Berry, J. W. (1991). Cultural variations in field dependence-independence. In S. Wapner & J. Derrick (Eds.), *Field dependence-independence cognitive style across the life span* (pp. 289–308). Hillsdale, NJ: Erlbaum.

Betancourt, J. R. (2003). Cross-cultural medical education: Conceptual approaches and frameworks for evaluation. *Academic Medicine, 78,* 560–569. doi:10.1097/00001888-200306000-00004

Betancourt, J. R., Green, A. R., Carrillo, J. E., & Ananch-Firempong, O. (2003, July–August). Defining cultural competence: A practical framework for addressing racial/ethnic disparities in health and health care. *Public Health Reports, 118,* 293–302. Retrieved from http://www.ncbi.nlm.nih.gov/pubmed/12815076

Bigfoot, D. (2008, March). *Adaptations and implementations for American Indians: Lessons learned.* Paper presented at the 2008 National Conference on Culturally Informed Evidence-Based Practice: Translating Research and Policy for the Real World, Bethesda, MD.

Bion, W. R. (1961). *Experiences in groups: And other papers.* London, England: Tavistock Publications.

Blair, Y. A., Gold, E. B., Greendale, G. A., Sternfeld, B., Adler, S. R., Azari, R., & Harkey, M. (2002). Ethnic differences in use of complementary and alternative medicine at midlife: Longitudinal results from SWAN participants. *American Journal of Public Health, 92,* 1832–1840.

Blanco, A. (1998). *Psicología de la liberación de Ignacio Martín-Baró* [Psychology of the Liberation of Ignacio Martín-Baró]. Madrid, Spain: Editorial Trotta.

Bolen, J. S. (1985). *Goddesses in everywoman: A new psychology of women.* New York, NY: Harper Colophon.

Bonitz, V. (2008). Use of physical touch in the "talking cure": A journey to the outskirts of psychotherapy. *Psychotherapy, 45,* 391–404. doi:10.1037/a0013311

Bordewich, F. M. (2005). *Bound for Canaan: The underground railroad and the war for the soul of America.* New York, NY: Amistad Press.

Borkan, J. M., & Neher, J. (1991). A developmental model of ethnosensitivity in family practice training. *Family Medicine, 23,* 212–217.

Boyd-Franklin, N. (2003). *Black families in therapy: Understanding the African American experience* (2nd ed.). New York, NY: Guilford Press.

Brewer, M. B., & Brown, R. J. (1998). Intergroup relations. In D. T. Gilbert & S. T. Fiske (Eds.), *The handbook of social psychology* (4th ed., Vol. 2, pp. 554–594). New York, NY: McGraw-Hill.

Brown, L. S. (1997). The private practice of subversion: Psychology as Tikkun Olam. *American Psychologist, 52,* 449–462. doi:10.1037/0003-066X.52.4.449

Brussat, F., & Brussat, M. (1996). *Spiritual literacy.* New York, NY: Simon & Schuster.

Burkard, A. W., & Knox, S. (2004). Effect of therapist color-blindness on empathy and attributions in cross-cultural counseling. *Journal of Counseling Psychology, 51,* 387–397.

Burnam, M. A., Hough, R. L., Karno, M., Escobar, J. I., & Telles, C. A. (1987). Acculturation and lifetime prevalence of psychiatric disorders among Mexican Americans in Los Angeles. *Journal of Health and Social Behavior, 28,* 89–102. doi:10.2307/2137143

Butcher, J. N., Dahlstrom, W. G., Graham, J. R., Tellegen, A., & Kaemmer, B. (1989).*The Minnesota Multiphasic Personality Inventory–2 (MMPI-2): Manual for administration and scoring.* Minneapolis, MN: University of Minnesota Press.

Byrne, D. (1997). An overview (and underview) of research and theory within the attraction paradigm. *Journal of Social and Personal Relationships, 14,* 417–431. doi:10.1177/0265407597143008

Caldwell-Colbert, A. T. (2003). Enhancing mental health service delivery to ethnically diverse populations: Introduction to the special series. *Clinical Psychology: Science and Practice, 10,* 439–443.

Callan, A., & Littlewood, R. (1998). Patient satisfaction: Ethnic origin or explanatory model? *International Journal of Social Psychiatry, 44,* 1–11. doi:10.1177/002076409804400101

Campinha-Bacote, J. (2002). Cultural competence in psychiatric nursing: Have you ASKED the right questions? *Journal of the American Psychiatric Nurses Association, 8,* 183–187. doi:10.1067/mpn.2002.130216

Campinha-Bacote, J. (2003). *The process of cultural competence in the delivery of healthcare services.* Cincinnati, OH: Transcultural C.A.R.E. Associates.

Campinha-Bacote, J. (2007). Becoming culturally competent in ethnic psychopharmacology. *Journal of Psychosocial Nursing and Mental Health Services, 45,* 27–33

Cane, P. (2000). *Trauma, healing, and transformation: Awakening a new heart with body mind spirit practices.* Watsonville, CA: Capacitar.

Carter, J. (2006). Theoretical pluralism and technical eclecticism. In C. Goodheart, R. J. Sternberg, & A. Kazdin (Eds.), *Evidence-based psychotherapy: Where practice and research meet* (pp. 63–79). Washington, DC: American Psychological Association. doi:10.1037/11423-003

Caspi, A., Taylor, A., Moffitt, T. E., & Plomin, R. (2000). Neighborhood deprivation affects children's mental health: Environmental risks identified in a genetic design. *Psychological Science, 11,* 338–342. doi:10.1111/1467-9280.00267

Cass, V. (1979). Homosexual identity formation: A theoretical model. *Journal of Homosexuality, 17,* 43–73.

Castillo, A. (1995). *Massacre of the dreamers: Essays on Xicanisma.* New York, NY: Plume.

Castillo, R. J. (1997). *Culture and mental illness: A client centered approach.* Pacific Grove, CA: Brooks/Cole.

Catrambone, R., Beike, D., & Niedenthal, P. (1996). Is the self-concept a habitual referent in judgments of similarity? *Psychological Science, 7,* 158–163. doi:10.1111/j.1467-9280.1996.tb00349.x

Cervantes, J. M. (2010). Mestizo spirituality: Toward an integrated approach to psychotherapy for Latina/os. *Psychotherapy, 47,* 527–539. doi:10.1037/a0022078

Cervantes, J. M., & Parham, T. A. (2005). Toward a meaningful spirituality for people of color: Lessons for the counseling practitioner. *Cultural Diversity and Ethnic Minority Psychology, 11,* 69–81. doi:10.1037/1099-9809.11.1.69

Chaudhry, I., Neelam, K., Duddu, V., & Husain, N. (2008). Ethnicity and psychopharmacology. *Journal of Psychopharmacology, 22,* 673–680. doi:10.1177/0269881107082105

Chao, C. (1992). The inner heart: Therapy with Southeast Asian families. In L. A. Vargas & J. Koss-Chioino (Eds.), *Working with culture: Psychotherapeutic interventions with ethnic minority children and adolescents* (pp. 157–181). San Francisco, CA: Jossey-Bass.

Chen, C., Lee, S., & Stevenson, H. W. (1995). Response style and cross-cultural comparisons of rating scales among East Asian and North American students. *Psychological Science, 6,* 170–175. doi:10.1111/j.1467-9280.1995.tb00327.x

Chen, M. L. (2006). Ethnic or racial differences revisited: impact of dosage regimen and dosage form on pharmacokinetics and pharmacodynamics. *Clinical Pharmacokinetics, 45,* 957–964. doi:10.2165/00003088-200645100-00001

Chen, S. W.-H. (2005). Cognitive-Behavioral Therapy With Chinese American Clients: Cautions and Modifications. *Psychotherapy, 42,* 101–110. doi:10.1037/0033-3204.42.1.101

Choi, I., Nisbett, R. E., & Norenzayan, A. (1999). Causal attribution across cultures: Variations and universality. *Psychological Bulletin, 125,* 47–63. doi:10.1037/0033-2909.125.1.47

Chu, J. A. (1998). *Rebuilding shattered lives: The responsible treatment of complex post-traumatic and dissociative disorders.* New York, NY: Wiley.

Church, A. T., & Lonner, W. J. (1998). The cross-cultural perspective in the study of personality. rationale and current research. *Journal of Cross-Cultural Psychology, 29,* 32–62. doi:10.1177/0022022198291003

Cienfuegos, A. J., & Monelli, C. (1983). The testimony of political repression as a therapeutic instrument. *American Journal of Orthopsychiatry, 53,* 43–51. doi:10.1111/j.1939-0025.1983.tb03348.x

Clark, R., Anderson, N. B., Clark, V. R., & Williams, D. R. (1999). Racism as a stressor for African Americans: A biopsychological model. *American Psychologist, 54,* 805–816. doi:10.1037/0003-066X.54.10.805

Clauss, C. S. (1998). Language: The unspoken variable in psychotherapy practice. *Psychotherapy, 35,* 188–196. doi:10.1037/h0087677

Cohen, K. (1998). Native American medicine. *Alternative Therapies in Health and Medicine, 4,* 45–57.

Comas-Díaz, L. (1981). Puerto Rican *espiritismo* and psychotherapy. *American Journal of Orthopsychiatry, 51,* 636–645. doi:10.1111/j.1939-0025.1981.tb01410.x

Comas-Díaz, L. (1992). The future of psychotherapy with ethnic minorities. *Psychotherapy, 29,* 88–94. doi:10.1037/0033-3204.29.1.88

Comas-Díaz, L. (2000). An ethnopolitical approach to working with people of color. *American Psychologist, 55,* 1319–1325. doi:10.1037/0003-066X.55.11.1319

Comas-Díaz, L. (2006a). Cultural variation in the therapeutic relationship. In C. Goodheart, A. Kazdin, & R. J. Sternberg (Eds.), *Evidence-based psychotherapy: Where practice and research meet* (pp. 81–105). Washington, DC: American Psychological Association. doi:10.1037/11423-004

Comas-Díaz, L. (2006b). Latino healing: The integration of ethnic psychology into psychotherapy. *Psychotherapy, 43,* 436–453. doi:10.1037/0033-3204.43.4.436

Comas-Díaz, L. (2007). Ethnopolitical psychology: Healing and transformation. In E. Aldarondo (Ed.), *Promoting social justice in mental health practice* (pp. 91–118). Mahwah, NJ: Erlbaum.

Comas-Díaz, L. (2008). *Spirita:* Reclaiming womanist sacredness in feminism. *Psychology of Women Quarterly, 32,* 13–21.

Comas-Díaz, L. (2011a). Interventions with culturally diverse populations. In D. Barlow (Ed.). *The Oxford handbook of clinical psychology* (pp. 868–887). New York, NY: Oxford University Press.

Comas-Díaz, L. (2011b). Multicultural approaches to psychotherapy. In N. Norcross, G. VandenBos, & D. K. Freedheim (Eds.), *History in psychotherapy:*

Continuity and change (2nd ed., pp. 243–267). Washington, DC: American Psychological Association. doi:10.1037/12353-008

Comas-Díaz, L. (in press). Colored spirituality: The centrality of Spirit among ethnic minorities. In L. Miller (Ed.), *The Oxford handbook of spirituality*. New York, NY: Oxford University Press.

Comas-Díaz, L., Arroyo, A., & Lovelace, J. C. (1982). Enriching self-concept through a Puerto Rican cultural awareness program. *The Personnel and Guidance Journal, 60,* 306–308.

Comas-Díaz, L., & Caldwell-Colbert, T. (2006). *Applying the APA multicultural guidelines to psychological practice.* Online continuing education course sponsored by Division 42 (Psychologists in Independent Practice) of the American Psychological Association. Retrieved from http://www.42online.org/continuing-education/multicultural

Comas-Díaz, L., & Duncan, J. W. (1985). The cultural context: A factor in assertiveness training with mainland Puerto Rican women. *Psychology of Women Quarterly, 9,* 463–476. doi:10.1111/j.1471-6402.1985.tb00896.x

Comas-Díaz, L., Geller, J. Melgoza, B., & Baker, R. (1982, August). *Ethnic minority clients' expectations of treatment and of their* therapists. Presentation made at the 90th Annual Convention of the American Psychological Association, Washington, DC.

Comas-Díaz, L., & Griffith, E. E. H. (Eds.). (1988). *Clinical guidelines in cross-cultural mental health.* New York, NY: Wiley.

Comas-Díaz, L., & Jacobsen, F. M. (1991). Ethnocultural transference and countertransference in the therapeutic dyad. *American Journal of Orthopsychiatry, 61,* 392–402. doi:10.1037/h0079267

Comas-Díaz, L., & Jacobsen, F. M. (1995a). The therapist of color and the White patient dyad: Contradictions and recognitions. *Cultural Diversity and Mental Health, 1,* 93–106. doi:10.1037/1099-9809.1.2.93

Comas-Díaz, L., & Jacobsen, F. M. (1995b). Women of color and psychopharmacology: An empowering perspective. *Women & Therapy, 16,* 85–112. doi:10.1300/J015v16n01_06

Comas-Díaz, L., & Jacobsen, F. M. (2001). Ethnocultural allodynia. *Journal of Psychotherapy Practice and Research, 10,* 246–252.

Comas-Díaz, L., Lykes, B., & Alarcon, R. (1998). Ethnic conflict and psychology of liberation in Guatemala, Perú, and Puerto Rico. *American Psychologist, 53,* 778–792.

Comas-Díaz, L., & Padilla, A. M. (1992). The English-only movement: Implications for mental health. *American Journal of Orthopsychiatry, 62,* 6. doi:10.1037/h0085023

Comas-Díaz & Ramos-Grenier. J. (1998). Migration and acculturation. In J. Sandoval, C. L. Frisby, K. F. Geisinger, J. D. Scheuneman, & J. Ramos-Grenier (Eds.), *Test interpretations and diversity: Achieving equity in assessment* (pp. 213–239). Washington, DC: American Psychological Association.

Congress, E. (1994). The use of culturagrams to assess and empower culturally diverse families. *Families in Society, 75,* 531–540.

Congress, E. (2002). Using culturagrams with culturally diverse families. In A. Roberts & G. Greene (Eds.), *Social desk reference* (pp. 57–61). New York, NY: Oxford University Press.

Constantine, M. G., Alleyne, V. L., Cladwell, L. D., McRae, M. B., & Suzuki, L. A. (2005). Coping responses of Asian, Black, and Latino/Latina New York residents following the September 11, 2001, terrorists attacks against the United States. *Cultural Diversity and Ethnic Minority Psychology, 11,* 293–308. doi:10. 1037/1099-9809.11.4.293

Cooper-Patrick, L., Gallo, J., Gonzales, J. J., Vu, H. T., Powe, N. E., Nelson, C., & Ford, D. (1999). Race, gender, and partnership in the patient–physician relationship. *JAMA, 282,* 583–589. doi:10.1001/jama.282.6.583

Costantino, G., Dana, R. H., & Malgady, R. G. (2007). *TEMAS (Tell-Me-A-Story) Assessment in multicultural societies.* New York, NY: Routledge.

Costantino, G., Malgady, R., & Rogler, L. (1986). *Cuento* therapy: A culturally sensitive modality for Puerto Rican children. *Journal of Consulting and Clinical Psychology, 54,* 639–645. doi:10.1037/0022-006X.54.5.639

Council of National Psychological Associations. (2003, November). *Psychological treatment of ethnic minority populations.* Washington, DC: Association of Black Psychologists.

Cowan, T. (1996). *Shamanism as a spiritual practice for daily life.* Freedom, CA: The Crossing Press.

Criswell, E. (2007). Yoga and mind–body medicine. In I. A. Serlin, K. Rockerfeller, & S. S. Brown (Eds.), *Whole person healthcare: Vol 2. Psychology, spirituality, and health* (pp. 191–210). Westport, CT: Praeger.

Crocker, J., & Major, B. (1989). Social stigma and self-esteem: The self-protective properties of stigma. *Psychological Review, 96,* 608–630. doi:10.1037/0033-295X.96.4.608

Cross, T., Bazron, B., Dennis, K., & Isaacs, M. (1989). *Toward a culturally competent system of care: A monograph on effective services for minority children who are severely emotionally disturbed* (pp. 13–17). Washington, DC: CASPP Technical Assistance Center, Georgetown University Child Development Center.

Cross, W. E., Jr. (1991). *Shades of Black: Diversity in African American identity.* Philadelphia, PA: Temple University Press.

Cuéllar, I., Arnold, B., & Maldonado, R. (1995). Acculturation rating scale for Mexican Americans-II: A revision of the original ARSMA Scale. *Hispanic Journal of Behavioral Sciences, 17,* 275–304. doi:10.1177/07399863950173001

Cunningham, P. B., Foster, S. L., & Warner, S. E. (2010). Culturally relevant family-based treatment for adolescent delinquency and substance abuse: Understanding within-session processes. *Journal of Clinical Psychology, 66,* 830–846. doi:10.1002/jclp.20709

Dana, R. H. (1993). *Multicultural assessment perspectives for professional psychology.* Boston, MA: Allyn & Bacon.

Danieli, Y. (Ed.). (1998). *International handbook of multigenerational legacies of trauma.* New York, NY: Plenum Press.

Dass-Brailsford, P. (2007). *A practical approach to trauma: Empowering interventions.* Thousand Oaks, CA: Sage.

Davis, G. Y., & Stevenson, H. C. (2006). Racial socialization experiences and symptoms of depression among Black youth. *Journal of Child and Family Studies, 15,* 303–317. doi:10.1007/s10826-006-9039-8

De Granda, G. (1968). *Transculturación e interferencia lingüística en el Puerto Rico contemporáneo* [Transculturation and linguistic interference in contemporary Puerto Rico]. Bogotá, Colombia: Ediciones Bogotá.

Deveaux, F. (1995). Intergenerational transmission of cultural family patterns. *Family Therapy, 22,* 17–23.

Devereux, G. (1953). Cultural factors in psychoanalytic therapy. *Journal of the American Psychoanalytic Association, 1,* 629–655. doi:10.1177/000306515300100403

Díaz, E., Woods, S. W., & Rosenheck, R. A. (2005). Effects of ethnicity on psychotropic medications adherence. *Community Mental Health Journal, 41,* 521–537. doi:10.1007/s10597-005-6359-x

Dobbie, A. E., Medrano, M., Tysinger, J., & Olney, C. (2003). The BELIEF intervention: A pre-clinical tool for eliciting patients' health beliefs. *Family Medicine, 35,* 316–319.

Dobbins, F., Kalev, A., & Kelly, E. (2007). Diversity management in corporate America. *Contexts, 6,* 21–27. doi:10.1525/ctx.2007.6.4.21

Dobkin De Rios, M. D. (1981). Saladerra: A culture-bound misfortune syndrome in the Peruvian Amazon. *Culture, Medicine and Psychiatry, 5,* 193–213. doi:10.1007/BF00055420

Dodge Rea, B. (2001). Finding our balance: The investigation and clinical application of intuition. *Psychotherapy, 38,* 97–106. doi:10.1037/0033-3204.38.1.97

Dovidio, J. F., & Gaertner, S. L. (1998). On the nature of contemporary prejudice: The causes, consequences and challenges of aversive racism. In J. L. Eberhardt & S. T. Fiske (Eds.), *Confronting racism: the problem and the response* (pp. 3–32). Thousand Oaks, CA: Sage.

Downing, N., & Roush, K. (1985). From passive acceptance to active commitment: A model of feminist identity development for women. *The Counseling Psychologist, 13,* 695–709. doi:10.1177/0011000085134013

Du Bois, W. E. B. (1996). *The souls of Black folk.* New York, NY: Penguin Books. (Original work published 1903)

Dudley-Grant, R., Comas-Díaz, L., Todd-Bazemore, B., & Hueston, J. D. (2004). *Fostering resilience in response to terrorism: For psychologists working with people of color.* Fact sheet from the American Psychological Association Practice Directorate's online help Center (http://www.APAHelpCenter.org).

Duran, E. (2006). *Healing the soul wound: Counseling with American Indians and other Native people.* New York, NY: Teachers College Press.

Duran, E., & Duran, B. (1995). *Native American postcolonial psychology.* Albany, NY: New York University Press.

Durana, C. (1998). The use of touch in psychotherapy: Ethical and clinical guidelines. *Psychotherapy, 35,* 269–280. doi:10.1037/h0087817

Early, C., & Ang, S. (2003). *Cultural intelligence: Individual interactions across cultures.* Stanford, CA: Stanford University Press.

Eisenberg, D. M., Davis, R. V., Ettner, S. L., Appel, S., Wilkey, S., Van Rompay, M., & Kessler, R. C. (1998). Trends in alternative medicine use in the United States. 1990–1997. *JAMA, 280,* 1569–1575. doi:10.1001/jama.280.18.1569

Ekman, P., Sorenson, E. R., & Freisen, W. V. (1969, April 4). Pan-cultural elements in facial display of emotions. *Science, 164,* 86–88. doi:10.1126/science.164.3875.86

Elder, G. (1979). Historical change in life patterns and personality. In P. Baltes & O. G. Brim (Eds.), *Life-span development behavior* (Vol. 2, pp. 117–159). New York, NY: Academic Press.

Elkins, G., Marcus, J., Rajab, M. H., & Durgam, S. (2005). Complementary and alternative therapy use by psychotherapy clients. *Psychotherapy, 42,* 232–235. doi:10.1037/0033-3204.42.2.232

Elsass, P. (1992). *Strategies for survival: The psychology of cultural resilience in ethnic minorities.* New York: New York University Press.

Epstein, M. (1995). *Thoughts without a thinker: Psychotherapy from a Buddhist perspective.* New York, NY: Basic Books.

Escobar, J. I., Burnan, A., & Karno, M. (1986). Use of the Mini-Mental State Examination (MMSE) in a community population of mixed ethnicity: Cultural and linguistic artifacts. *Journal of Nervous and Mental Disease, 174,* 607–614. doi:10.1097/00005053-198610000-00005

Espin, O. (1996). *Latina healers: Lives of power and tradition.* Encino, CA: Floricanto Press.

Espin, O. M. (1987). Psychological impact of migration on Latinas: Implications for psychotherapeutic practice. *Psychology of Women Quarterly, 11*, 489–503. doi:10.1111/j.1471-6402.1987.tb00920.x

Evans-Campbell, T. (2008). Historical trauma in American Indian/Native Alaska communities. *Journal of Interpersonal Violence, 23*, 316–338. doi:10.1177/0886260507312290

Factor-Litvak, P., Cushman, L. F., Kronenburg, F., Wade, C., & Kalmuss, D. (2001). Use of complementary and alternative medicine among women in New York City: A pilot study. *Journal of Alternative and Complementary Medicine, 7*, 659–666. doi:10.1089/10755530152755216

Falicov, C. J. (1998). *Latino families in therapy.* New York, NY: Guilford Press.

Falicov, C. J. (2001). The cultural meanings of money: The case of Latinos and Anglo-Americans. *American Behavioral Scientist, 45*, 313–328. doi:10.1177/00027640121957088

Fanon, F. (1967). *Black skin, White masks.* New York, NY: Grove Press.

Federal Indian Child Welfare Act of 1978, Pub. L. No. 95–608, 93 Stat. 3071 (1978).

Fernando, S. (2003). *Cultural diversity, mental health and psychiatry: The struggle against racism.* New York, NY: Brunner-Routledge. doi:10.4324/9780203420348

Fischman, Y., & Ross, J. (1990). Group treatment of exiled survivors of torture. *American Journal of Orthopsychiatry, 60*, 135–142. doi:10.1037/h0079191

Fisher, C. B. (2009). *Decoding the ethics code: A practical guide for psychologists* (2nd ed.). Thousand Oaks, CA: Sage Publications.

Fleming, C. (1992). American Indians and Alaska natives: Changing societies past and present. In M. A. Orlandi (Ed.), *Cultural competence for evaluators: A guide for alcohol and other drug abuse prevention practitioners working with ethnic/racial communities* (OSAP cultural Competence Series 1, pp. 147–171). Rockville, MD: Office for Substance Abuse Prevention.

Folstein, M. F., Folstein, S. E., & McHugh, P. R. (1975). "Mini-mental state": A practical method for grading the cognitive state of patients for the clinician". *Journal of Psychiatric Research, 12*, 189–198. doi:10.1016/0022-3956(75)90026-6

Foote, W. W. (1996). Guided-imagery therapy. In B. W. Scotton, A. B. Chien, & J. R. Battista (Eds.), *Textbook of transpersonal psychiatry and psychology* (pp. 355–365). New York, NY: Basic Books.

Foster, R. F., Moskowitz, M., & Javier, R. (Eds.). (1996). *Reaching across the boundaries of culture and class: Widening the scope of psychotherapy.* New York, NY: Jason Aronson.

Frank, J. (1973). *Persuasion and healing: a comparative study of psychotherapy.* Baltimore, MD: Johns Hopkins University Press.

Freire, P. (1970). *Pedagogy of the oppressed.* New York, NY: Seabury Press.

Freire, P., & Macedo, D. (2000). *The Paulo Freire reader.* New York, NY: Continuum.

Fuentes, C. (1999). *The buried mirror: Reflections on Spain and the new world.* Boston, MA: Mariner Books.

Fuller, K. (2002). Eradicating essentialism from cultural competency education. *Academic Medicine, 77,* 198–201. doi:10.1097/00001888-200203000-00004

Fullilove, M. T. (1996). Psychiatric implications of displacement: Contributions from the psychology of place. *The American Journal of Psychiatry, 153,* 1516–1523.

Galanter, M. (1993). Network Therapy for addiction: a model for office practice. *The American Journal of Psychiatry, 150,* 28–36.

Galinsky, A. D., & Moskowitz, G. B. (2000). Perspective-taking: Decreasing stereotype expression, stereotype accessibility, and in-group favoritism. *Journal of Personality and Social Psychology, 78,* 708–724. doi:10.1037/0022-3514.78.4.708

Gallardo, M. E., Parham, T. A., Johnson, J., & Carter, J. A. (2009). Ethics and multiculturalism: Advancing cultural and clinical responsiveness. *Professional Psychology: Research and Practice, 40,* 425–435. doi:10.1037/a0016871

Garcia, A. M. (Producer & Director) (1982). *La Operación.* [*The operation*] [Motion picture]. United States: Cinema.

Garcia Campayo, J. (2003). Basic elements of ethnopsychopharmacology. *Actas Españolas de Psiquiatría, 31,* 156–162.

Gawain, S. (2002). *Creative visualization: Use the power of your imagination to create what you want in your life.* Novato, CA: Nataraj.

Gehrie, M. J. (1979). Culture as an internal representation. *Psychiatry, Interpersonal, and Biological Processess, 42,* 165–170.

Gendlin, E. T. (1982). *Focusing* (2nd ed.). New York, NY: Bantam Books.

Gendlin, E. T. (2001). *Focusing oriented psychotherapy: A manual of the experiential method.* New York, NY: Guilford Press.

Genopro.com (n.d.). *Rules to build genograms.* Retrieved from http://www.genopro.com/genogram/rules/

Gilbert, D. T. (1998). Ordinary personology. In D. T. Gilbert & S. T. Fiske (Eds.), *The handbook of social psychology* (4th ed., Vol. 2, pp. 89–150). New York, NY: McGraw-Hill.

Gillem, A. R., Cohn, L. R., & Throne, C. (2001). Black identity in biracial Black/White people: A comparison of Jaqueline who refuses to be exclusively Black and Adolphus who wishes he were. *Cultural Diversity and Ethnic Minority Psychology, 7,* 182–196. doi:10.1037/1099-9809.7.2.182

Golby, A. J., Gabrielli, J. D. E., Chiao, J. Y., & Eberhardt, J. (2001). Differential responses in the fusiform region to same race and other race faces. *Nature Neuroscience, 4,* 845–850. doi:10.1038/90565

Gonzalez-Wippler, M. (1974). *Santería: African magic in Latin America.* New York, NY: Doubleday.

Gonzalez-Wippler, M. (1989). *Santería: The religion.* New York, NY: Harmony Books.

Green, A. R., Carney, D. R., Pallin, D. J., Ngo, L. H., Raymond, K. L., Iezzoni, L. I., & Banaji, M. R. (2007). Implicit bias among physicians and its prediction of thrombolysis decisions for Black and White Clients. *Journal of General Internal Medicine, 22,* 1231–1238. doi:10.1007/s11606-007-0258-5

Grenier, L. (1998). *Working with indigenous knowledge: A guide for researchers.* Ottawa, Canada: International Developmental Research Centre.

Gudykunst, W., & Kim, Y. Y. (1995). Communicating with strangers: An approach to intercultural communication. In J. Stewart (Ed.), *Bridges not walls* (6th ed., pp. 429–442). New York, NY: McGraw-Hill.

Halifax, J. (1982). *Shaman: The wounded healer.* London, England: Thames and Hudson.

Hall, C. I. (1997). Cultural malpractice: The growing obsolescence of psychology with the changing U.S. population. *American Psychologist, 52,* 642–651. doi:10.1037/0003-066X.52.6.642

Hall, E. T. (1976). *Beyond culture.* Garden City, NY: Anchor Press/Doubleday.

Hall, G. C. N. (2001). Psychotherapy research with ethnic minorities: Empirical, ethical, and conceptual issues. *Journal of Consulting and Clinical Psychology, 69,* 502–510. doi:10.1037/0022-006X.69.3.502

Hall, R. L., & Greene, B. (1995). Cultural competence in feminist family therapy: An ethical mandate. *Journal of Feminist Family Therapy, 6,* 5–28. doi:10.1300/J086v06n03_02

Hamilton, J. A., Jensvold, M. F., Rothblum, E. D., & Cole, E. (Eds.). (1995). *Psychopharmacology from a feminist perspective.* Binghamton, NY: Haworth Press.

Hammer, L. (1990). *Dragon rises, red bird lies: Psychology, energy, and Chinese medicine.* Barrytown, NY: Station Hill Press.

Hansen, N. D., Pepitone-Arreola-Rockwell, F., & Greene, A. F. (2000). Multicultural competence: Criteria and case examples. *Professional Psychology: Research and Practice, 31,* 652–660. doi:10.1037/0735-7028.31.6.652

Harding, S. (1999). *Curanderas* in the Americas. *Alternative and Complementary Therapies, 5,* 309–316. doi:10.1089/act.1999.5.309

Hardy, K. V., & Laszloffy, T. (1995). The cultural genogram: Key to training culturally competent family clinicians. *Journal of Marital and Family Therapy, 21,* 227–237.

Hart, A. J., Whalen, P. J., Shin, L. M., McInerney, S. C., Fisher, M., & Rauch, S. L. (2000). Differential responses in the human amygdala to social outgroup vs. ingroup face stimuli. *Neuroreport, 11,* 2351–2354. doi:10.1097/00001756-200008030-00004

Harwood, A. (1971). The hot/cold theory of disease. *JAMA, 216,* 1153–1158. doi:10.1001/jama.216.7.1153

Harwood, A. (1977). *Rx: Spiritualists as needed. A study of a Puerto Rican community mental health resource.* New York, NY: Wiley.

Hatch, M. L., Friedman, S., & Paradis, C. M. (1996). Behavioral treatment of obsessive disorder in African Americans. *Cognitive and Behavioral Practice, 3,* 303–315. doi:10.1016/S1077-7229(96)80020-4

Hayden, E. C. (2010). Sex bias blights drug studies: Omission of females is skewing results. *Nature, 464,* 332–333. doi:10.1038/464332b

Hayes, S. C. Strosahl, K. D., & Wilson, G. (2003). *Acceptance and commitment therapy: An experiential approach to behavior change.* New York, NY: Guilford Press.

Hays, P. (2001). *Addressing cultural complexities in practice: Assessment, diagnosis, and therapy.* Washington, DC: American Psychological Association.

Hays, P. (2008). *Addressing cultural complexities in practice: Assessment, diagnosis and therapy* (2nd ed.). Washington, DC: American Psychological Association. doi:10.1037/11650-000

Hedden, T., Ketay, S., Aron, A., Markus, H. R., & Gabrieli, J. (2008). Cultural influences on neural substrates of attentional control. *Psychological Science, 19,* 12–17. doi:10.1111/j.1467-9280.2008.02038.x

Hellinger, B., Weber, G., & Beaumont, H. (1998). *Love's hidden symmetry: What makes love in relationships.* Phoenix, AZ: Zeig, Tucker & Theisen.

Hellriegel, D., Slocum, J. W., & Woodman, R. W. (1998). *Organizational behavior* (5th ed.). Cincinnati, OH: South-Western College.

Helms, J. (1990a). *Black and White racial identity: Theory and research.* Westport, CT: Greenwood.

Helms, J. (1990 b). *Training manual for diagnosing racial identity in social interactions.* Topeka, KS: Content Communications.

Helms, J. E. (1992). Why is there no study of cultural equivalence in standardized cognitive ability testing? *American Psychologist, 47,* 1083–1101. doi:10.1037/0003-066X.47.9.1083

Henrich, J., Heine, S., & Norenzayan, A. (2010). Most people are not WEIRD. *Nature, 466.* doi:10.1038/466029a

Herlihy, B., & Corey, G. (1997). *Boundary issues in counseling: Multiple roles and responsibilities* (pp. 100–109). Alexandria, VA: American Counseling Association Press.

Hersen, M., Hilsenroth, M. J., & Segal, D. L. (Eds.). (2004). *Comprehensive handbook of psychological assessment: Personality assessment.* New York, NY: Wiley.

Hersoug, A. G., Hoglend, P., Monsen, J. T., & Havik, O. E. (2001). Quality of working alliance in psychotherapy: Therapist variables and patient/therapist similarity as predictors. *Journal of Psychotherapy Practice and Research, 10,* 205–216.

Hilliard, A. G. (1996). Either a paradigm shift or no mental measurement: The non-science of *The Bell Curve*. *Cultural Diversity and Mental Health, 2,* 1–20. doi:10.1037/1099-9809.2.1.1

Ho, M. K. (1987). *Family therapy with ethnic minorities*. Newbury Park, CA: Sage.

Hoffman, E. (1989). *Lost in translation: A life in a new language*. New York, NY: Penguin Books.

Holdstock, T. L. (2000). *Re-examining psychology: Critical perspectives and African insights*. London, England: Routledge.

Holmes, D. E. (1992). Race and transference in psychoanalysis and psychotherapy. *The International Journal of Psychoanalysis, 73,* 1–11.

Hong, Y., Morris, M., Chiu, C., & Benet-Martínez, V. (2000). Multicultural minds: A dynamic constructivist approach to culture and cognition. *American Psychologist, 55,* 709–720.

Horrell, S. C. V. (2008). Effectiveness of cognitive–behavioral therapy with adult ethnic minority clients: A review. *Professional Psychology: Research and Practice, 39,* 160–168. doi:10.1037/0735-7028.39.2.160

Howard-Hamilton, M. F., Phelps, R. E., & Torres, V. (1998). *Meeting the needs of all student s and staff members: The challenge of diversity. New directions for student services*. San Francisco, CA: Jossey-Bass.

Hughes, D., Rodriguez, J., Smith, E. P., Johnson, D. J., Stevenson, H. C., & Spicer, P. (2006). Parents' ethnic-racial socialization practices: A review of research and direction for future study. *Developmental Psychology, 42,* 747–770. doi:10.1037/0012-1649.42.5.747

Jacobs, G. (2003). *The ancestral mind*. New York, NY: Viking.

Jacobsen, F. M. (1988). Ethnocultural assessment. In L. Comas-Díaz & E. H. Griffith (Eds.), *Clinical guidelines in cross-cultural mental health* (pp. 135–147). New York, NY: Wiley.

Jacobsen, F. M., & Comas-Díaz, L. (1999). Psychopharmacological treatment of Latinas. *Essential Psychopharmacology, 3,* 29–42.

Jalali, B. (1988). Ethnicity, cultural adjustment, and behavior: Implications for family therapy. In L. Comas-Díaz & E. E. H. Griffith (Eds.), *Clinical guidelines in cross-cultural mental health* (pp. 9–32). New York, NY: Wiley.

Javier, R. A. (1995). Vicissitudes of autobiographical memories in a bilingual analysis. *Psychoanalytic Psychology, 12,* 429–438. doi:10.1037/h0079703

Javier, R. A. (2007). *The bilingual mind: Thinking, feeling, and speaking in two languages*. New York, NY: Springer Verlag.

Jewish Virtual Library. (2011). *Ashkenazi Jewish genetic diseases*. Retrieved from http://www.jewishvirtuallibrary.org/jsource/Health/genetics.html

Jones, E. E. (1985). Psychotherapy and counseling with Black clients. In P. Pedersen (Ed.), *Handbook of cross-cultural counseling and therapy* (pp. 173–179). Westport, CT: Greenwood Press.

Jones, J. H. (1981). *Bad blood: The Tuskegee syphilis experiment.* New York, NY: Free Press.

Kabat-Zinn, J. (2003). Mindfulness-based interventions in context: Past, present, and future. *Clinical Psychology: Science and Practice, 10,* 144–156. doi:10.1093/clipsy.bpg016

Kakar, S. (1982). *Shamans, mystics, and doctors: A psychological inquiry into India and its healing traditions.* New Delhi, India: Oxford University Press.

Kakar, S. (1985). Psychoanalysis and non-Western cultures. *The International Review of Psychoanalysis, 12,* 441–448.

Kalweit, H. (1989). When insanity is a blessing: The message of shamanism. In S. Grof & C. Grof (Eds.), *Spiritual emergency: When personal transformation becomes a crisis* (pp. 77–97). New York, NY: Tarcher/Putnam.

Kaplan, A. (1991). The self in relation: Implications for depression in women. In J. V. Jordan. A. G. Kaplan, J. B. Miller, I. P. Stiver, & J. I. Surrey (Eds.), *Women's growth in connection: Writings from the Stone Center* (pp. 206–222). New York, NY: Guilford Press.

Kaptchuk, T. J., & Eisenberg, D. M. (1998). The persuasive appeal of alternative medicine. *Annals of International medicine, 129.* 1061–1065.

Kardec, A. (1957). *El libro de los espíritus [The book of the spirits].* Mexico City, Mexico: Editorial Diana.

Kardiner, A., & Ovesey, L. (1951). *The mark of oppression.* New York, NY: Norton.

Karlsson, R. (2005). Ethnic matching between therapist and patient in psychotherapy: An overview of findings, together with methodological and conceptual issues. *Cultural Diversity and Ethnic Minority Psychology, 11,* 113–129. doi:10.1037/1099-9809.11.2.113

Katz, J. K. (1985). The sociopolitical nature of counseling. *The Counseling Psychologist, 13,* 615–624. doi:10.1177/0011000085134005

Kay, A. (1998). Generativity in the shadow of genocide: The Holocaust experience and generativity. In D. P. McAdams & E. de St. Aubin (Eds.), *Generativity and adult development: How and why we care for the next generation* (pp. 335–359). Washington, DC: American Psychological Association. doi:10.1037/10288-010

Keller, H. (2002). Culture and development: Developmental pathways to individualism and interrelatedness. In W. J. Lonner, D. L. Dinnel, S. A. Hayes, & D. N. Sattler (Eds.), *Online readings in psychology and culture* (Unit 11, Chapter 1). Center for Cross-Cultural Research, Western Washington University, Bellingham. Retrieved from http://www.wwu.edu/~culture

Kiev, A. (1968). Curanderismo: *Mexican American folk psychiatry*. New York, NY: Free Press.

Kleinman, A. (1980). *Patients and healers in the context of culture: An exploration of the borderland between anthropology, medicine, and psychiatry*. Berkeley: University of California Press.

Kleinman, A. (1988). *Rethinking psychiatry: From cultural category to personal experience*. New York, NY: Free Press.

Klerman, G. L., Weissman, M. M., Rounsanville, B., & Chevron, E. (1984). *Interpersonal psychotherapy of depression*. New York, NY: Basic Books.

Knipscheer, J. W., & Kleber, R. J. (2004). A need for ethnic similarity in the therapist–patient interaction? Mediterranean migrants in Dutch mental health care. *Journal of Clinical Psychology, 60,* 543–554. doi:10.1002/jclp.20008

Kluckholn, F. R., & Strodtbeck, F. L. (1961). *Variations in value orientations*. Evanston, IL: Row Patterson.

Kohn, L. P., Oden, T., Muñoz, R. F., Robinson, A., & Leavitt, D. (2002). Adapted cognitive behavioral group therapy for depressed low-income African American women. *Community Mental Health Journal, 38,* 497–504. doi:10.1023/A:1020884202677

Kornfield, J. (2008). *The wise heart: A guide to the universal teachings of Buddhist psychology*. New York, NY: Bantam Books.

Koss-Chioino, J. D. (1992). *Women as healers, women as patients: Mental health care and traditional healing in Puerto Rico*. Boulder, CO: Westview Press.

Koss-Chioino, J. D. (2006). Spiritual transformation, relation, and radical empathy: Core components of the ritual healing process. *Transcultural Psychiatry, 43,* 652–670. doi:10.1177/1363461506070789

Koss-Chioino, J. D., & Vargas, L. (1992). Through the cultural looking glass: A model for understanding culturally responsive psychotherapies. In L. A. Vargas (Ed.), *Working with culture: Psychotherapeutic interventions with ethnic minority, children and adolescents* (pp. 1–22). San Francisco, CA: Jossey Bass.

Kraut, A. M. (1994). *Silent travelers: Germs, genes and the "immigrant menace."* New York, NY: Basic Books.

Krieger, N. (1999). Embodying inequality: A review of concepts, measures, and methods for studying health consequences of discrimination. *International Journal of Health Services, 29,* 295–352. doi:10.2190/M11W-VWXE-KQM9-G97Q

Kritzberg, N. I. (1980). On patients' gift-giving. *Contemporary Psychoanalysis, 16,* 98–118.

Kühnen, U., Hannover, B., & Schubert, B. (2001). The semantic–procedural interface model of the self: The role of self-knowledge for context-dependent versus context-independent models of thinking. *Journal of Personality and Social Psychology, 80,* 397–409. doi:10.1037/0022-3514.80.3.397

Kumagai, A. K., & Lypson, M. L. (2009). Beyond cultural competence: Critical consciousness, social justice, and multicultural education. *Academic Medicine, 84,* 782–787. doi:10.1097/ACM.0b013e3181a42398

Kurtz, S. N. (1992). *All mothers are one: Hindu India and the cultural reshaping of psychoanalysis.* New York, NY: Columbia University Press.

Lad, V. (1993). *Ayurveda, a practical guide: The science of self-healing.* Twin Lakes, WI: Lotus Press.

La Fromboise, T., Trimble, J. E., & Mohatt, G. V. (1990). Counseling intervention and American Indian tradition. *American Psychologist, 19,* 628–654.

Lalonde, R., Taylor, D., & Moghaddam, F. (1992). The process of social identification for visible immigrant women in a multicultural context. *Journal of Cross-Cultural Psychology, 23,* 25–39. doi:10.1177/0022022192231002

Lam, Y., Castro, D., & Dunn, J. (1991). Drug metabolizing capacity in Mexican Americans. *Clinical Psychopharmacology and Therapeutics, 49,* 159.

Landrine, H., & Klonoff, E. A. (1996). The Schedule of Racist Events: A measure of racist discrimination and a study of its negative physical and mental health consequence. *Journal of Black Psychology, 22,* 144–168. doi:10.1177/00957984960222002

Landrine, H., & Klonoff, E. A. (1997). *Discrimination against women: Prevalence, consequences, remedies.* Thousand Oaks, CA: Sage.

Lawson, W. B. (1996). Clinical issues in pharmacotherapy of African Americans. *Psychopharmacological Bulletin, 32,* 275–81.

Lawson, W. B. (2000). Issues in pharmacotherapy for African Americans. In P. Ruiz (Ed.), *Ethnicity and psychopharmacology* (pp. 37–47). Washington, DC: American Psychiatric Press.

Leininger, M. (1978). Changing foci in American nursing education: Primary and transcultural nursing care. *Journal of Advanced Nursing, 3,* 155–166. doi:10.1111/j.1365-2648.1978.tb00840.x

Leung, A. K.-y., Maddux, W., Galinsky, A., & Chiu, C.-y. (2008). Multicultural experience enhances creativity: The when and how. *American Psychologist, 63,* 169–181. doi:10.1037/0003-066X.63.3.169

Levin, S. J., Like, R. C., & Gottlieb, J. E. (2000). ETHNIC: A framework for culturally competent clinical practice. *Patient Care, 34,* 188–189.

Levine, P. A. (1997). *Waking the tiger: Healing trauma.* Berkeley, CA: North Atlantic Books.

Levy, D. A. (2010). *Tools of critical thinking: Metathoughts for psychology* (2nd ed.). Long Grove, IL: Waveland Press.

Lewis-Fernández, R., & Díaz, N. (2002). The cultural formulation: A method for assessing cultural factors affecting the clinical encounter. *Psychiatric Quarterly, 73,* 271–295. doi:10.1023/A:1020412000183

Lewis-Fernández, R., Garrido-Castillo, P., Bennasar, M. C., Parrilla, E. M., Laria, A. J., Ma, G., & Petkova, E. (2002). Dissociation, childhood trauma, and ataque de nervious among Puerto Rican psychiatric outpatients. *American Journal of Psychiatry, 159,* 1603–1605. doi:10.1176/appi.ajp.159.9.1603

Lieberman, J. A., & Stuart, M. R. (1999). The BATHE Method: Incorporating counseling and psychotherapy into the everyday management of clients. *Primary Care Companion Journal Clinical Psychiatry, 1,* 35–39.

Liebowitz, M. R., Salman, E., Jusino, C. M., Garfinkel, R., Street, L., Cardenas, D. L., . . . Davies, S. (1994). Ataques de nervios and panic disorders. *The American Journal of Psychiatry, 151,* 871–875.

Lin, K.-M. (2010, January 12). Cultural and ethnic issues in psychopharmacology: Addressing both instrumental and symbolic effects of treatment. *Psychiatric News, 27.* Retrieved from http://www.psychiatrictimes.com/display/article/10168/1505053

Lin, K.-M., Anderson, D., & Poland, R. E. (1995). Ethnicity and psychopharmacology: Bridging the gap. *Psychiatric Clinics of North America, 18,* 635–647.

Lin, K.-M., & Cheung, F. (1999). Mental health issues for Asian Americans. *Psychiatric Services, 50,* 774–780.

Lin, K.-M., Poland, R. E., & Anderson, D. (1995). Psychopharmacology, ethnicity, and culture. *Transcultural Psychiatric Research Review, 32,* 3–40

Lin, K.-M., Smith, M. W., & Ortiz, V. (2001). Culture and psychopharmacology. *Psychiatric Clinics of North America, 24,* 523–538. doi:10.1016/S0193-953X(05)70245-8

Linehan, M. M. (1993). *Cognitive–behavioural treatment of borderline personality disorder.* New York, NY: Guilford Press.

Lloyd, K. R., Jakob, K. S., Patel, V., St. Louis, L., Bhugra, D., & Mann, A. H. (1998). The development of the Short Explanatory Model Interview (SEMI) and its use among primary-attenders with common mental disorders. *Psychological Medicine, 28,* 1231–1238. doi:10.1017/S0033291798007065

Lo, H.-T., & Fung, K. P. (2003). Culturally competent psychotherapy. *The Canadian Journal of Psychiatry/La Revue Canadienne de Psychiatrie, 48,* 161–170.

Locke, D. C. (1992). *Increasing multicultural understanding: A comprehensive model.* Newbury Park, CA: Sage.

Lonner, W. I., & Ibrahim, F. A. (1996). Appraisal and assessment in cross-cultural counseling. In P. B. Pedersen, J. G. Draguns, W. J. Lonner, & J. E. Trimble (Eds.), *Counseling across cultures* (pp. 293–322). Thousand Oaks, CA: Guilford Press.

Lopez, E. C., Lamar, D., & Scully-DeMartini, D. (1997). The cognitive assessment of limited-English-proficient children: Current problems and practical recommendations. *Cultural Diversity and Mental Health, 3,* 117–130. doi:10.1037/1099-9809.3.2.117

López, S. R. (1989). Patient variables biases in clinical judgment: Conceptual overview and methodological considerations. *Psychological Bulletin, 106,* 184–203. doi:10.1037/0033-2909.106.2.184

López, S. R. (1997). Cultural competence in psychotherapy: A guide for clinicians and their supervisors. In C. E. Watkins (Ed.), *Handbook of psychotherapy supervision* (pp. 570–588). New York, NY: Wiley.

López, S. R., & Taussig, F. M. (1991). Cognitive–intellectual functioning of Spanish-speaking impaired and nonimpaired elderly: Implications for culturally sensitive-psychological assessment. *Psychological Assessment: A Journal of Consulting and Clinical Psychology, 3,* 448–454.

López-Muñoz, F., Garcia-Garcia, P., & Alamo, C. (2007). The virtue of that precious balsam approach to Don Quixote from the psychopharmacological perspective. *Actas Españolas de Psiquiatría, 35,* 149–161.

Lu, F. G. (2004). Culture and inpatient psychiatry. In W.-S. Tseng & J. Streltzer (Eds.), *Cultural competence in clinical psychiatry* (pp. 21–36). Washington, DC: American Psychiatric Publishing.

Lu, F. G., Lim, R. F., & Mezzich, J. E. (1995). Issues in assessment and diagnosis of culturally diverse individuals. In J. M. Oldham, & M. Riba (Eds.). *Review of psychiatry* (pp. 477–510). Washington, DC: American Psychiatric Press.

Lubchansky, I., Egri, G., & Strokes, J. (1970). Puerto Rican spiritualists view mental illness: The faith healer as a paraprofessional. *The American Journal of Psychiatry, 127,* 312–321.

Luna, D., Ringberg, T., & Peracchio, L. A. (2008). One individual, two identities: Frame-switching among biculturals. *Journal of Consumer Research, 35,* 279–293. doi:10.1086/586914

Maduro, R. J. (1982). Working with Latinos and the use of dream analysis. *Journal of the American Academy of Psychoanalysis, 10,* 609–628.

Maduro, R. J. (1983). Curanderismo and Latino views of disease and curing. *The Western Journal of Medicine, 139,* 868–874.

Management Sciences for Health. (n.d.). *The Cultural Competence Self Assessment Protocol for Health Care Organizations and Systems.* Retrieved from http://erc.msh.org/mainpage.cfm?file=9.1g.htm&module=provider&language=English

Mandell, D. (1998). Therapist self-disclosure can be a balancing act. *Traumatic Stress Points, 12,* 6.

Marcos, L. R. (1979). Effects of interpreters on the evaluation of psychopathology in non-English speaking patients. *The American Journal of Psychiatry, 136,* 171–174.

Marin, G., & Marin, B. V. (1991). *Research with Hispanic populations.* Newbury Park, CA: Sage.

Marmar, C. R., Horowitiz, M. J., Weiss, D. S., & Marziali, E. (1986). The development of the therapeutic alliance rating system. In L. S. Grenber & W. M. Pinsof (Eds.), *The psychotherapeutic process: A research handbook* (pp. 367–390). New York, NY: Guilford Press.

Marsella, A. J., Bornemann, T., Ekblad, S., & Orley, J. (Eds.). (1994). *Amidst peril and pain: The mental health and well-being of the world's refugees.* Washington, DC: American Psychological Association. doi:10.1037/10147-000

Marsh, A. A., Elenbein, H. A., & Ambady, N. (2003). Nonverbal "accents": Cultural differences in facial expressions of emotion. *Psychological Science, 14,* 373–376. doi:10.1111/1467-9280.24461

Martin, L. (2002, May). Sirimbas, serenos, and teleles. *Latina Magazine,* 65–66.

Mason, J. L. (1995). *Cultural competence self-assessment questionnaire: A manual for users.* Oregon: Portland State University, Research and Training Center on Family Support and Children's Mental Health.

Mattelaer, J. J., & Jilek, W. (2007). Koro—the psychological disappearance of the penis. *Journal of Sexual Medicine, 4,* 1509–1515. doi:10.1111/j.1743-6109.2007.00586.x

Mayfield, D., McLeod, G., & Hall, P. (1974). The CAGE questionnaire: Validation of a new alcoholism screening instrument. *The American Journal of Psychiatry, 131,* 1121–1123.

McGill, D. W. (1992). The cultural story in multicultural family therapy. *Families in Society, 73,* 339–349.

McGoldrick, M., Gerson, R., & Petry, S. (2008). *Genograms: Assessment and intervention* (3rd ed.). New York, NY: Norton.

McGoldrick, M., Gerson, R., & Shellenberger, S. (1999). *Genograms: Assessment and intervention.* New York, NY: Norton.

McGoldrick, M., Giordano, J., & Garcia-Preto, N. (Eds.). (2005). *Ethnicity and family therapy* (3rd ed.). New York, NY: Guilford Press.

McIntosh, P. (1988). *White privilege and male privilege: A personal account of coming to see correspondences through work in women's studies.* Wellesley, MA: Wellesley College Center for Research on Women.

McKinley, J. C, & Hathaway, S. R. (1944). A multiphasic personality schedule (Minnesota): V. Hysteria, hypomania, and psychopathic deviate. *Journal of Applied Psychology, 28,* 153–174.

Mehl-Madrona, L. (2003). *Coyote healing: Miracles in Native medicine.* Rochester, Vermont: Bear & Company.

Melfi, C. A., Croghan, T. W., Hanna, M. P., & Robinson, R. (2000). Racial variation in antidepressant treatment in a Medicaid population. *Journal of Clinical Psychiatry, 61,* 16–21. doi:10.4088/JCP.v61n0105

Mendoza, R., & Smith, M. W. (2000). The Hispanic response to psychotropic medications. In P. Ruiz (Ed.), *Ethnicity and psychopharmacology* (pp. 55–89). Washington, DC: American Psychiatric Press.

Merrill, M. D. (1991). Constructivism and instructional design. *Educational Technology, 31,* 45–53.

Mezzich, J. F., Caracci, G., Fabrega, H., Jr., & Kirmayer, L. J. (2009). Cultural formulation guidelines. *Transcultural Psychiatry, 46,* 383–405.

Minnesota Department of Health and Human Services. (2004). *Guidelines for culturally competent organizations.* Retrieved from http://www.dhs.state.mn.us/main/idcplg?IdcService=GET_DYNAMIC_CONVERSION&RevisionSelectionMethod=LatestReleased&dDocName=id_016415

Minnesota Indian Family Preservation Act, Minn. Stat. § 260.751–260.835 (1999).

Miranda, J., Bernal, G., Lau, A., Kohn, L., Hwang, W.-C., & La Framboise, T. (2005). State of the science on psychosocial interventions for ethnic minorities. *Annual Review of Clinical Psychology, 1,* 113–142. doi:10.1146/annurev.clinpsy.1.102803.143822

Mogil, J. S., & Chanda, M. L. (2005). The case for the inclusion of female subjects in basic science studies of pain. *Pain, 117,* 1–5.

Mollica, R. F., & Lavalle, J. P. (1988). Southeast Asian refugees. In L. Comas-Díaz & E. E. H. Griffith (Eds.), *Clinical guidelines in cross-cultural mental health* (pp. 262–304). New York, NY: Wiley.

Montuori, A., & Fahim, U. (2004). Cross-cultural encounter as an opportunity for personal growth. *Journal of Humanistic Psychology, 44,* 243–265. doi:10.1177/0022167804263414

Moodley, R. (1998). Cultural returns to the subject: Traditional healing in counseling and therapy. *Changes: International Journal of Psychoanalytic Psychotherapy, 16,* 45–56.

Moodley, R., & West, W. (2006). *Integrating traditional healing practices into counseling and psychotherapy.* Thousand Oaks, CA: Sage.

Morales, E., & Norcross, J. C. (2010). Evidence-based practices with ethnic minorities: Strange bedfellows no more. *Journal of Clinical Psychology, 66,* 821–829. doi:10.1002/jclp.20712

Morita, S. (1998). *Morita therapy and the true nature of anxiety-based disorders (Shinkeishitsu).* New York: State University of New York Press.

Moya, P. M. L. (2001). Chicana feminism and postmodernist theory. *Signs, 26,* 441–483. doi:10.1086/495600

Muñoz, R. F. (1996). *The healthy management of reality.* Retrieved from http://www.medschool.ucsf.edu/latino/pdf/healthy_management.pdf

Muñoz, R. F., & Mendelson, T. (2005). Toward evidence-based interventions for diverse populations: The San Francisco General Hospital Prevention and Treatment Manuals. *Journal of Consulting and Clinical Psychology, 73*, 790–799. doi:10.1037/0022-006X.73.5.790

Murray, H. A. (1943). *Thematic Apperception Test.* Cambridge, MA: Harvard University Press.

Musil, C. M. (2003). Educating for citizenship. *Peer Review, 5*, 4–8.

Nápoles, A. M., Chadiha, L., Eversley, R., & Moreno-John, G. (2010). Developing culturally sensitive dementia caregiver interventions: Are we there yet? *American Journal of Alzheimer's Disease and Other Dementias, 25*, 389–406. doi:10.1177/1533317510370957

National Association of Social Workers. (2001). *NASW standards for cultural competence in social work practice.* Retrieved from http://www.naswdc.org/practice/standards/NASWculturalstandards.pdf

National Center for Complementary and Alternative Medicine. (n.d.). *What is complementary and alternative medicine?* Retrieved from http://nccam.nih.gov/health/whatiscam/

Neumann, D. A., & Gamble, S. J. (1995). Issues in professional development of psychotherapists: Countertransference and vicarious traumatization in the new trauma therapist. *Psychotherapy, 32*, 341–347. doi:10.1037/0033-3204.32.2.341

Nieves-Grafals, S. (1995). Psychological testing as a diagnostic and therapeutic tool in the treatment of traumatized Latin American and African refugees. *Cultural Diversity and Mental Health, 1*, 19–27. doi:10.1037/1099-9809.1.1.19

Ng, C. H., Lin, K.-M. Singh B. S., & Chiu, E. Y. K. (Eds.) (2008). *Ethnopsychopharmacology: Advances in current practice.* Cambridge, MA: Cambridge University Press.

Norcross, J. C. (Ed.). (2002). *Psychotherapy relationships that work: Therapist contributions and responsiveness to patients.* New York, NY: Oxford University Press.

Norcross, J. C., Koocher, G. P., & Garofalo, A. (2006). Discredited psychological treatments and tests: A Delphi poll. *Professional Psychology: Research and Practice, 37*, 515–522. doi:10.1037/0735-7028.37.5.515

Nuñez, L. M (1992). *Santería: A practical guide to Afro-Caribbean magic.* New York, NY: Spring Publications. Retrieved from http://w3.iac.net/~moonweb/Santeria/Intro.html

Ochoa, S. H., Powell, M. P., & Robles-Piña, R. (1996). School psychologists' assessment practices with bilingual and limited English proficient students. *Journal of Psychoeducational Assessment, 14*, 250–275. doi:10.1177/073428299601400306

Olmos, M. F., & Paravisini-Gebert, L. (1997). *Sacred possessions, Voodoo, Santería, Obeah, and the Caribbean.* Piscataway, NJ: Rutgers University Press.

Omer, H. (1993). Short-term psychotherapy and the rise of the life sketch. *Psychotherapy, 30*, 668–673. doi:10.1037/0033-3204.30.4.668

Organista, K. C., Muñoz, R. F., & Gonzales, G. (1994). Cognitive behavioral therapy for depression in low-income and minority medical outpatients: Description of a program and exploratory analyses. *Cognitive Therapy and Research, 18*, 241–259. doi:10.1007/BF02357778

Ornstein, R. E. (1972). *The psychology of consciousness.* San Francisco, CA: Freeman.

Ortiz, B. I., Shields, K. M., Clauson, K. A., & Clay, P. G. (2007). Complementary and alternative medicine use among Hispanics. *The Annals of Pharmacotherapy, 41*, 994–1004.

Page, E. (2007). Bisexual women's and men's experiences of psychotherapy. In B. Firestein (Ed.), *Becoming invisible: Counseling bisexuals across the lifespan* (pp. 52–71). New York, NY: Columbia University Press.

Painter, N. I. (2010). *The history of White people.* New York, NY: Norton.

Paniagua, F. A. (1994). *Assessing and treating culturally diverse clients: A practical guide.* Thousand Oaks, CA: Sage.

Parham, T. A., White, J. L., & Ajamu. A (1999). *The psychology of Blacks: An African-centered perspective* (3rd ed.). Englewood Cliffs, NJ: Prentice-Hall.

Parks, F. M. (2007). Working with narratives: Coping strategies in African American folk beliefs and traditional healing practices. *Journal of Human Behavior in the Social Environment, 15*, 135–147. doi:10.1300/J137v15n01_07

Papakostas, G. I., Mischoulon, D., Shyu, I., Alpert, J. E., & Fava, M. (2010). S-adenosyl methionine (SAMe) augmentation of serotonin reuptake inhibitors for antidepressant nonresponders with major depression disorder: A double-blind, randomized clinical trial. *The American Journal of Psychiatry, 167*, 942–948. doi:10.1176/appi.ajp.2009.09081198

Pedersen, P. (2000). *A handbook for developing multicultural awareness* (3rd ed.). Alexandria, VA: American Counseling Association.

Peltzer, K. ((1995). *Psychology and health in African cultures: Examples of ethnopsychotherapeutic practice.* Frankfurt, Germany: IKO-Verlag.

Penninx, B. W. J. H., Beekman, A. T. F., Honig, A., Deeg, D. J. H., Schoevers, R. A., Van Eijk, T. M., & van Tilburg, W. (2001). Depression and cardiac mortality: Results from a community-based longitudinal study. *Archives of General Psychiatry, 58*, 221–227. doi:10.1001/archpsyc.58.3.221

Pi, E. H., & Gray, G. E. (2000). Ethnopharmacology for Asians. In P. Ruiz (Ed.), *Ethnicity and psychopharmacology* (pp. 91–113). Washington, DC: American Psychiatric Press.

Pierce, C. M. (1995). Stress analogs of racism and sexism: Terrorism, torture, and disaster. In C. V. Willie, P. P. Reiker, & B. S. Brown (Eds.), *Mental health, racism, and sexism* (pp. 277–293). Pittsburgh, PA: University of Pittsburgh Press.

Pierre, J. M. (2010). Hallucinations in nonpsychotic disorders: Toward a differential diagnosis of "hearing voices." *Harvard Review of Psychiatry, 18,* 22–35. doi:10.3109/10673220903523706

Pinderhughes, E. (1989). *Understanding race, ethnicity, and power: The key to efficacy in clinical practice.* New York, NY: The Free Press.

Pinderhughes, E. (1994). Empowerment as an intervention goal: Early ideas. In L. Gutierrez & P. Nurius (Eds.), *Education and research for empowerment practice* (pp. 17–31). Seattle: University of Washington School of Social Work, Center for Policy and Practice Research.

Portela, J. M. (1971). Social aspects of transference and countertransference in the patient–psychiatrist relationship in an underdeveloped country: Brazil. *International Journal of Social Psychiatry, 17,* 177–188. doi:10.1177/002076407101700302

Poston, W. C. (1990). The biracial identity development model: A needed addition. *Journal of Counseling & Development, 69,* 152–155.

Prince, R. (1980). Variations in psychotherapeutic procedures. In H. C. Triandis & J. Draguns (Eds.), *Handbook of cross-cultural psychology* (Vol. 6, pp. 314–321). Boston, MA: Allyn & Bacon.

Quinn, A. (2007). Reflections on intergenerational trauma: Healing as a critical intervention. *First Peoples Child and Family Review, 3,* 72–82.

Radloff, L. S. (1977). The CES-D scale: A self-report depression scale for research in the general population. *Applied Psychological Measurement, 1,* 385–401.

Ragins, R. (1995). Diversity, power, and mentorship in organizations: A cultural, structural and behavioral perspective. In M. M. Cheners, S. Oskamp., & M. A. Costano (Eds.), *Diversity in organizations* (pp. 91–132). Thousand Oaks, CA: Sage.

Ramirez, M. (1991). *Psychotherapy and counseling with minorities: A cognitive approach to individual and cultural differences.* New York, NY: Pergamon.

Regier, D. A., Myers, J. K., Kramer, M., Robbins, L. N., Blazer, D. G., Hough, R. L., . . . Locke, B. Z. (1984). The NIMH Epidemiologic Catchment Area (ECA) program: Historical context, major objectives and study population characteristics. *Archives of General Psychiatry, 41,* 934–941.

Regional Office for Culture in Latin America and the Caribbean. (n.d.). *Introduction: Breaking the silence, the case of Aruba.* Retrieved from http://www.lacult.org/sitios_memoria/Aruba.php?lan=en

Remen, R. N. (1989). The search for healing. In R. Carlson & B. Shield (Eds.), *Healers on healing* (pp. 91–96). New York, NY: Putnam.

Rey, J. A. (2006). Interface of multiculturalism and psychopharmacology. *Journal of Pharmacy Practice, 19,* 379–385. doi:10.1177/0897190007300734

Reynolds, D. K. (1980). *The quiet therapies: Japan pathways to personal growth.* Honolulu: The University Press of Hawaii.

Rhee, E., Uleman, J. S., Lee, H. K., & Roman, R. J. (1995). Spontaneous self-descriptions and ethnic identities in individualistic and collectivistic cultures. *Journal of Personality and Social Psychology, 69,* 142–152. doi:10.1037/0022-3514.69.1.142

Rhode, D. L., & Williams, J. C. (2007). Legal perspectives on employment discrimination. In F. J. Crosby, M. S. Stockdale, & S. A. Ropp (Eds.), *Sex discrimination in the workplace* (pp. 235–270). Malden, MA: Blackwell.

Richeson, J. A., & Shelton, J. N. (2003). When prejudice does not pay: Effects of interracial contact on executive function. *Psychological Science, 14,* 287–290.

Ridley, C. (1985). Imperatives for ethnic and cultural relevance in psychology training programs. *Professional Psychology: Research and Practice, 16,* 611–622. doi:10.1037/0735-7028.16.5.611

Ridley, C., & Lingle, D. W. (1996). Cultural empathy in multicultural counseling: A multidimensional process model. In P. B. Pedersen, J. G. Draguns, W. J. Lonner, & J. E. Trimble (Eds.), *Counseling across cultures* (4th ed., pp. 21–46). Thousand Oaks, CA: Sage.

Rittenhouse, J. (2000). Using Eye Movement Desensitization and Reprocessing to treat complex PTSD in a biracial client. *Cultural Diversity and Ethnic Minority Psychology, 6,* 399–408. doi:10.1037/1099-9809.6.4.399

Robbins, L. N., Helzer, J. E., Croughan, J. L., & Ratcliff, K. S. (1981). National Institute of Mental Health diagnostic schedule: Its history, characteristics, and validity. *Archives of General Psychiatry, 38,* 381–389.

Rogers, W. A. (2004). Evidence medicine and justice: A framework for looking at the impact of EBM upon vulnerable and disadvantage groups. *Journal of Medical Ethics, 30,* 141–145. doi:10.1136/jme.2003.007062

Rogers-Sirin, L. (2008). Approaches to multicultural training for professionals: A guide for choosing an appropriate program. *Professional Psychology: Research and Practice, 39,* 313–319. doi:10.1037/0735-7028.39.3.313

Rogler, L. H. (1999). Methodological sources of cultural insensitivity in mental health research. *American Psychologist, 54,* 424–433. doi:10.1037/0003-066X.54.6.424

Root, M. M. P. (1990). Resolving the "other" status: Identity development of biracial individuals. In L. S. Brown & M. M. P. Root (Eds.), *Diversity and complexity in feminist therapy* (pp. 185–205). New York, NY: Harworth Press.

Root, M. M. P. (Ed.). (1992). *Racially mixed people in America.* Thousand Oaks, CA: Sage.

Root, M. M. P. (2004). From exotic to a dime a dozen. In A. Gillen & C. Thompson (Eds.), *Biracial women in therapy: Between the rock of gender and the hard place of race* (pp. 19–31). New York, NY: Harworth Press.

Rosselló, J., & Bernal, G. (1999). The efficacy of cognitive–behavioral and interpersonal treatments for depression in Puerto Rican adolescents. *Journal of Consulting and Clinical Psychology, 67,* 734–745. doi:10.1037/0022-006X.67.5.734

Rossman, M. L. (2000). *Guided imagery for self-healing: An essential resource for anyone seeking wellness* (2nd ed.). Tiburon, CA: Kramer.

Roysircar-Sodowsky, G., & Kuo, P. Y. (2001). Determining cultural validity of personality assessment: Some guidelines. In D. Pope-Davis & H. L. D. Coleman (Eds.), *The intersection of race, class and gender in multicultural counseling* (pp. 213–240). Thousand Oaks, CA: Sage.

Rubik, B. (2007). *Qigong* for health and wellness. In I. A. Serlin (Ed.), *Whole person healthcare. Vol. 2: Psychology, spirituality, and health* (pp. 211–233). Westport, CT: Praeger.

Ruiz, P. (Ed.). (2000). *Ethnicity and psychopharmacology.* Washington, DC: American Psychiatric Press.

Ruiz, P., & Langrod, J. (1976). The role of folk healers in community mental health. *Community Mental Health Journal, 12,* 392–398. doi:10.1007/BF01411078

Rupert, P., & Baird, R. (2004). Managed care and the independent practice of psychology. *Professional Psychology: Research and Practice, 35,* 185–193. doi:10.1037/0735-7028.35.2.185

Rust, P. C. (2002). Bisexuality: The state of the union. *Annual Review of Sex Research, 13,* 180–240.

Sakauye, K. (1996). Ethnocultural aspects. In J. Sadavoy. L. W. Lazarus, L. F. Jarvik, & G. T. Grossberg (Eds.), *Comprehensive review of geriatric psychiatry* (2nd ed., pp. 197–221). Washington, DC: American Psychiatric Press.

Sanderson, W. C., Rue, P. J., & Wetzler, S. (1998). The generalization of cognitive behavior therapy for panic disorder. *Journal of Cognitive Psychotherapy, 12,* 323–330.

Sandoval, C. (1998). *Mestizaje* as method: Feminists-of-color challenge the canon. In C. Trujillo (Ed.), *Living Chicana theory* (pp. 352–370). Berkeley, CA: Third Woman Press.

Sandoval, J. (1998). Critical thinking in test interpretation. In J. Sandoval, C. L. Frisby, K. Geisinger, J. D. Scheuneman, & J. R. Grenier (Eds.), *Test interpretation and diversity: Achieving equity in assessment* (pp. 31–49). Washington, DC: American Psychological Association. doi:10.1037/10279-002

Santería religion—What is Santería? (2010, August 9). Retrieved from http://boricua.com/features/santeria religion—what is santeria?

Santiago-Rivera, A. L., & Altarriba, J. (2002). The role of language in therapy with the Spanish-English bilingual client. *Professional Psychology: Research and Practice, 33,* 30–38. doi:10.1037/0735-7028.33.1.30

Sardar, Z., & Van Loon, B. (2004). *Introducing cultural studies.* Crows Nest, Australia: Allen & Unwin.

Satcher, D. (2001) *Mental health: Culture, race, and ethnicity. A report of the Surgeon General Disparities in mental health care for racial and ethnic minorities.* U.S. Department of Health and Human Services, 2001. Rockville, MD: Office of the Surgeon General. Retrieved from: http://www.surgeongeneral.gov/library/mentalhealth/cre/execsummary-1.html

Schank, J. A., Helbok, C. M., Haldeman, D. C., & Gallardo, M. E. (2010). Challenges and benefits of ethical small-community practice. *Professional Psychology: Research and Practice, 41,* 502–510. doi:10.1037/a0021689

Schofield, W. (1964). *Psychotherapy: The purchase of friendship.* Englewood Cliffs, NJ: Prentice-Hall.

Scotton, B. W. (1996). Introduction and definition of transpersonal psychiatry. In B. W. Scotton, A. B. Chinen, & J. R. Battista (Eds.), *Textbook of transpersonal psychiatry and psychology* (pp. 3–8) New York, NY: Basic Books.

Seeley, K. M. (2000). *Cultural psychotherapy: Working with culture in the clinical encounter.* Northvale, New Jersey: Jason Aronson.

Segal, Z. V., Williams, J. M., & Teasdale, J. D. (2002). *Mindfulness-based cognitive therapy for depression: A new approach to preventing relapse.* New York, NY: Guilford Press.

Semmler, P. L., & Williams, C. B. (2000). Narrative therapy: A storied context for multicultural counseling. *Journal of Multicultural Counseling and Development, 28,* 51–62.

Shapiro, E. R. (1994). *Grief as a family process: A developmental approach to clinical practice.* New York, NY: Guilford Press.

Shapiro, E. R. (1998). The healing power of culture stories: What writers can teach psychotherapies. *Cultural Diversity and Mental Health, 4,* 91–101. doi:10.1037/1099-9809.4.2.91

Shapiro, F. (1995). *Eye movement desensitization and reprocessing: Basic principles, protocols, and procedures.* New York, NY: Guilford Press.

Shon, S., & Ja, D. Y. (1982). Asian families. In M. McGoldrick, J. K. Pearce, & J. Giordano (Eds.), *Ethnicity and family therapy* (pp. 208–228). New York, NY: Guilford Press.

Shorter-Gooden, K. (1996). The Simpson trial: Lessons for mental health practitioners. *Cultural Diversity and Mental Health, 2,* 65–68. doi:10.1037/1099-9809.2.1.65

Shweder, R. A., & Bourne, E. J. (1982). Does the concept of person vary cross culturally? In A. J. Marsella & G. M. White (Eds.), *Cultural conceptions of mental health and therapy* (pp. 97–137). Dordrecht, The Netherlands: Reidel.

Simoni, J. M., & Perez, L. (1995). Latinos and mutual support groups: A case for considering culture. *American Journal of Orthopsychiatry, 65,* 440–445. doi:10.1037/h0079697

Simonton, O. C., Creighton, J., & Simonton, S. M. (1978). *Getting well again: A step by step, self-help guide to overcoming cancer for patients and their families.* New York, NY: Bantam.

Smith, M., & Mendoza, R. (1996). Ethnicity and psychopharmacogenetics. *The Mount Sinai Journal of Medicine, 63,* 285–290.

Smolan, R., Moffitt, P., & Naythons, M. (1990). *The power to heal: Ancient arts and modern medicine.* New York, NY: Prentice-Hall.

Snyderman, R., & Weil, A. T. (2002). Integrative medicine: Bringing medicine back to its roots. *Archives of Internal Medicine, 162,* 395–397. doi:10.1001/archinte.162.4.395

Sollod, R. (1993). Integrating spiritual healing approaches and techniques into psychotherapy. In G. Stricker & J. Gold (Eds.), *Comprehensive handbook of psychotherapy integration* (pp. 237–248). New York, NY: Plenum.

Speck, R. V., & Attneave, C. L. (1973). *Family networks.* New York, NY: Pantheon Books.

Spradley, J. P. (1990). *Participant observation.* New York, NY: Holt, Rinehart and Winston.

Stake, J. E., & Oliver, J. (1991). Sexual contact and touching between therapist and client: A survey of psychologists' attitudes and behavior. *Professional Psychology: Research and Practice, 22,* 297–307. doi:10.1037/0735-7028.22.4.297

St. Onge, P., Applegate, B., Asakura, V., Moss, M. K., Vergara-Lobo, A., & Rouson, B. (2009). *Embracing cultural competency: A roadmap for nonprofit capacity builders.* St. Paul, MN: Fieldstone Alliance.

Stein, R. (2008, December 11). 38% of adults use alternative medicine. *Washington Post,* pp. A2.

Steele, C. M., & Aronson, J. (1995). Stereotype threat and the intellectual test performance of African Americans. *Journal of Personality and Social Psychology, 69,* 797–811. doi:10.1037/0022-3514.69.5.797

Stern, D. (1985). *The interpersonal world of the infant: A view from psychoanalysis and developmental psychology.* New York, NY: Basic Books.

Stephens, N. M., Hamedani, M. Y., Markus, H. R., Bergsicker, H. B., & Eloul, L. (2009). Why did they "choose" to stay? Perspectives of Hurricane Katrina observers and survivors. *Psychological Science, 20,* 878–886. doi:10.1111/j.1467-9280.2009.02386.x

Steward, E., & Bennett, A. (1991). *American cultural patterns: A cross-cultural perspective* (2nd ed.). Yarmouth, ME: Intercultural Press.

Strickland, T. L., Ranganath, V., & Lin, K-M. (1991). Psychopharmacologic considerations in the treatment of Black American populations. *Psychopharmacology Bulletin, 27,* 441–448.

Suárez-Orozco, C., & Suárez-Orozco, M. (2001). *Children of immigration.* Cambridge, MA: Harvard University Press.

Suchman, A. L., Markakis, K., Beckman, H. B., & Frankel, R. (1997). A model of empathic communication in the medical interview. *JAMA, 277,* 678–682. doi:10.1001/jama.277.8.678

Sue, D. W. (2001). The superordinate nature of cultural competence. *The Counseling Psychologist, 29,* 850–857. doi:10.1177/0011000001296006

Sue, D. W., Arredondo, P., & McDavis, R. J. (1992). Multicultural counseling competencies and standards: A call to the profession. *Journal of Counseling & Development, 70,* 477–483.

Sue, D. W., Bingham, R. P., Porche-Burke, L., & Vasquez, M. (1999). The diversification of psychology: A multicultural revolution. *American Psychologist, 54,* 1061–1069. doi:10.1037/0003-066X.54.12.1061

Sue, D. W., Capodilupo, C. M., & Holder, A. M. B. (2008). Racial microaggressions in the life experience of Black Americans. *Professional Psychology: Research and Practice, 39,* 329–336. doi:10.1037/0735-7028.39.3.329

Sue, D. W., Capodilupo, C. M., Torino, G. C., Bucceri, J. M., Holder, A. M., Nadal, K. L., & Esquilin, M. (2007). Racial microaggressions in everyday life: Implications for clinical practice. *American Psychologist, 62,* 271–286. doi:10.1037/0003-066X.62.4.271

Sue, D. W., & Sue, D. (2008). *Counseling the culturally diverse: Theory and practice* (5th ed.). New York, NY: Wiley.

Sue, S. (1998). In search of cultural competence in psychotherapy and counseling. *American Psychologist, 53,* 440–448. doi:10.1037/0003-066X.53.4.440

Sue, S., & Zane, N. (1987). The role of culture and cultural techniques in psychotherapy. A critique and reformulation. *American Psychologist, 42,* 37–45. doi:10.1037/0003-066X.42.1.37

Suinn, R. M., Rickard-Figueroa, K., Lew, S., & Vigil, P. (1987). The Suinn-Lew Asian self-identity acculturation scale. *Educational and Psychological Measurement, 47,* 401–407. doi:10.1177/0013164487472012

Talmon, J. E. (1991). *Single session therapy.* San Francisco, CA: Jossey Bass.

Tamasese, K., & Waldegrave, C. (1994). Cultural and gender accountability in the "just therapy" approach. *Journal of Feminist Family Therapy, 5,* 29–45. doi:10.1300/J086v05n02_03

Tamura, T., & Lau, A. (1992). Connectedness versus separateness: Applicability of family therapy to Japanese families. *Family Process, 31,* 319–340. doi:10.1111/j.1545-5300.1992.00319.x

Tan, S.-Y., & Dong, N. J. (2000). Psychotherapy with members of Asian American churches and spiritual traditions. In P. S. Richards & A. E. Bergin (Eds.), *Handbook of psychotherapy and religious diversity* (pp. 421–444). Washington, DC: American Psychological Association. doi:10.1037/10347-017

Tedlock, B. (2005). *The woman in the shaman's body: Reclaiming the feminine in religion and medicine.* New York, NY: Bantam Dell.

Tervalon, M., & Murray-Garcia, J. (1998). Cultural humility versus cultural competence: A critical distinction in defining physician training outcomes in multicultural education. *Journal of Health Care for the Poor and Underserved, 9,* 117–125.

Textor, E. (1966). Cultural confrontation in the Philippines. In E. Textor (Ed.), *Cultural frontiers of the Peace Corps* (pp. 35–61). Cambridge, MA: MIT Press.

Thomas, M. B., & Dansby, P. G. (1985). Black clients: Family structures, therapeutic issues, and strengths. *Psychotherapy, 22,* 398–407. doi:10.1037/h0085521

Tien, L. (1994). Southeast Asian American women. In L. Comas-Díaz & B. Greene (Eds.), *Women of color: Integrating ethnic and gender identities in psychotherapy* (pp. 479–503). New York, NY: Guilford Press.

Toossi, M. (2006). A new look at a long-term labor force projections to 2050. *Monthly Labor Review, 129,* 19–39.

Torrey, E. F. (1986). *Witchdoctors and psychiatrists: The common roots of psychotherapy and its future.* New York, NY: Harper Row.

Treiber, F. A., McCaffrey, F., Musante, L., Rhodes, T., Davis, H., Strong, W. B., & Levy, M. (1993). Ethnicity and family history of hypertension and patterns of hemodynamic reactivity in boys. *Psychosomatic Medicine, 55,* 70–77.

Triandis, H. (1995). *Individualism and collectivism.* Boulder, CO: Westview Press.

Trimble, J. E., Fleming, C. M., Beauvais, F., & Jumper-Thurman, P. (1996). Essential cultural and social strategies for counseling Native American Indians. In P. B. Pedersen, G. G. Draguns, P. B. Lonner, & J. E. Trimble (Eds.), *Counseling across cultures* (4th ed., pp. 177–209). Thousand Oaks, CA: Sage.

Trujillo, A. (2000). Psychotherapy with Native Americans: A view into the role of religion and spirituality. In P. S. Richards & A. E. Bergin (Eds.), *Handbook of psychotherapy and religious diversity* (pp. 445–466). Washington, DC: American Psychological Association. doi:10.1037/10347-018

Tseng, W.-S. (2001). *Handbook of cultural psychiatry.* San Diego, CA: Academic Press.

Tseng, W.-S., & McDermott, J. F. (1975). Psychotherapy: Historical roots, universal elements and cultural variations. *The American Journal of Psychiatry, 132,* 378–384.

Tseng, W.-S., & Streltzer, J. (2004). Introduction: Culture and psychiatry. In W.-S. Tseng & J. Streltzer (Eds.), *Cultural competence in clinical psychiatry* (pp. 1–20). Washington, DC: American Psychiatric Publishing.

Tummala-Narra, P. (2004). Mothering in a foreign land. *The American Journal of Psychoanalysis, 64,* 167–182. doi:10.1023/B:TAJP.0000027271.27008.60

U.S. Department of Health and Human Services, Office of Minority Health. (2001). *National standards for culturally and linguistically appropriate services in health care (CLAS).* Washington, DC: Author. Retrieved from http://minorityhealth. hhs.gov/templates/browse.aspx?lvl=2&lvlID=15

U.S. General Accounting Office. (2000). *Women's health: NIH has increased its efforts to include women in research. Report to Congressional Requesters.* Retrieved from http://www.gao.gov/archive/2000/he00096.pdf

van de Vijver, F. J. R., & Hambleton, R. K. (1996). Translating tests: Some practical guidelines. *European Psychologist, 1,* 89–99. doi:10.1027/1016-9040.1.2.89

Valenstein, M., Adler, D. A., Berlant, J., Dixon, L. B., Dulit, R. A., Goldman, B., ... Sonis, W. A. (2009). Implementing standardized assessments in clinical care: now's the time. *Psychiatric Services, 60,* 1372–1375. doi:10.1176/ appi.ps.60.10.1372

Varghese, F. T. (1983). The racially different psychiatrist: Implications for psychotherapy. *Australian and New Zealand Journal of Psychiatry, 17,* 329–333.

Vasquez, C., & Javier, C. A. (1991). The problem with interpreters: Communicating with Spanish-speaking patients. *Hospital & Community Psychiatry, 42,* 163–165.

Vasquez, M., & Comas-Díaz, L. (2007). Feminist leadership among Latinas. In J. L. Chin, B. Lott, J. Rice, & J. Sanchez-Hucles (Eds.), *Transforming leadership: Diverse visions and women's voices* (pp. 264–280). Malden, MA: Blackwell.

Vasquez, M. J. (1998). Latinos and violence: Mental health implications and strategies for clinicians. *Cultural Diversity and Mental Health, 4,* 319–334. doi:10.1037/1099-9809.4.4.319

Vázquez, L. A., Garcia-Vasquez, E., Bauman, S. A., & Sierra, A. S. (1997). Skin color, acculturation, and community interest among Mexican American students: A research note. *Hispanic Journal of Behavioral Sciences, 19,* 377–386. doi:10.1177/07399863970193009

Villoldo, A. (2000). *Shaman, healer, sage: How to heal yourself and others with energy medicine of the Americas.* New York, NY: Harmony Books.

Walsh, R. (1999). *Essential spirituality: The seven central principles.* New York, NY: Wiley.

Walsh, R. (2011). Contemplative psychotherapies. In R. J. Corsini & D. Wedding (Eds.), *Current psychotherapies* (9th ed., pp. 437–480). Belmont, CA: Brooks/Cole.

Walsh, R., & Shapiro, S. (2006). The meeting of meditative disciplines and Western psychology: A mutually enriching dialogue. *American Psychologist, 61,* 227–239. doi:10.1037/0003-066X.61.3.227

Warnecke, A. M., Masters, R. D., & Kempter, G. (1992). The roots of nationalism: Nonverbal behavior and xenophobia. *Ethology and Sociobiology, 13,* 267–282. doi:10.1016/0162-3095(92)90026-Z

Wampold, B. E. (2007). Psychotherapy: The humanist (and effective) treatment. *American Psychologist, 62,* 857–873.

Washington, H. A. (2007). *Medical apartheid: The dark history of medical experimentation on Black Americans from colonial times to the present.* New York, NY: Doubleday.

Watson, W. H. (Ed.). (1984). *Black folk medicine: the therapeutic significance of faith and trust.* New Brunswick, NJ: Transaction Books.

Watts, A. W. (1961). *Psychotherapy East & West.* New York, NY: Ballantine Books.

Weahkee, R. L. (2008). American Indian women and spirituality. In C. Rayburn & L. Comas-Díaz (Eds.), *WomanSoul: The inner life of woman's spirituality* (pp. 107–118). New York, NY: Praeger/Greenwood.

Weaver, G. R. (1998). Contrasting and comparing cultures. In G. R. Weaver (Ed.), *Culture, communication and conflict. Readings in intercultural relations* (2nd ed., pp. 72–77). Needham Heights, MA: Simon & Schuster.

Weinreich, P., & Saunderson, W. (2003). *Analyzing identity: Cross-cultural, societal, and clinical contexts.* New York, NY: Routledge.

Weinreich, U. (1953). *Languages in contact.* The Hague, The Netherlands: Mouton.

Westermeyer, J. J. (1990). Working with an interpreter in psychiatric assessment and treatment. *Journal of Nervous and Mental Disease, 178,* 745–749. doi:10.1097/00005053-199012000-00003

Westermeyer, J. J. (1993). Cross-cultural psychiatric assessment. In A. Gaw (Ed.), *Culture, ethnicity, and mental illness* (pp. 125–144). Washington, DC: American Psychiatric Press.

Westermeyer, J. J. (2004). Culture and addiction psychiatry. In W.-S. Tseng & J. Streltzer (Eds.), *Cultural competence in clinical psychiatry* (pp. 85–106). Washington, DC: American Psychiatric Press.

Whaley, A. L. (1998). Racism in the provision of mental health services: A social–cognitive analysis. *American Journal of Orthopsychiatry, 68,* 47–57. doi:10.1037/h0080269

Whaley, A. L., & Davis, K. E. (2007). Cultural competence and evidence-based practice in mental health services: A complementary perspective. *American Psychologist, 62,* 563–574. doi:10.1037/0003-066X.62.6.563

Wilber, K. (2000). *Integral psychology.* Boston, MA: Shambhala.

Williams, D. R., Neighbors, H. W., & Jackson, J. S. (2008) Racial/ethnic discrimination and health: Findings from community studies. *American Journal of Public Health, 98* (Suppl. 1), 29–39.

Williams, D. R., Yu, Y., Jackson, J., & Anderson, N. (1997). Racial differences in physical and mental health: Socioeconomic status, stress, and discrimination. *Journal of Health Psychology, 2,* 335–351. doi:10.1177/135910539700200305

Wimberly, E. P. (1991). *African American pastoral care.* Nashville, TN: Abingdon Press.

Wrenn, C. G. (1985). The culturally encapsulated counselor revisited. In P. Pedersen (Ed.), *Handbook of cross-cultural counseling and therapy* (pp. 323–329). Westport, CT: Greenwood.

Wong, T. M. Strickland, T. L., Fletcher-Janzen, E., Ardila, A., & Reynolds, C. R. (2000). Theoretical and practical issues in the neuropsychological assessment and treatment of culturally dissimilar patients. In E. Fletcher-Janzen, T. L. Strickland, & C. R. Reynolds (Eds.), *Handbook of cross cultural neuropsychology* (pp. 3–18). New York, NY: Kluwer Academic/Plenum.

Worell, J., & Remer, P. (2003). *Feminist perspectives in therapy* (2nd ed.). New York, NY: Wiley.

Wu, E., & Martinez, M. (2006, October). *Taking cultural competence from theory to action.* Retrieved from http://www.commonwealthfund.org/Content/Publications/Fund-Reports/2006/Oct/Taking-Cultural-Competency-from-Theory-to-Action.aspx

Yeh, C. J., Hunter, C. D., Madan-Bahel, A., Chiang, L., & Arora, A. K. (2004). Indigenous and interdependent perspectives of healing: Implications for counseling and research. *Journal of Counseling & Development, 82,* 410–419.

Yi, K. (1995). Psychoanalytic psychotherapy with Asian clients: Transference and therapeutic considerations. *Psychotherapy, 32,* 308–316. doi:10.1037/0033-3204.32.2.308

Yontz, V. (2009, December 9). *Introduction to cultural and ethical considerations: Presentation made at the case management and social workers training.* Available from http://hepatitis.idlinks.com/hepatitis/media/20091203Case_managment_training_Cultural_consideration.ppt

Young, M. I. (1990). *Justice and the politics of difference.* Princeton, NJ: Princeton University Press.

Zaphiropoulos, M. L. (1982). Transcultural parameters in the transference and countertransference. *Journal of the American Academy of Psychoanalysis, 10,* 571–584.

Zuñiga, M. E. (1991). *Dichos* as metaphorical tools for resistant Latino clients. *Psychotherapy, 28,* 480–483. doi:10.1037/0033-3204.28.3.480

Zuñiga, M. E. (1992). Using metaphors in therapy: *Dichos* and Latino clients. *Social Work, 37,* 55–60.

Index

APA Multicultural Guidelines. See
    Guidelines on Multicultural
    Education, Training, Research,
    Practice, and Organizational
    Change for Psychologists
Apartheid, medical, 130–131
Appearance, physical, 64–65
Applegate, B., 229, 232, 233, 240–241
"Applying the APA Multicultural
    Guidelines to Psychological
    Practice" (L. Comas-Diaz &
    T. Caldwell-Colbert), 7–8
Aron, A., 104–105
ASDAH (Association of Size Diversity
    and Health), 134
Asian Americans, 153
ASKED method, 28
Assessment. See also Cultural self-
    assessment; Multicultural
    assessment
  of acculturation, 82
  bias in instruments for, 162–163
  of clinician by client, 35
  of cultural competence, 27–28
  of cultural translocation, 79–80
  in diagnosis and treatment, 93–94
  diagnostic errors in, 161–162
  neuropsychological, 167–168
  translocation narrative in, 74, 76–79
Associate languages, 20
Association of Size Diversity and
    Health (ASDAH), 134
Assumptions, 19–22
Ataque de nervios, 213
Atkinson, D. R., 137
Attack of nerves, 213
Attitude, 23, 124
Attneave, C., 223
Attunement, affective, 140–141
Aversive racism, 124, 127
Awareness
  in aversive racism, 124
  cultural, 6, 24–25

in cultural competence, 23
multicultural, 14, 28–30
of racial bias, 124

Baker, R., 137
Balance, 137
Basic assumption group, 231
BATHE model, 37–38, 51–52
Bazron, B., 238
Behaviors, 23
BELIEF model, 38, 53
Beliefs
  about health and mental health, 63
  and behaviors, 23
  of clinician, 124
  folk, 62
  and psychotic symptoms, 162
Bellido, C., 173–174
Benet-Martínez, V., 105
Bennet, M. J., 26
Bennett, A., 19–20
Bergsicker, H. B., 21
Berlin, E. A., 38
Bernal, G., 173–174
Bias
  in assessment instruments, 162–163
  in assessment methods, 161–162
  in psychological testing, 164–169
  racial, 129
  in test result interpretation,
      168–169
Biblical proverbs, 222
Bile, 213
Bilingualism, 45, 164, 236
Bilis, 213
Biocultural factors, 60, 70–72
Biological factors
  in exposure to racism, 182, 183
  in multicultural assessment, 71
  in psychopharmacotherapy treat-
      ment, 152–156
Bion, W. R., 231
Bisexual individuals, 97–98

Ingroup favoritism, 123–125
Initial contact, 34–36, 53–54
Integration, 27, 244
Intelligence, 162–163, 244–246
Interactions, 81
Interdependence, 102
Internal monologue, 198
Interpersonal inventory,
    multicultural, 83–85
Interpretation, cultural, 109–110,
    160–163
Interpreters, 164
Interracial families, 126–127
Interrogation, 203–204
Introspection, 96
Intuitive empathy, 141
Invitations, 117
IQ tests, 162
Isaacs, M., 238

Jacobs, G., 197–198
Jacobsen, F, M., 143
Johnson, J., 114–115
Jung, C., 197
Jungian approach, 109–110

Kakar, S., 175
Kardec, A., 206
Ketay, S., 104–105
King, Rodney, 68
Kleinman, A., 37, 47
Klerman, G. L., 85
Kluckholn, F. R., 16
Knowledge, 23
Knowledge, indigenous, 202
Koro, 214, 218
Koss-Chioino, J. D., 141
Kumagai, A. K., 239
Kurtz, S. N., 102

Lalonde, R., 99
Lam, Y., 155

Language
    associate, 20
    in engagement, 45–46
    heterosexist, 128
    in multicultural assessment, 63
    in organizational cultural compe-
        tence, 234–236
    and psychological testing, 163–164
    sexist, 128
    in White U.S. culture, 20
Laszloffy, T., 73, 85
Latino/a individuals
    acculturative stress in, 82
    drug metabolism by, 155
    expectations for therapeutic
        relationship in, 135
    plática in, 43
    psychological testing for, 166
    psychopharmacotherapy for, 153
    spirituality of, 204–206, 225
    touch norms of, 118–119
    and White privilege, 126–127
    xenophobia toward, 130
Latino folk healing
    ataque de nervios in, 213
    cuentos, 222–223
    culture-bound syndromes in,
        215–216
    emotions in, 218
    ethnic psychotherapies in,
        220–223
    nervios in, 214
    rootwork in, 214
    syncretistic approach in, 208–209
LEARN model, 38, 52
Lebron, Delia, 242
Left brain hemisphere, 197, 198
Length of treatment, 53
Lesbian, gay, bisexual, and
    transgender (LGBT), 97–98
Lesbian identity, 97
Leung, A. K.-y, 244
Levels of functioning, 93

Worldview. *See also* Sociocentric
   worldview
  of collectivistic approach, 16–17
  and cultural context, 58
  in cultural identity, 95
  in cultural self-assessment, 15–17
  of folk healing traditions, 199–201
  multicultural sociocentric, 101–114
  of shamanism, 203
  of Western healing tradition,
   199–201

Wounded healer syndrome,
   210–211

Xenophobia, 130

YAVIS clients, 124–125
Yontz, V., 243
Yoshimoto, Ishin, 224

Zar, 215
Zen healing approach, 224

About the Author

Lillian Comas-Díaz, PhD, is a clinical psychologist in full-time private practice and a clinical professor in the George Washington University Department of Psychiatry and Behavioral Sciences. Previously, she was a faculty member of the Yale University Department of Psychiatry, where she also directed its Hispanic Clinic. The author of more than 100 publications, Dr. Comas-Díaz is the coeditor of *Clinical Guidelines in Cross-Cultural Mental Health* (with Ezra Griffith, 1988), *Women of Color: Integrating Ethnic and Gender Identities in Psychotherapy* (with Beverly Greene, 1994), *WomanSoul: The Inner Life of Women's Spirituality* (with Carole A. Rayburn, 2008), and *Women Psychotherapists: Journeys in Healing* (with Marcella Bakur Weiner, 2011). She is the founding editor of *Cultural Diversity and Ethnic Minority Psychology,* the official journal of the Society for the Psychological Study of Ethnic Minority Issues (Division 45 of the American Psychological Association [APA]). In addition, she serves on several editorial boards and is an associate editor of *American Psychologist.* Dr. Comas-Díaz is a past president of Psychologists in Independent Practice (Division 42 of APA) and former director of the APA Office of Ethnic Minority Affairs.